Here's a powerful collection of interviews with leading experts on some of the toughest objections to Christianity. Lee Strobel uses his skills as an award-winning investigative reporter to crisscross the country and elicit compelling answers to the objections that hinder many people from putting their faith in Christ. This is nothing short of a masterpiece of apologetics! Highly recommended for Christians and for anyone who is spiritually curious.

> MARK MITTELBERG, bestselling author of *Contagious Faith* and *The Questions Christians Hope No One Will Ask (with Answers)*

Lee Strobel has given both believers and skeptics alike a gift in this book. He does not avoid asking the most difficult questions imaginable—questions about God and suffering, about divine judgment and hell, about injustice, and about the exclusivity of Christ. He dares to deal with complexity too, thus refusing to pander to readers or provide simplistic answers that do more harm than good. Yet his style of writing—by recording interviews with experts who address these difficult questions—makes the book surprisingly accessible and winsome. I found it both helpful and captivating.

> JERRY SITTSER, professor of theology,
> senior fellow in the Office of Church Engagement,
> Whitworth College, and author of *A Grace Disguised*

Everyone—seekers, doubters, fervent believers—benefits when Lee Strobel hits the road in search of answers, as he does again in *The Case for Faith*. In the course of his probing interviews, some of the toughest intellectual obstacles to faith fall away.

> LUIS PALAU, president, Luis Palau Evangelistic Association

With intellectual depth and honesty, Lee Strobel investigates and then nullifies the toughest arguments against Christianity. A perfect book for the intellectual, the doubter, and the inquisitive. A great faith builder.

> DR. BILL BRIGHT, founder and president,
> Campus Crusade for Christ International

THE CASE FOR
Faith

Resources by Lee Strobel

THE CASE FOR
Faith

A Journalist Investigates the Toughest
Objections to Christianity

UPDATED AND EXPANDED

LEE
STROBEL

NEW YORK TIMES BESTSELLING AUTHOR

ZONDERVAN
BOOKS

ZONDERVAN BOOKS

The Case for Faith
Copyright © 2000, 2004, 2021 by Lee Strobel

Requests for information should be addressed to:
Zondervan, *3900 Sparks Dr. SE, Grand Rapids, Michigan 49546*

Zondervan titles may be purchased in bulk for educational, business, fundraising, or sales promotional use. For information, please email SpecialMarkets@Zondervan.com.

ISBN 978-0-310-36427-6 (softcover)
ISBN 978-0-310-36458-0 (audio)
ISBN 978-0-310-36428-3 (ebook)

Published in association with Don Gates of the literary agency The Gates Group, www .the-gates-group.com.

Cover design: Faceout Studio
Cover photo: Shutterstock
Interior typesetting: Kait Lamphere

Contents

The Challenge of Faith

*Christian theism must be rejected by any person
with even a shred of respect for reason.*

GEORGE H. SMITH, ATHEIST

*Christian faith is not an irrational leap. Examined
objectively, the claims of the Bible are rational
propositions well supported by reason and evidence.*

CHARLES COLSON, CHRISTIAN

William Franklin Graham steadied himself by gripping both sides of the podium. He was eighty years old, fighting Parkinson's disease, but he stared intently at the throngs inside the RCA Dome in Indianapolis and spoke in a steady, forceful voice. There was no hint of hesitation, no uncertainty or ambiguity. His sermon was essentially the same simple and direct message he had been preaching for fifty years.

He referenced the chaos and violence around the world, and he zeroed in on the anguish, pain, and confusion in the hearts of individuals. He talked about sin, about forgiveness, about redemption, and about the loneliness, despair, and depression that weigh so many people down.

"All of us want to be loved," he said in his familiar North Carolina cadence as he approached the conclusion of his talk. "All of us want somebody to love us. Well, I want to tell you that God

1

loves you. He loves you so much that he gave us his Son to die on the cross for our sins. And he loves you so much that he will come into your life and change the direction of your life and make you a new person, whoever you are.

"Are you sure that you know Christ? There comes a moment in which the Spirit of God convicts you, calls you, speaks to you about opening your heart and making certain of your relationship to God. And hundreds of you here tonight are not sure. You'd like to be sure. You'd like to leave here tonight knowing that if you died on the way home, you would be ready to meet God."[1]

So he urged them to come. And they did—at first, there was a trickle of people, and then the floodgates opened, with individuals, couples, and entire families pouring into the empty space in front of the platform. Soon they were shoulder to shoulder, the crowd wrapping around the sides of the stage, nearly three thousand in all. Some were weeping, gripped by somber conviction; others stared downward, still stewing in shame over their past; many were smiling from ear to ear—liberated, joyous . . . home, finally.

The response of one married woman was typical. "My mom died of cancer when I was young, and at the time I thought I was being punished by God," she told a counselor. "Tonight I realized that God loves me—it is something I've known but couldn't really grasp. Tonight a peacefulness came into my heart."[2]

What is faith? There would have been no need to define it for these people on that sultry June night. Faith was almost palpable to them. They reached out to God almost as if they were expecting to physically embrace him. Faith drained them of the guilt that had oppressed them. Faith replaced despondency with hope. Faith infused them with new direction and purpose. Faith unlocked heaven. Faith was like cool water soaking their parched souls.

But faith isn't always that easy, even for people who desperately want it. Some people hunger for spiritual certainty, yet something hinders them from experiencing it. They wish they could taste that kind of freedom, but obstacles block their paths. Objections pester them. Doubts mock them. Their hearts want to soar to God; their intellects keep them securely tied down.

They see the television coverage of the crowds that have come forward to pray with Billy Graham, and they shake their heads. *If it were only that simple*, they sigh to themselves. *If only there weren't so many questions.*

For Charles Templeton—ironically, once Billy Graham's pulpit partner and close friend—questions about God have hardened into bitter opposition toward Christianity. Like Graham, Templeton once spoke powerfully to crowds in vast arenas and called for people to commit themselves to Jesus Christ. Some even predicted Templeton would eventually eclipse Graham as an evangelist.

But that was a long time ago. That was before the crippling questions. Today Templeton's faith—repeatedly punctured by persistent and obstinate doubts—has leaked away. Maybe forever.

Maybe.

From Faith to Doubt

The year was 1949. Thirty-year-old Billy Graham was unaware that he was on the brink of being catapulted into worldwide fame and influence. Ironically, as he readied himself for his breakthrough crusade in Los Angeles, he found himself grappling with uncertainty—not over the existence of God or the divinity of Jesus, but over the fundamental issue of whether he could totally trust what his Bible was telling him.

In his autobiography, Graham said he felt as if he were being stretched on a rack. Pulling him toward God was Henrietta Mears, the bright and compassionate Christian educator who had a thorough understanding of modern scholarship and an abounding confidence in the reliability of the Scriptures. Yanking him the other way was Graham's close companion and preaching colleague, thirty-three-year-old Charles Templeton.[3]

According to Templeton, he became a Christian fifteen years

earlier when he found himself increasingly disgusted with his life-style on the sports staff of the Toronto *Globe*. Fresh from a night out at a sleazy strip joint, feeling shoddy and unclean, he went to his room and knelt by his bed in the darkness.

"Suddenly," he would recall later, "it was as though a black blanket had been draped over me. A sense of guilt pervaded my entire mind and body. The only words that would come were, 'Lord, come down. Come down . . .'" And then:

> Slowly, a weight began to lift, a weight as heavy as I. It passed through my thighs, my torso, my arms and shoulders, and lifted off. An ineffable warmth began to suffuse my body. It seemed that a light had turned on in my chest and that it had cleansed me . . .
>
> I hardly dared breathe, fearing that I might alter or end the moment. And I heard myself whispering softly over and over again, "Thank you, Lord. Thank you. Thank you. Thank you."
>
> Later, in bed, I lay quietly at the center of a radiant, over-whelming, all-pervasive happiness.[4]

After abandoning journalism for the ministry, Templeton met Graham in 1945 at a Youth for Christ rally. They were roommates and constant companions during an adventurous tour of Europe, alternating in the pulpit as they preached at rallies. Templeton founded a church that soon overflowed its 1,200-seat sanctuary. *American Magazine* said he "set a new standard for mass evange-lism."[5] His friendship with Graham grew. "He's one of the few men I have ever loved in my life," Graham once told a biographer.[6]

But soon doubts began gnawing at Templeton. "I had gone through a conversion experience as an incredibly green youth," he recalled later. "I lacked the intellectual skills and the theological training needed to buttress my beliefs when—as was inevitable—questions and doubts began to plague me . . . My reason had begun to challenge and sometimes to rebut the central beliefs of the Christian faith."[7]

A Triumph of Faith

Now, there was the skeptical Templeton, a counterpoint to the faith-filled Henrietta Mears, tugging his friend Billy Graham away from her repeated assurances that the Scriptures are trustworthy. "Billy, you're fifty years out of date," he argued. "People no longer accept the Bible as being inspired the way you do. Your faith is too simple."

Templeton seemed to be winning the tug-of-war. "If I was not exactly doubtful," Graham would recall, "I was certainly disturbed."[8] He knew that if he could not trust the Bible, he could not go on. The Los Angeles crusade—the event that would open the door to Graham's worldwide ministry—was hanging in the balance.

Graham searched the Scriptures for answers, he prayed, he pondered. Finally, in a heavy-hearted walk in the moonlit San Bernardino Mountains, everything came to a climax. Gripping a Bible, Graham dropped to his knees and confessed he couldn't answer some of the philosophical and psychological questions that Templeton and others were raising.

"I was trying to be on the level with God, but something remained unspoken," he wrote. "At last the Holy Spirit freed me to say it. 'Father, I am going to accept this as Thy Word—by *faith*! I'm going to allow faith to go beyond my intellectual questions and doubts, and I will believe this to be Your inspired Word.'"

Rising from his knees, tears in his eyes, Graham said he sensed the power of God as he hadn't felt it for months. "Not all my questions were answered, but a major bridge had been crossed," he said. "In my heart and mind, I knew a spiritual battle in my soul had been fought and won."[9]

For Graham, it was a pivotal moment. For Templeton, though, it was a bitterly disappointing turn of events. Templeton said Graham was committing "intellectual suicide" when Graham declared, "I've decided, once and for all, to stop questioning and accept the Bible as God's Word."[10] The emotion he felt most toward his friend was pity. Now on different paths, their lives began to diverge.

History knows what would happen to Graham in the succeeding years. He would become the most persuasive and effective evangelist of modern times and one of the most admired men in the world. But what would happen to Templeton? Decimated by doubts, he resigned from the ministry and moved back to Canada, where he became a commentator and novelist.

Templeton's reasoning had chased away his faith. But are faith and intellect really incompatible? Is it possible to be a thinker and a Bible-believing Christian at the same time? Some don't believe so.

"Reason and faith are opposites, two mutually exclusive terms: there is no reconciliation or common ground," asserts atheist George Smith. "Faith is belief without, or in spite of, reason."[11]

Christian educator W. Bingham Hunter takes the opposite view. "Faith," he said, "is a rational response to the evidence of God's self-revelation in nature, human history, the Scriptures and his resurrected Son."[12]

For me, having lived much of my life as an atheist, the last thing I want is a naive faith built on a paper-thin foundation of wishful thinking or make-believe. I need a faith that is consistent with reason, not contradictory to it; I want beliefs that are grounded in reality, not detached from it. I need to find out once and for all whether the Christian faith can stand up to scrutiny.

It was time for me to talk face-to-face with Charles Templeton.

From Minister to Agnostic

Some five hundred miles north of where Billy Graham was staging his Indianapolis campaign, I tracked Templeton to a modern highrise building in a middle-class neighborhood of Toronto. Taking the elevator to the twenty-fifth floor, I went to a door marked "Penthouse" and used the brass knocker.

Under my arm I carried a copy of Templeton's latest book, whose title leaves no ambiguity concerning his spiritual perspective. It's called *Farewell to God: My Reasons for Rejecting the Christian*

Faith. The often-acerbic tome seeks to eviscerate Christian beliefs, attacking them with passion for being "outdated, demonstrably untrue, and often, in their various manifestations, deleterious to individuals and to society."[13]

Templeton draws on a variety of illustrations as he strives to undermine faith in the God of the Bible. But I was especially struck by one moving passage in which he pointed to the horrors of Alzheimer's disease, describing in gripping detail the way it hideously strips people of their personal identity by rotting their minds and memories. How, he demanded, could a compassionate God allow such a ghastly illness to torture its victims and their loved ones?

The answer, he concluded, is simple: Alzheimer's would not exist if there were a loving God. And because it does exist, that's one more bit of persuasive evidence that God does not.[14] For someone like me, whose wife's family has endured the ugly ravages of Alzheimer's, it was an argument that carried considerable emotional punch.

I wasn't sure what to expect as I waited at Templeton's door. Would he be as combative as he was in his book? Would he be bitter toward Billy Graham? Would he even go through with our interview? When he had consented in a brief telephone conversation two days earlier, he had said vaguely that his health was not good.

Templeton's third wife, Madeleine, fresh from tending flowers in her rooftop garden, opened the door and greeted me warmly. "I know you've come all the way from Chicago," she said, "but Charles is very sick, I'm sorry to say."

"I could come back another time," I offered.

"Well, let's see how he's feeling," she said. She led me up a red-carpeted staircase into their luxury apartment, two large and frisky poodles at her heels. "He's been sleeping . . ."

At that moment, her eighty-three-year-old husband emerged from his bedroom. He was wearing a dark brown, lightweight robe over similarly colored pajamas. Black slippers were on his feet. His thinning gray hair was a bit disheveled. He was gaunt and pale, although his blue-gray eyes appeared alert and expressive. He politely extended his hand to be shaken.

"Please excuse me," he said, clearing his throat, "but I'm not well." Then he added matter-of-factly, "Actually, I'm dying."

"What's wrong?" I asked.

His answer almost knocked me on my heels. "Alzheimer's disease," he replied.

My mind raced to what he had written about Alzheimer's being evidence for the nonexistence of God; suddenly, I had an insight into at least some of the motivation for his book.

"I've had it . . . let's see, has it been three years?" he said, furrowing his brow and turning to his wife for help. "That's right, isn't it, Madeleine?"

She nodded. "Yes, dear, three years."

"My memory isn't what it was," he said. "And as you may know, Alzheimer's is always fatal. Always. It sounds melodramatic, but the truth is I'm doomed. Sooner or later, it will kill me. But first it will take my mind." He smiled faintly. "It's already started, I'm afraid. Madeleine can attest to that."

"Look, I'm sorry to intrude," I said. "If you're not feeling up to this . . ."

But Templeton insisted. He ushered me into the living room, brightly decorated in a contemporary style and awash in afternoon sunshine, which poured through glass doors that offered a breathtaking panoramic view of the city. We sat on adjacent cushioned chairs, and in a matter of minutes Templeton seemed to have mustered fresh energy.

"I suppose you want me to explain how I went from the ministry to agnosticism," he said. With that, he proceeded to describe the events that led to the shedding of his faith in God.

That was what I had expected. But I could never have anticipated how our conversation would end.

The Power of a Picture

Templeton was fully engaged now. Occasionally, I could see evidence of his Alzheimer's, such as when he was unable to recall a precise sequence of events or when he'd repeat himself. But for the most part, he spoke with eloquence and enthusiasm, using an impressive vocabulary, his rich and robust voice rising and lowering for emphasis. He had an aristocratic tone that sounded nearly theatrical at times.

"Was there one thing in particular that caused you to lose your faith in God?" I asked at the outset.

He thought for a moment. "It was a photograph in *Life* magazine," he said finally.

"Really?" I said. "A photograph. How so?"

He narrowed his eyes a bit and looked off to the side, as if he were viewing the photo afresh and reliving the moment. "It was a picture of a black woman in northern Africa," he explained. "They were experiencing a devastating drought. And she was holding her dead baby in her arms and looking up to heaven with the most forlorn expression. I looked at it and I thought, *Is it possible to believe there is a loving or caring Creator when all this woman needed was* rain?"

As he emphasized the word *rain*, his bushy gray eyebrows shot up and his arms gestured toward heaven as if beckoning for a response.

"How could a loving God *do this* to that woman?" he implored as he got more animated, moving to the edge of his chair. "Who runs the rain? I don't; you don't. *He* does—or that's what I thought. But when I saw that photograph, I immediately knew it is not possible for this to happen and for there to be a loving God. There was no way. Who else but a fiend could destroy a baby and virtually kill its mother with agony—when all that was needed was *rain?*"

He paused, letting the question hang heavily in the air. Then he settled back into his chair. "That was the climactic moment," he said. "And then I began to think further about the world being the creation of God. I started considering the plagues that sweep across parts of the planet and indiscriminately kill—more often than not, painfully—all kinds of people, the ordinary, the decent, and the rotten. And it just became crystal clear to me that it is not possible for an intelligent person to believe there is a deity who loves."

Templeton was tapping into an issue that had vexed me for years. In my career as a newspaper reporter, I hadn't merely seen photos of intense suffering; I was a frequent firsthand observer of the underbelly of life where tragedy and suffering festered—the rotting inner cities of the United States, the filthy slums of India, Cook County Jail and the major penitentiaries, the hospice wards for the hopeless . . . all sorts of disaster scenes. More than once, my mind reeled at trying to reconcile the idea of a loving God with the depravity, heartache, and anguish before my eyes.

But Templeton wasn't done. "My mind then went to the whole concept of hell. My goodness," he said, his voice infused with astonishment, "I couldn't hold someone's hand to a fire for a moment. Not an instant! How could a loving God, just because you don't obey him and do what he wants, torture you forever—not allowing you to die, but to continue in that pain for eternity? There is no criminal who would do this!"

"So these were the first doubts you had?" I asked.

"Prior to that, I had been having more and more questions. I had preached to hundreds of thousands of people the antithetical message, and then I found to my dismay that I could no longer believe it. To believe it would be to deny the brain I had been given. It became quite clear that I had been wrong. So I made up my mind that I would leave the ministry. That's essentially how I came to be agnostic."

"Define what you mean by that," I said, since various people have offered different interpretations of that term.

"The atheist says there is no God," he replied. "The Christian and Jew say there is a God. The agnostic says, 'I cannot know.' Not *do not* know but *cannot* know. I never would presume to say flatly that there is no God. I don't know everything; I'm not the embodiment of wisdom. But it is not possible for me to believe in God."

I hesitated to ask the next question. "As you get older," I began in a tentative tone, "and you're facing a disease that's always fatal, do you—"

"Worry about being wrong?" he interjected. He smiled. "No, I don't."

"Why not?"

"Because I have spent a lifetime thinking about it. If this were a simplistic conclusion reached on a whim, that would be different. But it's impossible for me—*impossible*—to believe that there is any thing or person or being that could be described as a loving God who could allow what happens in our world daily."

"Would you *like* to believe?" I asked.

"Of course!" he exclaimed. "If I could, I would. I'm eighty-three years old. I've got Alzheimer's. I'm dying, for goodness' sake! But I've spent my life thinking about it, and I'm not going to change now. Hypothetically, if someone came up to me and said, 'Look, old boy, the reason you're ill is God's punishment for your refusal to continue on the path your feet were set in'—would that make any difference to me?"

He answered himself emphatically: "No," he declared. "*No*. There cannot be, in our world, a loving God."

His eyes locked with mine. "*Cannot* be."

The Illusion of Faith

Templeton ran his fingers through his hair. He had been talking in adamant tones, and I could tell he was beginning to tire. I wanted to be sensitive to his condition, but I had a few other questions I wanted to pursue. With his permission, I continued.

"As we're talking, Billy Graham is in the midst of a series of rallies in Indiana," I told Templeton. "What would you say to the people who've stepped forward to put their faith in Christ?"

Templeton's eyes got wide. "Why, I wouldn't interfere in their lives at all," he replied. "If a person has faith and it makes them a better individual, then I'm all for that—even if I think they're nuts. Having been a Christian, I know how important it is to people's lives—how it alters their decisions, how it helps them deal with difficult problems. For most people, it's a boon beyond description. But is it because there is a God? No, it's not."

Templeton's voice carried no condescension, and yet the implications of what he was saying were thoroughly patronizing. Is that what faith is all about—fooling yourself into becoming a better person? Convincing yourself there's a God so that you'll become motivated to ratchet up your morality a notch or two? Embracing a fairy tale so you'll sleep better at night? *No, thank you,* I thought to myself. If that's faith, I wasn't interested.

"What about Billy Graham himself?" I asked. "You said in your book that you feel sorry for him."

"Oh, no, no," he insisted, contrary to his writings. "Who am I to feel sorry for what another man believes? I may regret it on his behalf, if I may put it that way, because he has closed his mind to reality. But would I wish him ill? Not for anything at all!"

Templeton glanced over to an adjacent glass coffee table where Billy Graham's autobiography was sitting.

"Billy is pure gold," he remarked fondly. "There's no feigning or fakery in him. He's a first-rate human being. Billy is profoundly Christian—he's the genuine goods, as they say. He sincerely believes—unquestionably. He is as wholesome and faithful as anyone can be."

And what about Jesus? I wanted to know what Templeton thought of the cornerstone of Christianity. "Do you believe Jesus ever lived?" I asked.

"No question," came the quick reply.

"Did he think he was God?"

He shook his head. "That would have been the last thought that would have entered his mind."

"And his teaching—did you admire what he taught?"

"Well, he wasn't a very good preacher. What he said was too simple. He hadn't thought about it. He hadn't agonized over the biggest question there is to ask."

"Which is?"

"Is there a God? How could anyone believe in a God who does, or allows, what goes on in the world?"

"And so how do you assess this Jesus?" It seemed like the next logical question—but I wasn't ready for the response it would evoke.

The Allure of Jesus

Templeton's body language softened. It was as if he suddenly felt relaxed and comfortable in talking about an old and dear friend. His voice, which at times had displayed such a sharp and insistent edge, now took on a melancholy and reflective tone. His guard seemingly down, he spoke at an unhurried pace, almost nostalgically, carefully choosing his words as he talked about Jesus.

"He was," Templeton began, "the greatest human being who has ever lived. He was a moral genius. His ethical sense was unique. He was the intrinsically wisest person I've ever encountered in my life or in my readings. His commitment was total and led to his own death, much to the detriment of the world. What could one say about him except that this was a form of greatness?"

I was taken aback. "You sound like you really care about him," I said.

"Well, yes, he's the most important thing in my life," came his reply. "I . . . I . . . I," he stuttered, searching for the right word, "I know it may sound strange, but I have to say . . . I *adore* him!"

I wasn't sure how to respond. "You say that with some emotion," I said.

"Well, yes. Everything good I know, everything decent I know, everything pure I know, I learned from Jesus. Yes . . . yes. And tough! Just look at Jesus. He castigated people. He was angry. People don't think of him that way, but they don't read the Bible. He had a righteous anger. He cared for the oppressed and the exploited. There's no question he had the highest moral standard, the least duplicity, the greatest compassion, of any human being in history. There have been many other wonderful people, but Jesus is Jesus."

"And so the world would do well to emulate him?"

"Oh, my goodness, yes! I have tried—and try is as far as I can go—to act as I have believed he would act. That doesn't mean I could read his mind, because one of the most fascinating things about him was that he often did the opposite thing you'd expect—"

Abruptly, Templeton cut short his thoughts. There was a brief pause, almost as if he was uncertain whether he should continue. "Uh . . . but . . . no," he said slowly, "he's the most . . ." He stopped, then started again. "In my view," he declared, "he is the most important human being who has ever existed."

That's when Templeton uttered the words I never expected to hear from him. "And if I may put it this way," he said as his voice began to crack, *"I . . . miss . . . him!"*

With that, tears flooded his eyes. He turned his head and looked downward, raising his left hand to shield his face from me. His shoulders bobbed as he wept.

What was going on? Was this an unguarded glimpse into his soul? I felt drawn to him and wanted to comfort him; at the same time, the journalist in me wanted to dig to the core of what was prompting this reaction. Missed him *why?* Missed him *how?*

In a gentle voice, I asked, "In what way?"

Templeton fought to compose himself. I could tell it wasn't like him to lose control in front of a stranger. He sighed deeply and wiped away a tear. After a few more awkward moments, he waved his hand dismissively. Finally, quietly but adamantly, he insisted, "Enough of that."

He leaned forward to pick up his coffee. He took a sip, holding the cup tightly in both hands as if drawing warmth from it. It was obvious he wanted to pretend this unvarnished look into his soul had never happened.

But I couldn't let it go. Nor could I gloss over Templeton's pointed but heartfelt objections about God. Clearly they demanded a response.

For him, as well as for me.

On the Road to Answers

*1.6 billion [Christians] can be wrong . . . My claim is
simply that . . . rational people should give up these beliefs.*
MICHAEL MARTIN, ATHEIST

*Today, it seems to me, there is no good reason for
an intelligent person to embrace the illusion of atheism
or agnosticism, to make the same intellectual mistakes
I made. I wish . . . I had known then what I know now.*
PATRICK GLYNN, ATHEIST-TURNED-CHRISTIAN

A short time after the interview with Charles Templeton, my
wife, Leslie, and I began driving back to Chicago, spending
much of the way in an animated discussion about my enigmatic
encounter with the former evangelist.

Frankly, I needed some time to process the experience. It had
been an unusual interview, ranging all the way from the resolute
rejection of God to an emotional desire to reconnect with the Jesus
he used to worship.

"It sounds like you really like Templeton," Leslie remarked at
one point.

"I do," I said.

The truth is that my heart went out to him. He hungers for
faith; he conceded as much. As someone facing death, he has every
incentive to want to believe in God. There's an undeniable pull

toward Jesus that clearly comes from deep inside him. But then there are those formidable intellectual barriers that stand squarely in his path.

Like Templeton, I've always been someone who has grappled with questions. In my former role as legal affairs editor at the *Chicago Tribune*, I had been notorious for raising what I called "Yes, but" objections. *Yes*, I could see that the evidence in a trial was pointing toward a certain verdict, *but* what about that inconsistency or this flaw or that weak link? *Yes*, the prosecutor may have presented a convincing case for the defendant's guilt, *but* what about their alibi or the lack of fingerprints?

And the same was true of my personal investigation of Jesus. I started out as an atheist, utterly convinced that God didn't create people but that people created God in a pathetic effort to explain the unknown and temper their overpowering fear of death. My previous book, *The Case for Christ*, described my nearly two-year-long examination of the historical evidence that pointed me toward the verdict that God really exists and that Jesus actually is his unique Son. (For a summary of those findings, please see the appendix.)

But that hadn't been enough by itself to completely settle the matter for me. There were still those nagging objections. *Yes*, I could see how the historical evidence for Jesus' resurrection can support a verdict that he's divine, *but* what about the flurry of problems that raises? I called these conundrums "the Big Eight":

- If there is a loving God, why does this pain-wracked world groan under so much suffering and evil?
- If the miracles of God contradict science, how can any rational person believe they're true?
- If God really created the universe, why does the persuasive evidence of science compel so many to conclude that the unguided process of evolution accounts for life?
- If God is morally pure, how could he sanction the slaughter of innocent children, as the Old Testament says he did?

- If Jesus is the only way to heaven, what about the millions of people who have never heard of him?
- If God cares about the people he created, how could he consign so many of them to an eternity of torture in hell just because they didn't believe the right things about him?
- If God is the ultimate overseer of the church, why has it been rife with hypocrisy and brutality throughout the ages?
- If I'm still plagued by doubts, then is it still possible to be a Christian?

These are among the most commonly posed questions about God. In fact, they were some of the very issues discussed by Charles Templeton in my interview with him and in his book. And as it was with Templeton, these obstacles also once stood solidly between me and faith.

Overcoming Objections

While I could relate to many of the objections that Templeton had raised, at the same time I wasn't naive enough to accept each of them at face value. It was clear that some of his obstacles to faith shouldn't be impediments at all.

For example, Templeton was plain wrong about Jesus considering himself to be a mere human being. Even if you go back to the earliest and most primitive information about him, you find that Jesus undoubtedly saw himself in transcendent, divine, and messianic terms.[1]

In fact, here's an irony: the very historical documents that Templeton relied on for his information about the inspiring moral life of Jesus are actually the exact same records that repeatedly affirm his deity. So if Templeton is willing to accept their accuracy concerning Jesus' character, he also ought to consider them trustworthy when they assert that Jesus claimed to be divine and then backed up that assertion by rising from the dead.

In addition, the idea that the resurrection of Jesus could be a legend, as Templeton claimed, seemed highly implausible to me. That's because the apostle Paul preserved a creed of the early church that reported eyewitnesses to Jesus' return from the dead—and which various scholars have dated to as early as twenty-four to thirty-six months after Jesus' death.[2] It's unlikely that legend or mythology could develop that quickly and wipe out a solid core of historical truth.[3]

As I systematically documented in *The Case for Christ*, the eyewitness evidence, the corroborating evidence, the documentary evidence, the scientific evidence, the psychological evidence, the "fingerprint" or prophetic evidence, and other historical data point powerfully toward the conclusion that Jesus really is God's one and only Son.

Yes, but . . .

What about those nettlesome issues that hindered Templeton from embracing the faith he admittedly desires so much to have? They haunted me. They were the same issues that had once perplexed me—and as Leslie and I drove along the interstate toward home, some of them began to nag at me anew.

Traveling the Same Path

Leslie and I were quiet for a while. I gazed out the window at the undulating meadows of the Canadian countryside. Finally, Leslie said, "It sounds like your interview ended a little abruptly. What did Templeton say before you left?"

"Actually, he was very warm. He even gave me a tour of his apartment," I told her. "It was like he didn't want me to leave. But no matter how much I tried, I couldn't get him to reengage in discussing his feelings about Jesus."

I thought for a moment before continuing. "He did say one other thing that struck me. Just as I was getting ready to leave, he looked me in the eyes—very intensely—and shook my hand and said with great sincerity, 'We've been on the same path.'"

Leslie nodded. "You *have* been," she said. "You're both writers; you've both been skeptics." Then she added with a smile, "And you're both too hardheaded to buy into faith until you're sure it's not riddled with holes."

She was right. "But, you know, his mind seemed so closed," I said. "He insisted there *cannot* be a loving God. And yet at the same time, his heart seemed so open. In a way, I think he wants Jesus just as much as the people who came forward in Indianapolis. Only he can't have him. At least, he doesn't think so. Not with his objections."

Leslie and I spent the night in a Michigan hotel and finally arrived home before noon the following day. I lugged our suitcase up the stairs and tossed it onto the bed. Leslie unzipped it and began taking out clothes.

"At least we're home for a while," she remarked.

"Well, not quite," I said.

I couldn't let Templeton's questions go. They resonated too deeply with my own. So I decided to retrace and expand on my spiritual journey in a different direction than I had pursued when I wrote *The Case for Christ*, which was an investigation of the historical evidence for the life, death, and resurrection of Jesus Christ. I wanted to determine once again whether there are soul-satisfying responses when Christianity is confronted with life's harshest and most perplexing questions that send nagging doubts into our hearts and minds. Can faith really stand up to reason? Or will rigorous intellectual scrutiny chase God away?

I resolved to track down the most knowledgeable and ardent defenders of Christianity. My intent was not to take a cynical or confrontational approach by badgering them with nitpicky questions or seeing whether I could trick them into painting themselves into a rhetorical corner. This wasn't a game to me.

I was sincerely interested in determining whether they had rational answers to "the Big Eight." I wanted to give them ample opportunity to spell out their reasoning and evidence in detail so that, in the end, I could evaluate whether their positions made sense. Most of all, I wanted to find out whether God was telling the truth when he said, "You will seek me and find me when you seek me with all your heart."[4]

I picked up the telephone. It was time to make plans to hit the road in search of answers.

Charles Templeton would have expected nothing less.

OBJECTION #1

Since Evil and Suffering Exist, a Loving God Cannot

Either God wants to abolish evil, and cannot; or he can,
but does not want to; or he cannot, and does not want to.
If he wants to, but cannot, he is impotent. If he can, and
does not want to, he is wicked. But, if God both can and
wants to abolish evil, then how comes evil in the world?

EPICURUS, PHILOSOPHER

The fact of suffering undoubtedly constitutes the single
greatest challenge to the Christian faith, and has been in
every generation. Its distribution and degree appear to be
entirely random and therefore unfair. Sensitive spirits ask if
it can possibly be reconciled with God's justice and love.

JOHN STOTT, THEOLOGIAN

As an idealistic young reporter fresh out of journalism school, one of my first assignments at the *Chicago Tribune* was to write a thirty-part series in which I would profile destitute families living in the city. Having been raised in the homogenized suburbs, where being "needy" meant having only one Cadillac, I quickly found myself immersed in Chicago's underbelly of deprivation and desperation. In a way, my experience was akin to Charles Templeton's reaction to the photo of the African woman with her deceased baby.

Just a short drive from Chicago's Magnificent Mile, where the stately Tribune Tower rubs shoulders with elegant fashion boutiques and luxury hotels, I walked into the tiny, dim, and barren hovel being shared by sixty-year-old Perfecta de Jesus and her two granddaughters. They had lived there about a month, ever since their previous cockroach-infested tenement erupted in flames.

Perfecta, frail and sickly, had run out of money weeks earlier and had received a small amount of emergency food stamps. She stretched the food by serving only rice and beans with bits of meat for meal after meal. The meat ran out quickly. Then the beans. Now all that was left was a handful of rice. When the overdue public-aid check would finally come, it would be quickly consumed by the rent and utility bills, and the family would be right back where it started.

The apartment was almost completely empty, without furniture, appliances, or carpets. Words echoed off the bare walls and cold wooden floor. When her eleven-year-old granddaughter, Lydia, would set off for her half-mile walk to school on the biting-cold winter mornings, she would wear only a thin gray sweater over her short-sleeved print dress. Halfway to school, she would give the sweater to her shivering thirteen-year-old sister, Jenny, clad in just a sleeveless dress, who would wrap the sweater around herself for the rest of the way. Those were the only clothes they owned.

"I try to take care of the girls as best I can," Perfecta explained to me in Spanish. "They are good. They don't complain."[1]

Hours later, safely back in my plush lakefront high-rise with an inspiring view of Chicago's wealthiest neighborhoods, I felt staggered by the contrast. If there is a God, why would kind and decent people like Perfecta and her grandchildren be cold and hungry in the midst of one of the greatest cities in the world? Day after day as I conducted research for my series, I encountered people in circumstances that were similar or even worse. My response was to settle deeper into my atheism.

Hardships, suffering, heartbreak, man's inhumanity to man—those were my daily diet as a journalist. This wasn't looking at magazine photos from faraway places; this was the grit and pain of life, up close and personal.

I've looked into the eyes of a young mother who had just been told that her only daughter had been molested, mutilated, and murdered. I've listened to courtroom testimony describing gruesome horrors perpetrated against innocent victims. I've visited noisy and chaotic prisons, the trash heaps of society; low-budget nursing homes where the elderly languish after being abandoned by their loved ones; pediatric hospital wards where emaciated children fight vainly against the inexorable advance of cancer; and crime-addled inner cities where drug trafficking and drive-by shootings are all too common.

But nothing shocked me as much as my visit to the slums of Bombay, India. Lining both sides of the noisy, filthy, congested streets, as far as the eye could see, were small cardboard and burlap shanties, situated right next to the road where buses and cars would spew their exhaust and soot. Naked children played in the open sewage ditches that coursed through the area. People with missing limbs or bodies contorted by deformities sat passively in the dirt. Insects buzzed everywhere. It was a horrific scene, a place where, one taxi driver told me, people are born on the sidewalk, live their entire lives on the sidewalk, and die a premature death on the sidewalk.

Then I came face-to-face with a ten-year-old boy, about the same age as my son, Kyle, at the time. The Indian child was scrawny and malnourished, his hair filthy and matted. One eye was diseased and half closed; the other stared vacantly. Blood oozed from scabs on his face. He extended his hand and mumbled something in Hindi, apparently begging for coins. But his voice was a dull, lifeless monotone, as if he didn't expect any response. As if he had been drained of all hope.

Where was God in that festering hellhole? If he had the power to instantly heal that youngster, why did he turn his back? If he loved these people, why didn't he show it by rescuing them? *Is this, I wondered, the real reason: because the very presence of such awful, heart-wrenching suffering actually disproves the existence of a good and loving Father?*

Making Sense of Suffering

Everyone has encountered pain and sorrow. Heart disease claimed my father when he should have had many years left to see his grand-children grow up. I kept a vigil at a neonatal intensive care unit as my newborn daughter battled a mysterious illness that both threatened her life and baffled her doctors. I've rushed to the hospital after the anguished call from a friend whose daughter had been hit by a drunk driver, and I was holding their hands at the moment life slipped away from her. I've had to break the news to a friend's two small children that their mother had committed suicide. I've seen childhood bud-dies succumb to cancer, to Lou Gehrig's disease, to heart ailments, to car accidents. I've seen Alzheimer's ravage the mind of a loved one. I'm sure you can tell similar stories of personal pain.

We recently emerged from a century unprecedented in its cru-elty and inhumanity, where victims of tyrants like Hitler, Stalin, Pol Pot, and Mao Tse-tung are numbered in the tens of millions. The vastness of the cruelty numbs our minds, but then occasionally we come across a story that personalizes the horror and makes us shudder anew.

Like the account I read recently of an Italian journalist during World War II who was visiting a smiling Ante Pavelić, the pro-Nazi leader of Croatia. Pavelić proudly showed him a basket of what looked like oysters. It was, he said, a gift from his troops—forty pounds of human eyes. A small memento from their slaughter of Serbs, Jews, and Gypsies.[2]

We read stories like that—horrible evils like the Holocaust, the Killing Fields of Cambodia, the genocide of Rwanda, and the torture chambers of South America—and we can't help but wonder, *Where is God?* We watch television coverage of earthquakes and hurricanes in which thousands perish, and we wonder, *Why didn't God stop it?* We read the statistic that one billion people in the world lack the basic necessities of life, and we wonder, *Why doesn't God care?* We may suffer ourselves with persistent pain or aching loss or seemingly hopeless circumstances, and we wonder, *Why doesn't God help?* If he is loving and if he is all-powerful and if he is good, then surely all this suffering should not exist. And yet it does.

What's worse, it's often the innocent who are victimized. "If only villains got broken backs or cancers, if only cheaters and crooks got Parkinson's disease, we should see a sort of celestial justice in the universe," wrote agnostic-turned-Christian Sheldon Vanauken.

> But, as it is, a sweet-tempered child lies dying of a brain tumor, a happy young wife sees her husband and child killed before her eyes by a drunken driver; and . . . we soundlessly scream at the stars, "Why? Why?" A mention of God—of God's will—doesn't help a bit. How could a good God, a loving God, do that? How could He even let it happen? And no answer comes from the indifferent stars.[3]

Christian author Philip Yancey begins his celebrated book on suffering with a chapter appropriately titled "A Problem That Won't Go Away."[4] This is not just an intellectual issue to be debated in sterile academic arenas; it's an intensely personal matter that can tie our emotions into knots and leave us with spiritual vertigo— disoriented, frightened, and angry. One writer referred to the problem of pain as "the question mark turned like a fishhook in the human heart."[5]

In fact, this is the single biggest obstacle for spiritual seekers. I commissioned George Barna, the public opinion pollster, to conduct a national survey in which he asked a scientifically selected cross section of adults, "If you could ask God only one question and you knew he would give you an answer, what would you ask?" The top response, offered by 17 percent of those who said they had a question, was, "Why is there pain and suffering in the world?"[6]

Charles Templeton also demanded an answer to that question. His retreat from faith began with that *Life* magazine photo of the African mother holding her child who had died because of a simple lack of rain. In his book denouncing Christianity, Templeton recounts a litany of tragedies from ancient and modern history and then declares:

> "A loving God" could not possibly be the author of the horrors we have been describing—horrors that continue every day, have continued since time began, and will continue as long as life exists. It is an inconceivable tale of suffering and death, and because the tale is fact—is, in truth, the history of the world—it is obvious that there cannot be a loving God.[7]

Cannot? Does the presence of suffering necessarily mean the absence of God? Is this obstacle to faith insurmountable? To believe wholeheartedly in a loving and omnipotent Father, do I have to paper over the reality of evil and pain around me? As a journalist, that was simply not an option. I had to account for all the facts, for all the evidence, minimizing nothing.

I was discussing these issues with Leslie at a sensitive time in her life. Her uncle had just died, and her aunt had been diagnosed with Alzheimer's disease and terminal cancer. Rocked by that turbulence, Leslie was wary of anyone who might try to give easy answers.

"If someone thinks they can wrap everything up in a neat little package and put a fancy theological bow on it," she cautioned, "go somewhere else."

I knew she was right. That's why I placed a call to Boston College and asked to make an appointment with the author of *Making Sense Out of Suffering*—a book whose title summed up exactly what I was seeking to do.

The First Interview: Peter John Kreeft, PhD

I like to refer to Peter Kreeft as "the un-philosopher." Not that he isn't a philosopher; in fact, he's a first-rate philosophical thinker, with a doctorate from Fordham University, postgraduate study at Yale

University, and thirty-eight years of experience as a philosophy professor at Villanova University and (since 1965) Boston College. He has taught such courses as metaphysics; ethics; mysticism; sexuality; and Oriental, Greek, medieval, and contemporary philosophy, earning such honors as the Woodrow Wilson and Yale-Sterling Fellowships.

Still, if you were to conjure up a mental image of a stereotypical philosopher, Kreeft would probably not come to mind. Unfairly or not, philosophers are generally imagined to be a bit boring, speaking in vague and convoluted sentences, residing in the cloistered ivory towers of academia, and being serious to the point of dour.

In contrast, Kreeft gives real-world answers in an engaging and even entertaining way; communicates crisply, often with a memorable twist of a phrase; wears a bemused grin and can't restrain himself from cracking jokes about even the most sacrosanct subject; and, although he's sixty-two years old, can frequently be found at any given beach pursuing his hobby of surfing. (One of Kreeft's books is titled *I Surf, Therefore I Am.*)

Kreeft, a Catholic also widely read by Protestants, has written more than forty books, including *Love Is Stronger Than Death*, *Heaven: The Heart's Deepest Longing*, *Prayer: The Great Conversation*, *A Refutation of Moral Relativism*, and *Handbook of Christian Apologetics*. His whimsical imagination is especially evident in *Between Heaven and Hell*, which envisions C. S. Lewis, John F. Kennedy, and Aldous Huxley, after death, arguing about Christ, and *Socrates Meets Jesus*, in which the ancient thinker becomes a Christian at Harvard Divinity School.

I encountered Kreeft's offbeat sense of humor even before I walked into his office. While the other sixteen office doors on his drab and dimly lit corridor were undefaced, Kreeft's was festooned with Doonesbury and Dilbert cartoons and other tongue-in-cheek mementos—a drawing of a bull with a slash through it, a photo of Albert Einstein playfully sticking out his tongue, and a cartoon in which Satan greets people in hell by saying, "You'll find that there's no right or wrong here—just what works for you."

What drew me to Kreeft was his insightful book about suffering, in which he skillfully weaves a journey of discovery through Socrates, Plato, and Aristotle; through Augustine, Kierkegaard, and Dostoyevsky; through *Star Trek*, *The Velveteen Rabbit*, and *Hamlet*; and through Moses, Job, and Jeremiah. All along the way, there are clues that eventually, ultimately, finally, converge on Jesus and the tears of God.

I got there early and waited for Kreeft in the hallway. He soon arrived fresh from a philosophical conclave being held elsewhere in Boston. His brown tweed jacket, thick glasses, and neatly combed dark gray hair gave him a fatherly appearance. He sat behind his desk (under a sign that read, "No Dumping"), and we started by casually chatting about his beloved Boston Red Sox—an appropriate subject given our topic of suffering.

But then I turned a corner. There was no other approach than to hit Kreeft head-on with Templeton's blunt objections to Christianity, embodied by that *Life* magazine photo of an anguished mother clutching her dead infant in drought-ravaged Africa.

A Bear, a Trap, a Hunter, and God

Confronting Kreeft with the same emotional intensity that Templeton had displayed to me, I described the photo and then quoted the former evangelist word for word:

> I thought, *Is it possible to believe there is a loving or caring Creator when all this woman needed was rain?* How could a loving God *do this* to that woman? Who runs the rain? I don't; you don't. *He* does—or that's what I thought. But when I saw that photograph, I immediately knew it is not possible for this to happen and for there to be a loving God. There was no way. Who else but a fiend could destroy a baby and virtually kill its mother with agony—when all that was needed was *rain?* . . . And then I began . . . considering the plagues that sweep across parts

of the planet and indiscriminately kill . . . and it just became crystal clear to me that it is not possible for an intelligent person to believe there is a deity who loves.

I looked up from my notes. The professor's eyes were riveted on me. Facing him squarely, leaning forward in my chair for emphasis, I said in a rather accusatory tone, "Dr. Kreeft, you're an intelligent person and you believe in a deity who loves. How in the world would you respond to Templeton?"

Kreeft cleared his throat. "First of all," he began, "I'd focus on his words, 'it is not possible.' Even David Hume, one of history's most famous skeptics, said it's just *barely* possible that God exists. That's at least a somewhat reasonable position—to say that there's at least a small possibility. But to say there's *no* possibility that a loving God who knows far more than we do, including about our future, could possibly tolerate such evil as Templeton sees in Africa—well, that strikes me as intellectually arrogant."

That took me aback. "Really?" I asked. "How so?"

"How can a mere finite human be sure that infinite wisdom would not tolerate certain short-range evils in order for more long-range goods we couldn't foresee?" he asked.

I could see his point but needed an example. "Elaborate a bit," I prodded.

Kreeft thought for a moment. "Look at it this way," he said. "Would you agree that the difference between us and God is greater than the difference between us and, say, a bear?"

I nodded.

"Okay, then, imagine a bear in a trap and a hunter who out of sympathy wants to liberate him. He tries to win the bear's confidence, but he can't do it, so he has to shoot the bear full of drugs. The bear, however, thinks this is an attack and that the hunter is trying to kill him. He doesn't realize this is being done out of compassion.

"Then in order to get the bear out of the trap, the hunter has to push him further into the trap to release the tension on the spring. If the bear were semiconscious at that point, he would be even more convinced that the hunter was his enemy who was out to cause him suffering and pain. But the bear would be wrong. He reaches this incorrect conclusion because he's not a human being."

Kreeft let the illustration soak in for a moment. "Now," he concluded, "how can anyone be certain that's not an analogy between us and God? I believe God does the same to us sometimes, and we can't comprehend why he does it any more than the bear can understand the motivations of the hunter. As the bear could have trusted the hunter, so we can trust God."

Faith and Prejudice

I paused to think about Kreeft's point, but he continued before I could reply.

"However," he said, "I certainly don't want to demean Templeton. He's responding in a very honest and heartfelt way to the fact that something counts against God. Only in a world where faith is difficult can faith exist. I don't have faith in two plus two equals four or in the noonday sun. Those are beyond question. But Scripture describes God as a hidden God. You have to make an effort of faith to find him. There are clues you can follow.

"And if that weren't so, if there were something more or less than clues, it's difficult for me to understand how we could really be free to make a choice about him. If we had absolute proof instead of clues, then we could no more deny God than we could deny the sun. If we had no evidence at all, we could never get there. God gives us just enough evidence so that those who want him can have him. Those who want to follow the clues will.

"The Bible says, 'Seek and you will find.'[8] It doesn't say everybody will find him; it doesn't say nobody will find him. *Some* will find. Who? Those who seek. Those whose hearts are set on finding him and who follow the clues."

I jumped in. "Wait a minute—a moment ago you admitted that 'something counts against God'—that evil and suffering *are* evidence against him," I pointed out. "Aren't you conceding, therefore, that evil disproves God's existence?" I thumped my hand on his desk. "Case closed!" I declared with a mock air of triumph.

Kreeft recoiled a bit at my outburst. "No, no," he insisted, shaking his head. "First of all, evidence is not necessarily certain or conclusive. I'm saying that in this world there is evidence against and evidence for God. Augustine put it very simply: 'If there is no God, why is there so much good? If there is a God, why is there so much evil?'

"There's no question that the existence of evil is one argument against God, but in one of my books I summarize twenty arguments that point persuasively in the other direction—in favor of the existence of God.[9] Atheists must answer all twenty arguments; theists must only answer one. However, each of us gets to cast a vote. Faith is active; it demands a response. Unlike reason, which bows down faithfully to the evidence, faith is prejudiced."

That last word jumped out at me. "What do you mean, 'prejudiced'?"

"Suppose a police officer came into this room and said they just captured my wife in the act of murdering thirteen neighbors by chopping off their heads, and they have witnesses. I would laugh at him. I would say, 'No, this cannot be. You do not know her as I do.' He would say, 'Where's your evidence?' I'd say, 'It's of a different kind than yours. But there is evidence that this could not be.' So I'm prejudiced.

"However, my prejudice is a *reasonable* prejudice because it's based on the evidence I've gathered in my very real experience. So someone who knows God has evidence—and therefore prejudices, which are based on that evidence—that someone who does not know God does not have."

Evil as Evidence for God

Kreeft stopped for a few seconds before adding this unexpected and counterintuitive remark: "Besides, the evidence of evil and suffering can go both ways—it can actually be used in *favor* of God."

I sat up straight in my chair. "How," I demanded, "is *that* possible?"

"Consider this," Kreeft said. "If Templeton is right in responding to these events with outrage, that presupposes there really is a difference between good and evil. The fact that he's using the standard of good to judge evil—the fact that he's saying, quite rightly, that this horrible suffering isn't what ought to be—means that he has a notion of what ought to be, that this notion corresponds to something real, and that there is therefore a reality called the Supreme Good. Well, that's another name for God."

That sounded suspiciously like philosophical sleight of hand. Warily, I summarized Kreeft's point to see if I understood it. "You mean that unintentionally Templeton may be testifying to the reality of God because by recognizing evil he's assuming there's an objective standard on which it's based?"

"Right. If I give one student a ninety and another an eighty, that presupposes that one hundred is a real standard. And my point is this: If there is no God, where did we get the standard of goodness by which we judge evil as evil?

"What's more, as C. S. Lewis said, 'If the universe is so bad . . . how on earth did human beings ever come to attribute it to the activity of a wise and good Creator?'[10] In other words, the very presence of these ideas in our minds—that is, the idea of evil, thus of goodness and of God as the origin and standard of goodness—needs to be accounted for."

An interesting counterpunch, I mused. "Are there any other ways in which you believe evil works against atheism?" I asked.

"Yes, there are," he replied. "If there is no Creator and therefore no moment of creation, then everything is the result of evolution.

If there was no beginning or first cause, then the universe must have always existed. That means the universe has been evolving for an infinite period of time—and, by now, everything should already be perfect. There would have been plenty of time for evolution to have finished and evil to have been vanquished. But there still is evil and suffering and imperfection—and that proves the atheist wrong about the universe."

"Then atheism," I said, "is an inadequate answer to the problem of evil?"

"It's an easy answer—maybe, if I may use the word, a *cheap* answer," he said. "Atheism is cheap on people, because it snobbishly says nine out of ten people through history have been wrong about God and have had a lie at the core of their hearts.

"Think about that. How is it possible that more than 90 percent of all the human beings who have ever lived—usually in far more painful circumstances than we—could believe in God? The objective evidence, just looking at the balance of pleasure and suffering in the world, would not seem to justify believing in an absolutely good God. Yet this has been almost universally believed.

"Are they all crazy? Well, I suppose you can believe that if you're a bit of an elitist. But maybe, like Leo Tolstoy, we have to learn from the peasants. In his autobiography, he wrestles with the problem of evil. He saw that life had more suffering than pleasure and more evil than good and was therefore apparently meaningless. He was so despairing that he was tempted to kill himself. He said he didn't know how he could endure.

"Then he said, in effect, 'Wait a minute—most people *do* endure. Most people have a life that's harder than mine, and yet they find it wonderful. How can they do that? Not with explanations, but with faith.' He learned from the peasants and found faith and hope.[11]

"So atheism treats people cheaply. Also, it robs death of meaning, and if death has no meaning, how can life ultimately have meaning? Atheism cheapens everything it touches—look at the results of Communism, the most powerful form of atheism on earth.

"And in the end, when the atheist dies and encounters God instead of the nothingness they had predicted, they'll recognize that atheism was a cheap answer because it refused the only thing that's not cheap—the God of infinite value."

A Problem of Logic

Kreeft had made some interesting initial points, but we had been dancing around the subject a bit. It was time to cut to the core of the issue. Pulling out some notes I had scrawled on the airplane, I challenged Kreeft with a question that crystallized the controversy.

"Christians believe in five things," I said. "First, God exists. Second, God is all-good. Third, God is all-powerful. Fourth, God is all-wise. And, fifth, evil exists. Now, how can all of those statements be true at the same time?"

An enigmatic smile crept onto Kreeft's face. "It looks like they can't be," he conceded. "I remember a liberal preacher who once tried to dissuade me from taking up with the fundamentalists. He said, 'There's a logical problem here—you can be intelligent, or you can be honest, or you can be a fundamentalist, or any two of the three, but not all three.' And my fundamentalist friend said, 'I'd say, you can be honest, or you can be intelligent, or you can be liberal, or any of the two, but not all three.'"

I laughed at the story. "We have the same kind of logical problem here," I said.

"That's right. It seems you have to drop one of those beliefs. If God is all-powerful, he can do anything. If God is all-good, he wants only good. If God is all-wise, he knows what is good. So if all of those beliefs are true—and Christians believe they are—then it would seem that the consequence is that no evil can exist."

"But evil *does* exist," I said. "Therefore, isn't it logical to assume that such a God doesn't exist?"

"No, I'd say one of those beliefs about him must be false, or we must not be understanding it in the right way."

It was time to find out. With a sweep of my hand, I invited Kreeft to examine these three divine attributes—God being all-powerful, all-good, and all-knowing—one at a time in light of the existence of evil.

Attribute #1: God Is All-Powerful

"What does it mean when we say that God is all-powerful?" Kreeft asked, and then he answered his own question: "That means he can do everything that is meaningful, everything that is possible, everything that makes any sense at all. God cannot make himself cease to exist. He cannot make good evil."

"So," I said, "there are some things he can't do, even though he's all-powerful."

"Precisely *because* he is all-powerful, he can't do some things. He can't make mistakes. Only weak and stupid beings make mistakes. One such mistake would be to try to create a self-contradiction, like two plus two equals five or a round square.

"Now, the classic defense of God against the problem of evil is that it's not logically possible to have free will and no possibility of moral evil. In other words, once God chose to create human beings with free will, it was up to them rather than to God as to whether there was sin or not. That's what free will means. Built into the situation of God deciding to create human beings is the chance of evil and, consequently, the suffering that results."

"Then God is the creator of evil."

"No, he created the *possibility* of evil; people actualized that potentiality. The source of evil is not God's power but mankind's freedom. Even an all-powerful God could not have created a world in which people had genuine freedom and yet there was no potentiality for sin, because our freedom includes the possibility of sin within its own meaning. It's a self-contradiction—a meaningless nothing—to have a world where there's real choice while at the same time no possibility of choosing evil. To ask why God didn't create such a world is like asking why God didn't create colorless color or round squares."

"Then why didn't God create a world without human freedom?"

"Because that would have been a world without humans. Would it have been a place without hate? Yes. A place without suffering? Yes. But it also would have been a world without love, which is the highest value in the universe. That highest good never could have been experienced. Real love—our love of God and our love of each other—must involve a choice. But with the granting of that choice comes the possibility that people would choose instead to hate."

"But look at Genesis," I said. "God did create a world where people were free, and yet there was no sin."

"That's precisely what he did," Kreeft said. "After creation, he declared that the world was 'good.' People were free to choose to love God or turn away from him. However, such a world is necessarily a place where sin is freely possible—and, indeed, that potentiality for sin was actualized not by God but by people. The blame, ultimately, lies with us. He did his part perfectly; we're the ones who messed up."

"Rabbi Harold Kushner reaches a different conclusion in his bestseller *When Bad Things Happen to Good People*," I pointed out. "He says God isn't all-powerful after all—that he would *like* to help, but he just isn't capable of solving all the problems in the world. He said, 'Even God has a hard time keeping chaos in check.'"[12]

Kreeft raised an eyebrow. "For a rabbi, that's hard to understand, because the distinctively Jewish notion of God is the opposite of that," he said. "Surprisingly—against the evidence, it seems—the Jews insisted that there is a God who is all-powerful and nevertheless all-good.

"Now, that doesn't seem as reasonable as paganism, which says if there is evil in the world, then there must be many gods, each of them less than all-powerful, some of them good and some of them evil, or if there's one God, then he's facing forces he can't quite control. Until Judaism's revelation of the true God, that was a very popular philosophy."

"You don't think much of Kushner's God," I said, more as a statement than a question.

"Frankly, that God is hardly worth believing in. Do I have a big brother who's doing what he can but it's not very much? Well, who cares?" he said, shrugging his shoulders. "Practically speaking, that's the same as atheism. Rely on yourself first and then maybe God, maybe not.

"No, the evidence is that God *is* all-powerful. The point to remember is that creating a world where there's free will and no possibility of sin is a self-contradiction—and that opens the door to people choosing evil over God, with suffering being the result. The overwhelming majority of the pain in the world is caused by our choices to kill, to slander, to be selfish, to stray sexually, to break our promises, to be reckless."

Attribute #2: God Is All-Knowing

I asked Kreeft to move on to the next divine quality—God's omniscience. He pushed back his chair to get more comfortable and then looked off to the side as he collected his thoughts once more.

"Let's begin this way," he said. "God, if he is all-wise, knows not only the present but the future. And he knows not only present good and evil but also future good and evil. If his wisdom vastly exceeds ours, as the hunter's exceeds the bear's, it is at least possible—contrary to Templeton's analysis—that a loving God could deliberately tolerate horrible things like starvation because he foresees that in the long run, more people will be better and happier than if he miraculously intervened. That's at least intellectually possible."

I shook my head. "That's still hard to accept," I said. "It sounds like a cop-out to me."

"Okay, then, let's put it to the test," Kreeft replied. "You see, God has specifically shown us very clearly how this can work. He has demonstrated how the very worst thing that has ever happened in the history of the world ended up resulting in the very best thing that has ever happened in the history of the world."

"What do you mean?"

"I'm referring to deicide," he replied. "The death of God himself on the cross. At the time, nobody saw how anything good could ever result from this tragedy. And yet God foresaw that the result would be the opening of heaven to human beings. So the worst tragedy in history brought about the most glorious event in history. And if it happened there—if the ultimate evil can result in the ultimate good—it can happen elsewhere, even in our own individual lives. Here God lifts the curtain and lets us see it. Elsewhere he simply says, 'Trust me.'

"All of which would mean that human life is incredibly dramatic, like a story for which you don't know the ending rather than a scientific formula. In fact, let's follow this dramatic story line for a minute.

"Suppose you're the devil. You're the enemy of God and you want to kill him, but you can't. However, he has this ridiculous weakness of creating and loving human beings, whom you *can* get at. Aha! Now you've got hostages! So you simply come down into the world, corrupt humankind, and drag some of them to hell. When God sends prophets to enlighten them, you kill the prophets.

"Then God does the most foolish thing of all—he sends his own Son, and he plays by the rules of the world. You say to yourself, 'I can't believe he's that stupid! Love has addled his brains! All I have to do is inspire some of my agents—Herod, Pilate, Caiaphas, the Roman soldiers—and get him crucified.' And that's what you do.

"So there he hangs on the cross—forsaken by humanity and seemingly by God, bleeding to death and crying, 'My God, my God, why have you forsaken me?' What do you feel now as the devil? You feel triumph and vindication! But of course you couldn't be more wrong. This is *his* supreme triumph and your supreme defeat. He stuck his heel into your mouth and you bit it, and that blood destroyed you.

"Now, if that is not a freak occurrence, but a paradigm of the human situation, then when we bleed and when we suffer, as Christ did, maybe the same thing is happening. Maybe this is God's way of defeating the devil.

"At the time of the crucifixion, the disciples couldn't see how anything good could result; similarly, as we face struggles and trials and suffering, we sometimes can't imagine good emerging. But we've seen how it did in the case of Jesus, and we can trust it will in our case too. For instance, the greatest Christians in history seem to say that their sufferings ended up bringing them the closest to God—so this is the best thing that could happen, not the worst."

Attribute #3: God Is All-Good

That left us with God's attribute of goodness.

"*Good* is a notoriously tricky word," Kreeft began, "because even in human affairs there's such a wide range of meaning. But the difference once again between us and God is certainly greater than the difference between us and animals, and since good varies enormously between us and animals, it must vary even more enormously between us and God."

"Granted," I said. "But if I sat there and did nothing while my child got run over by a truck, I wouldn't be good in any sense of the word. I'd be an evil father if I were to do that. And God does the equivalent of that. He sits by and refuses to perform miracles to take us out of dangers even greater than being hit by a truck. So why isn't he bad?"

Kreeft nodded. "It looks like he is," he said. "But the fact that God deliberately allows certain things, which if we allowed them would turn us into monsters, doesn't necessarily count against God."

I couldn't see his reasoning. "You'll have to explain why that is," I said.

"Okay, let me give you an analogy in human relationships," he replied. "If I said to my brother, who is about my age, 'I could bail you out of a problem but I won't,' I would probably be irresponsible and perhaps wicked. But we do that with our children all the time. We don't do their homework for them. We don't put a bubble around them and protect them from every hurt.

"I remember when one of my daughters was about four or five years old and was trying to thread a needle in Brownies. It was very difficult for her. Every time she tried, she hit herself in the finger, and a couple of times she bled. I was watching her, but she didn't see me. She just kept trying and trying.

"My first instinct was to go and do it for her, since I saw a drop of blood. But wisely I held back, because I said to myself, *She can do it*. After about five minutes, she finally did it. I came out of hiding, and she said, 'Daddy, Daddy—look at what I did! Look at what I did!' She was so proud she had threaded the needle that she had forgotten all about the pain.

"That time the pain was a good thing for her. I was wise enough to have foreseen it was good for her. Now, certainly God is much wiser than I was with my daughter. So it's at least possible that God is wise enough to foresee that we need some pain for reasons we may not understand but that he foresees as being necessary to some eventual good. Therefore, he's not being evil by allowing that pain to exist.

"Dentists, athletic trainers, teachers, parents—they all know that sometimes to be good is *not* to be kind. Certainly there are times when God allows suffering and deprives us of the lesser good of pleasure in order to help us toward the greater good of moral and spiritual education. Even the ancient Greeks believed the gods taught wisdom through suffering. Aeschylus wrote, 'And even in our sleep pain that cannot forget, falls drop by drop upon the heart, and in our own despite, against our will, comes wisdom to us by the awful grace of God.'[13]

"We know that moral character gets formed through hardship, through overcoming obstacles, through enduring despite difficulties. Courage, for example, would be impossible in a world without pain. The apostle Paul testified to this refining quality of suffering when he wrote that 'suffering produces perseverance; perseverance, character; and character, hope.'[14]

"Let's face it: we learn from the mistakes we make and the suffering they bring. The universe is a soul-making machine, and part of that process is learning, maturing, and growing through difficult, challenging, and painful experiences. The point of our lives in this world isn't comfort, but training and preparation for eternity. Scripture tells us that even Jesus learned obedience through suffering[15]—and if that was true for him, why wouldn't it be even more true for us?"

Kreeft let the question hang in the air for a moment while his mental gears whirred. Then he continued. "Suppose we didn't have any suffering at all," he added. "Suppose we had drugs for every pain, free entertainment, free love—everything but pain. No Shakespeare, no Beethoven, no Boston Red Sox, no death—no meaning. Impossibly spoiled little brats—that's what we'd become.

"It's like that old *Twilight Zone* television show where a gang of bank robbers gets shot and one of them wakes up walking on fluffy clouds at the golden gate of a celestial city. A kindly, white-robed man offers him everything he wants. But soon he's bored with the gold, since everything is free, and with the beautiful girls, who only laugh when he tries to hurt them, since he has a sadistic streak.

"So he summons the Saint Peter figure.

Bank robber: There must be some mistake.
Saint Peter: No, we make no mistakes here.
Bank robber: Can't you send me back to earth?
Saint Peter: Of course not! You're dead.
Bank robber: Well, then, I must belong with my friends in the Other Place. Send me there.
Saint Peter: Oh, no, we can't do that. Rules, you know.
Bank robber: What is this place anyway?
Saint Peter: This is the place where you get everything you want.

Bank robber: But I thought I was supposed to like heaven.
Saint Peter: Heaven? Who said anything about heaven?
      Heaven is the Other Place.[16]

"The point is that a world without suffering appears more like hell than heaven."

That seemed hyperbolic. "Do you really believe that?" I asked.

"Yes, I do. In fact, if you don't, then pretend you're God and try to create a better world in your imagination. Try to create Utopia. But you have to think through the consequences of everything you try to improve. Every time you use force to prevent evil, you take away freedom. To prevent all evil, you must remove all freedom and reduce people to puppets, which means they would then lack the ability to freely choose love.

"You may end up creating a world of precision that an engineer might like—*maybe*. But one thing's for sure: you'll lose the kind of world that a Father would want."

The Megaphone of Pain

Clue by clue, Kreeft was shedding more and more light on the mystery of suffering. But each new insight seemed to spawn new questions.

"Evil people get away with hurting others all the time. Certainly God can't consider that fair," I said. "How can he stand there and watch that happen? Why doesn't he intervene and deal with all the evil in the world?"

"People *aren't* getting away with it," Kreeft insisted. "Justice delayed is not necessarily justice denied. The day will come when God will settle accounts and people will be held responsible for the evil they've perpetrated and the suffering they've caused. Criticizing God for not doing it right now is like reading half a novel and criticizing the author for not resolving the plot. God will bring accountability at the right time—in fact, the Bible says one reason he's delaying is because some people are still following the clues and have yet to find him.[17] He's actually delaying the consummation of history out of his great love for them."

"But in the meantime, doesn't the sheer amount of suffering in the world bother you?" I asked. "Couldn't God curtail at least some of the more horrific evil? One philosopher formulated an argument against God this way: First, there is no reason that would justify God's permitting so much evil rather than a lot less; second, if God exists, then there must be such a reason; so, three, God does not exist."

Kreeft was sympathetic to the problem, but wasn't buying that solution. "That's like saying it's reasonable to believe in God if six Jews died in the Holocaust, but not seven. Or sixty thousand, but not sixty thousand and one, or 5,999,999, but not six million," he said. "When you translate the general statement 'so much' into particular examples like that, it shows how absurd it is. There can't be a dividing line.

"It's true that there are some instances where quantity does become quality. Take boiling water, for example. Once a temperature of 212 degrees is reached, you get a new state—gas—and gas laws rather than liquid laws apply. But suffering isn't like that. At what point does suffering disprove the existence of God? No such point can be shown. Besides, because we're not God, we can't say how much suffering is needed. Maybe every single element of pain in the universe is necessary. How can we know?"

I chuckled. "I suppose a person could say, 'If *I'm* having the pain, then that's too much suffering in the world!'"

Kreeft laughed. "Aha, of course!" he exclaimed. "That's the subjective 'too much.' That's a classic case of anthropomorphism. If I were God, I wouldn't allow this much pain; God couldn't possibly disagree with me; God did allow this pain; and therefore there is no God."

"You said a moment ago that some pain might be necessary. That indicates there is a meaning to suffering," I said. "If so, what is it?"

"One purpose of suffering in history has been that it leads to repentance," he said. "Only after suffering, only after disaster, did Old Testament Israel, do nations, do individual people, turn back to God. Again, let's face it, we learn the hard way. To quote C. S. Lewis: 'God whispers to us in our pleasures, speaks in our conscience, but shouts in our pains: it is His megaphone to rouse a deaf world.'[18] And, of course, repentance leads to something wonderful—to blessedness, since God is the source of all joy and all life. The outcome is good—in fact, better than good.

"Simply put, I believe that suffering is compatible with God's love if it is medicinal, remedial, and necessary—that is, if we are very sick and desperately need a cure. And that's our situation. Jesus said, 'It is not the healthy who need a doctor, but the sick . . . I have not come to call the righteous, but sinners.'"[19]

"But good people suffer just as much—or sometimes more—than the bad," I pointed out. "That's what's so striking about the title of Kushner's book: *When Bad Things Happen to Good People.* How is that fair?"

"Well, the answer to that is that there are no good people," Kreeft replied.

"What about that old saying, 'God don't make no junk'?'"

"Yes, we're ontologically good—we still bear God's image—but morally we're not. His image in us has been tarnished. The prophet Jeremiah said that 'from the least to the greatest, all are greedy for gain,'[20] and the prophet Isaiah said, 'All of us have become like one who is unclean, and all our righteous acts are like filthy rags.'[21] Our good deeds are stained with self-interest and our demands for justice are mixed with lust for vengeance. Ironically, it's the best people who most readily recognize and admit their own shortcomings and sin.

"We are good stuff gone bad, a defaced masterpiece, a rebellious child. Lewis pointed out that we're not just imperfect people who need growth, but we're rebels who need to lay down our arms.[22] Pain and suffering are frequently the means by which we become motivated to finally surrender to God and to seek the cure of Christ.

"That's what we need most desperately. That's what will bring us the supreme joy of knowing Jesus. Any suffering, the great Christians from history will tell you, is worth that result."

Bearing the Pain

I sat back in my chair and reflected on what Kreeft had said so far. Some of his arguments were stronger than others, but at least he wasn't merely offering canned explanations. The clues seemed to be leading somewhere.

I decided to ask him about a quote from Augustine: "Since God is the highest good, He would not allow any evil to exist in His works unless his omnipotence and goodness were such as to bring good even out of evil."[23] After reading him those words, I said, "Does that mean suffering and evil contain the potential for good?"

"Yes, I believe all suffering contains at least the opportunity for good," came his response, "but not everyone actualizes that potential. Not all of us learn and benefit from suffering; that's where free will comes in. One prisoner in a concentration camp will react quite differently from another, because of the choice each one makes to respond to the environment.

"But just about every human being can reflect on their past and say, 'I learned from that hardship. I didn't think I would at the time, but I'm a bigger and better person for having endured it and persevered through it.' Even people without religious faith are aware of that dimension of suffering. And if we can bring good out of evil even without bringing God into the picture, you can imagine how much more, with God's help, evil can work out for the greater good."

Bringing God into the picture, however, raised another issue: If he loves people, how can he emotionally tolerate the ongoing onslaught of pain and suffering? Wouldn't it overwhelm him? I pulled out Templeton's book and read Kreeft this quote:

Jesus said, "Are not five sparrows sold for a penny, and not one of them is forgotten before God; and are you not of more value than many sparrows?" But if God grieves over the death of one sparrow, how could even his eternal spirit bear the sickness, suffering, and death of the multiplied millions of men, women, children, animals, birds, and other sensate creatures, in every part of the world, in every century since time began?[24]

"I think Mr. Templeton is anthropomorphizing God by saying, 'I couldn't imagine how any intelligent being could bear this,'" Kreeft said. "And, yes, he's right—we *can't* imagine it. But we can believe it. God does, in fact, weep over every sparrow and grieve over every evil and every suffering. So the suffering that Jesus endured on the cross is literally unimaginable. It's not just what you and I would have experienced in our own finite human agony, physical and mental, but all the sufferings of the world were there.

"Let's go back to Templeton's photo of the starving woman in Africa—all she needed was rain. *Where is God?* He was entering into her agony. Not just her physical agony, but her moral agony. *Where is God? Why doesn't he send the rain?* God's answer is the incarnation. He himself entered into all that agony; he himself bore all of the pain of this world. And that's unimaginable and shattering and even more impressive than the divine power of creating the world in the first place.

"Just imagine every single pain in the history of the world, all rolled together into a ball, eaten by God, digested, fully tasted, eternally. In the act of creating the world, God not only said, 'Let there be pretty little bunny rabbits and flowers and sunsets, but also let there be blood and guts and the buzzing flies around the cross.' In a sense, Templeton is right. God is intimately involved in the act of creating a world of suffering. He didn't do it—we did it—yet he did say, 'Let this world be.'

"And if he did that and then just sat back and said, 'Well, it's your fault after all'—although he'd be perfectly justified in doing that—I don't see how we could love him. The fact that he went beyond justice and quite incredibly took all the suffering upon himself, makes him so winsome that the answer to suffering is—" Kreeft's eyes darted around the room as he searched for the right words. "The answer," he said, "is . . . how could you not love this being who went the extra mile, who practiced more than he preached, who entered into our world, who suffered our pains, who offers himself to us in the midst of our sorrows? What more could he do?"

I said, "In effect, then, the answer to Templeton's question about how God could bear all that suffering is—he did."

"He did!" Kreeft declared. "God's answer to the problem of suffering is that he came right down into it. Many Christians try to get God off the hook for suffering; God put himself on the hook, so to speak, on the cross. And therefore the practical conclusion is that if we want to be with God, we have to be with suffering; we have to not avoid the cross, either in thought or in fact. We must go where he is, and the cross is one of the places where he is. And when he sends us the sunrises, we thank him for the sunrises; when he sends us sunsets and deaths and sufferings and crosses, we thank him for that."

I bristled. "Is it possible, really, to thank God for the pain that befalls us?"

"Yes. In heaven, we will do exactly that. We will say to God, 'Thank you so much for this little pain I didn't understand at the time and that little pain that I didn't understand at the time; these I now see were the most precious things in my life.'

"Even if I don't find myself emotionally capable of doing that right now, even if I cannot honestly say to God in the middle of pain, 'God, thank you for this pain,' but have to say instead, 'Deliver me from evil,' that's perfectly right and perfectly honest—yet I believe that's not the last word. The last words of the Lord's Prayer aren't 'deliver us from evil'; the last words are, 'Yours is the kingdom and the power and the glory forever.'

"I do think that any fairly mature Christian can look back on their life and identify some moment of suffering that drew them much closer to God than they had ever thought possible. Before this happened, they would have said, 'I don't really see how this can accomplish any good at all,' but after they emerge from the suffering, they say, 'That's amazing. I learned something I never thought I could have learned. I didn't think that my weak and rebellious will was capable of such strength, but God, with his grace, gave me the strength for those moments.' If it weren't for suffering, it wouldn't have been possible.

"The closeness to God, the similarity to God, the conformity to God, not just the feeling of being close to God but the ontological real closeness to God, the Godlikeness of the soul, emerges from suffering with remarkable efficiency."

"You mentioned heaven," I said. "And the Bible does talk about our sufferings in this world being light and momentary compared to what God's followers will experience in heaven.[25] How does the heaven part play into all this story?"

Kreeft's eyes widened. "If it weren't for that, there would hardly be a story," he said. "Excise all the references to heaven from the New Testament, and you have very little left. Teresa of Ávila is reported to have said, 'In light of heaven, the worst suffering on earth, a life full of the most atrocious tortures on earth, will be seen to be no more serious than one night in an inconvenient hotel.'[26] That's a challenging or even an outrageous statement! But she didn't speak from the kind of insulated bubble that so many of us live in; she spoke from a life that was full of suffering.

"The apostle Paul uses another outrageous word in a similar context when he's comparing earthly pleasures with the pleasure of knowing Christ. He said the privileges of Roman citizenship, of being a Pharisee of the Pharisees, of being highly educated, of being blameless in regard to the law—all of this, as compared to knowing Christ Jesus, is 'dung.'[27] That's a very bold word!

"Similarly, compared with knowing God eternally, compared to the intimacy with God that Scripture calls a spiritual marriage, nothing else counts. If the way to that is through torture, well, torture is nothing compared with that. Yes, it's enormous in itself, but compared to that, it's nothing.

"So the answer to Templeton is, yes, you're perfectly right in saying that this photograph of the African woman is outrageous. This lack of rain, this starvation, is indeed outrageous in itself. And in one sense, the answer is not to figure it out; one answer is to look into the face of God and compare those two things.

"On the one side of the scale, this torture or all the tortures of the world; on the other side of the scale, the face of God—the God available to all who seek him in the midst of their pain. The good of God, the joy of God, is going to infinitely outweigh all of the sufferings—and even the joys—of this world."

The Power of God's Presence

I was glad that Kreeft had brought the conversation back around to the woman from Templeton's photograph. I didn't want the interview to get too far afield from her. She personalized the issue of suffering, standing as a powerful representative of the world's one billion destitute people.

"If she were here right now," I said to Kreeft, "what would you say to her?"

Kreeft didn't hesitate. "Nothing," he said simply.

I blinked in disbelief. *"Nothing?"*

"Not at first, anyway," he said. "I'd let her talk to me. The founder of an organization for those with multiple disabilities says he works with this population for a very selfish reason: they teach him something much more valuable than he could ever teach them—namely, who he is. That sounds sentimental, but it's true.

"One of my four children has moderate disabilities, and I've learned more from her than from the other three. I've learned that

I'm disabled and that we're all disabled, and listening to her helps me understand myself.

"So the first thing we need to do with this woman is listen to her. Be aware of her. See her pain. Feel her pain. We live in a relative bubble of comfort, and we look at pain as an observer, as a philosophical puzzle or theological problem. That's the wrong way to look at pain. The thing to do with pain is to enter it, be one with her, and then you learn something from it.

"In fact, it's significant that most objections to the existence of God from the problem of suffering come from outside observers who are quite comfortable, whereas those who actually suffer are, as often as not, made into stronger believers by their suffering."

That's a phenomenon many writers have noted. After wide-ranging research into the topic of suffering, Philip Yancey wrote, "As I visited people whose pain far exceeded my own . . . I was surprised by its effects. Suffering seemed as likely to reinforce faith as to sow agnosticism."[28] Scottish theologian James S. Stewart said, "It is the spectators, the people who are outside, looking at the tragedy, from whose ranks the skeptics come; it is not those who are actually in the arena and who know suffering from the inside. Indeed, the fact is that it is the world's greatest sufferers who have produced the most shining examples of unconquerable faith."[29]

"Why is that?" I asked Kreeft.

His response was crisp. "Free will," he said. "There's a story of two rabbis in a concentration camp. One had lost his faith and said there is no God; the other had kept his faith and said, 'God will rescue us.' Both were in a line to enter the death showers. The believer looked around and said, 'God will rescue us,' but when his turn came to go in, his last words were, 'There is no God.'

"Then the unbelieving rabbi, who had constantly heckled the other rabbi's faith, entered the gas chamber with the prayer 'Shema, Israel' on his lips. He became a believer. Free will, both ways. Why do some people in starving Africa or concentration camps become believers and some lose their faith? That's a mystery of human unpredictability."

"Let's go back to the woman," I replied. "You said we should listen and react to her, which sounds like a good thing. But there must be more."

"Yes," he said. "We would want to be Jesus to her, to minister to her, to love her, to comfort her, to embrace her, to weep with her. Our love—a reflection of God's love—should spur us to help her and others who are hurting."

Kreeft gestured toward the hallway. "On my door there's a cartoon of two turtles. One says, 'Sometimes I'd like to ask why he allows poverty, famine, and injustice when he could do something about it.' The other turtle says, 'I'm afraid God might ask me the same question.' Those who have Jesus' heart toward hurting people need to live out their faith by alleviating suffering where they can, by making a difference, by embodying his love in practical ways."

"That cartoon reminds me of the way God likes to turn questions around," I commented.

"Yes, he's constantly doing that. This happened to Job. Job was wondering who God was, because it looked as if God was a cosmic sadist. At the end of the book of Job, the all-time classic reflection on the problem of suffering, God finally shows up with the answer—and the answer is a question.

"He says to Job, 'Who are you? Are you God? Did you write this script? Were you there when I laid the foundations of the earth?' And Job realizes the answer is no. Then he's satisfied. Why? *Because he sees God!* God doesn't write him a book. He could have written the best book on the problem of evil ever written. Instead, he shows himself to Job."

"And that satisfied him—"

"Yes! It *has* to—that's what's going to satisfy us forever in heaven. I think Job gets a foretaste of heaven at the end of the book of Job, because he meets God. If God had given him only words, it would mean that Job could dialogue and ask God another question and God would give a good answer and Job would ask another question the next day and the next day, because Job was a very demanding philosopher. This would go on and on and never end. What could make it end? God's presence!

"God didn't let Job suffer because he lacked love, but because he *did* love, in order to bring Job to the point of encountering God face-to-face, which is humanity's supreme happiness. Job's suffering hollowed out a big space in him so that God and joy could fill it.

"As we look at human relationships, what we see is that lovers don't want explanations, but presence. And what God is, essentially, is presence—the doctrine of the Trinity says God is three persons who are present to each other in perfect knowledge and perfect love. That's why God is infinite joy. And insofar as we can participate in that presence, we too have infinite joy. So that's what Job has—even on his dung heap, even before he gets any of his worldly goods back—once he sees God face-to-face.

"As I said, this makes sense even among human beings. Let's say Romeo and Juliet have a much deeper and more mature love than in Shakespeare's play. Let's say that what Romeo wants most in all the world is Juliet. And let's say that he has lost all his friends and possessions, and he's bleeding and he thinks Juliet is dead.

"Then he sees Juliet rise up and say, 'Romeo, where are you? I'm not dead; are you?' Is Romeo completely happy? Yes. *Completely* happy? Yes. Does he mind at all that he's bleeding and tattered and poor? Not at all! He would much rather be in love in the South Bronx than divorced in Honolulu."

Every Tear, His Tear

We were clearly moving toward the climax of our discussion. The clues Kreeft had mentioned at the outset of our interview were converging, and I could sense an increasing passion and conviction in his voice. I wanted to see more of his heart—and I wouldn't be disappointed.

"The answer, then, to suffering," I said in trying to sum up where we'd come, "is not an answer at all."

"Correct," he emphasized, leaning forward as he pleaded his case. "It's the Answerer. It's Jesus himself. It's not a bunch of words; it's *the* Word. It's not a tightly woven philosophical argument; it's a person. *The* person. The answer to suffering cannot just be an abstract idea, because this isn't an abstract issue; it's a personal issue. It requires a personal response. The answer must be someone, not just something, because the issue involves someone—*God, where are you?*"

That question almost echoed in his small office. It demanded a response. To Kreeft, there is one—a very real one. A living One.

"Jesus is there, sitting beside us in the lowest places of our lives," he said. "Are we broken? He was broken, like bread, for us. Are we despised? He was despised and rejected by mankind. Do we cry out that we can't take any more? He was a man of sorrows and acquainted with grief. Do people betray us? He himself was sold out. Are our tenderest relationships broken? He too loved and was rejected. Do people turn from us? They hid their faces from him as from a leper.

"Does he descend into all of our hells? *Yes*, he does. From the depths of a Nazi death camp, Corrie ten Boom wrote, 'There is no pit so deep that Jesus is not deeper still.'[30] He not only rose from the dead; he changed the meaning of death and therefore of all the little deaths—the sufferings that anticipate death and make up parts of it.

"He is gassed in Auschwitz. He is sneered at in Soweto. He is mocked in Northern Ireland. He is enslaved in Sudan. He's the one we love to hate, yet to us he has chosen to return love. Every tear we shed becomes his tear. He may not wipe them away yet, but he will."

He paused, his confident tone downshifting to tentative. "In the end, God has only given us partial explanations," he said slowly, a shrug in his voice. "Maybe that's because he saw that a better explanation wouldn't have been good for us. I don't know why. As a philosopher, I'm obviously curious. Humanly, I wish he had given us more information."

With that, he looked fully into my face.

"But he knew Jesus was more than an explanation," he said firmly. "*He* is what we really need. If your friend is sick and dying, the most important thing they want is not an explanation; they want you to sit with them. They're terrified of being alone more than anything else. So God has not left us alone."

Kreeft leaned back in his chair and let himself relax. There was only one more thing he wanted me to know.

"And for that," he said, "*I love him.*"

Drawing Good from Evil

Less than an hour later, everything was quiet in the car as it snaked through Boston's rain-slickened streets on the way back to the airport. My friend Marc Harrienger, a longtime Boston resident, had graciously volunteered to drive me to and from Kreeft's office. Looking out the window at nothing in particular, I was reviewing the interview in my mind. Most of all, I was wondering how the African woman would have responded to the philosopher's earnest words.

Marc had sat through the interview, listening intently from a wooden chair propped against the wall. This was not a topic of idle speculation to him.

He broke the silence in the car. "It's true," he said.

"What's true?" I asked.

"What Kreeft said—it's true. I know it. I've lived it."

Several years earlier, Marc had been shoveling snow on his driveway when his wife said she was going to move the car and asked him to watch their young daughter. As the car backed out, they were suddenly thrust into the worst nightmare parents can imagine: their toddler was crushed beneath a wheel.

Like the African woman, Marc has known what it's like to hold a dying child in his arms. While I wasn't able to talk with that grieving mother, I could converse with him.

So deep was Marc's initial despair that he had to ask God to help him breathe, to help him eat, to help him function at the most fundamental level. Otherwise, he was paralyzed by the emotional pain. But he increasingly felt God's presence, his grace, his warmth, and his comfort, and very slowly, over time, his wounds began to heal.

Having experienced God at his point of greatest need, Marc would emerge from this crucible a changed person, abandoning his career in business to attend seminary. Through his suffering—though he never would have chosen it, though it was horribly painful, though it was life-shattering at the time—Marc has been transformed into someone who would devote the rest of his life to bringing God's compassion to others who are alone in their desperation.

In the pulpit for the first time, Marc was able to draw on his own experiences with God in the depths of sorrow. People were captivated because his own loss had given him special insights, empathy, and credibility. In the end, dozens responded by saying they too wanted to know this Jesus, this God of tears. Now other hearts were being healed because Marc's had been broken. From one couple's despair emerged new hope for many.

"Sometimes skeptics scoff at the Bible telling us that God can cause good to emerge from our pain if we run toward him instead of away from him," Marc said. "But I've watched it happen in my own life. I've experienced God's goodness through deep pain, and no skeptic can dispute that. The God the skeptic denies is the same God who held our hands in the deep, dark places; who strengthened our marriage; who deepened our faith; who increased our reliance on him; who gave us two more children; and who infused our lives with new purpose and meaning so that we can make a difference to others."

I asked gently, "Do you wish you had more answers about why suffering happens in the first place?"

"We live in a broken world; Jesus was honest enough to tell us we'd have trials and tribulations.[31] Sure, I'd like to understand more about why. But Kreeft's conclusion was right—the ultimate answer is Jesus' presence. That sounds sappy, I know. But just wait—when your world is rocked, you don't want philosophy or theology as much as you want the reality of Christ. He *was* the answer for me. He was the very answer we needed."

The existence of pain and suffering is a powerful accusation against God. The question, however, is whether the evidence succeeds in convicting him. I thought Kreeft's deft analysis and analogies went a long way toward undermining this formidable obstacle to faith, but many other kinds of objections remained. This was just the beginning of a long journey of discovery, and I decided to withhold my final verdict until all the obstacles to faith were confronted and all the facts were in.

In the meantime, prominent British pastor John R. W. Stott, who acknowledged that suffering is "the single greatest challenge to the Christian faith," has reached his own conclusion:

> I could never myself believe in God, if it were not for the cross . . . In the real world of pain, how could one worship a God who was immune to it? I have entered many Buddhist temples in different Asian countries and stood respectfully before the statue of Buddha, his legs crossed, arms folded, eyes closed, the ghost of a smile playing round his mouth, a remote look on his face, detached from the agonies of the world. But each time after a while I have had to turn away. And in imagination I have turned instead to that lonely, twisted, tortured figure on the cross, nails through hands and feet, back lacerated, limbs wrenched, brow bleeding from thorn-pricks, mouth dry and intolerably thirsty, plunged in Godforsaken darkness. That is the God for me! He laid aside his immunity to pain. He entered

our world of flesh and blood, tears and death. He suffered for us. Our sufferings become more manageable in light of his. There is still a question mark against human suffering, but over it we boldly stamp another mark, the cross that symbolizes divine suffering. "The cross of Christ . . . is God's only self-justification in such a world" as ours.[32]

Deliberations
Questions for Reflection or Group Study

1. How have difficulties, challenges, and even pain shaped your character and values? How are you different today as a result of the problems you've had to face in life? Can you ever imagine thanking God someday for how suffering has molded you? Kreeft said, "I believe all suffering contains at least the opportunity for good." Was that true in your case?

2. What were Kreeft's strongest points? What were his weakest? If you had an opportunity to question him, what would you ask? Based on his other observations, how do you think he might respond to your question?

3. If you were God, how would you have designed the world differently? As you remove suffering or evil and tinker with people's free will, think through the consequences that would result. How would people form character in your Utopia? Would they be motivated to seek God in the midst of their pleasures? If you supernaturally intervened to eliminate evil, where would you draw the line to prevent murder? Child abuse? Theft? Slander? Evil thoughts that may prompt evil actions? At what point are people turned into puppets who lack free will and are therefore unable to truly express love?

4. If Marc were to sit down with the woman in the *Life* magazine photo, what three things do you think he would say to her? How do you believe she might respond?

For Further Evidence
More Resources on This Topic

Geisler, Norman. *If God, Why Evil? A New Way to Think about the Question.* Minneapolis: Bethany House, 2011.

Greig, Pete. *God on Mute: Engaging the Silence of Unanswered Prayer.* Grand Rapids: Zondervan, 2020.

Jones, Clay. *Why Does God Allow Evil? Compelling Answers for Life's Toughest Questions.* Eugene, OR: Harvest House, 2017.

Keller, Timothy. *Walking with God through Pain and Suffering.* New York: Penguin, 2015.

Kreeft, Peter. *Making Sense Out of Suffering.* Ann Arbor, MI: Servant, 1986.

Lewis, C. S. *The Problem of Pain.* 1940. Reprint, New York: HarperCollins, 2001.

Meister, Chad. *Evil: A Guide for the Perplexed.* 2nd ed. New York: Bloomsbury Academic, 2018.

Orr-Ewing, Amy. *Where Is God in All the Suffering?* Charlotte, NC: Good Book, 2020.

Palau, Luis. *Where Is God When Bad Things Happen? Finding Solace in Times of Trouble.* New York: Doubleday, 1999.

Wright, N. T. *Evil and the Justice of God.* Downers Grove, IL: InterVarsity, 2013.

Since Miracles Contradict Science, They Cannot Be True

The Virgin Birth, the Resurrection, the Raising of
Lazarus . . . even the Old Testament miracles, all are
freely used for religious propaganda, and very effective they
are with an audience of unsophisticates and children.

RICHARD DAWKINS, ATHEIST

It is not just a provocative rumor that God has acted in history,
but a fact worthy of our intellectual conviction. The miracles
of Christianity are not an embarrassment to the Christian
worldview. Rather, they are testimony to the compassion of
God for human beings benighted by sin and circumstance.

GARY HABERMAS, CHRISTIAN

I've seen guilty defendants squirm and sweat on the witness stand as they feel the noose of justice slowly tightening around their necks. They try to lie their way out of their predicament. They concoct improbable stories in a futile effort to explain away incriminating evidence. They manufacture transparently false alibis; they cast blame on innocent people; they attempt to discredit police and prosecutors; they rewrite history; they deny and obfuscate and try to hoodwink the judge and jurors.

But there's one tactic I've never seen: a defendant claiming that the reason his fingerprints ended up on the murder weapon is that somehow, for some inexplicable reason, an act of God occurred, a mysterious, unrepeatable, supernatural event that made his fingerprints suddenly appear somewhere he had never touched.

Once a defendant tried a "Twinkie defense" by making the dubious assertion that his elevated sugar levels were somehow responsible for his criminal behavior, but not even the most audacious defendant would try a "miracle defense."

Why? Because nobody would believe them! After all, we're modern and scientific people living in the third millennium. We don't subscribe to superstition, sorcery, or direct intervention from some unseen divine source. Claiming a miracle would be so blatantly silly that even the most desperate defendant wouldn't resort to that strategy.

One time I saw Penn and Teller, the comedian-magicians, select a ten-year-old boy named Isaiah from the audience and show him a long strip of polyester, which they proceeded to knot and cut in the middle. Then with a big flourish they shook out the cloth and—voilà!—it was in one piece again.

"What do you think?" Penn asked little Isaiah. "Was that a miracle or a magic trick?"

Isaiah didn't hesitate. "A magic trick," he replied with confidence.

A mere child, it seems, is smart enough to know that when we can't quite understand what might have caused a mysterious event, there's still undoubtedly a reasonable explanation apart from the miraculous.

I knew from my conversation with agnostic Charles Templeton that he had shed his belief in miracles many years ago. "Our early forefathers sought within the limits of their experience to interpret life's imponderables, usually attributing the inexplicable to the intervention of one or more of their gods, demi-deities, and evil spirits," he wrote. "But surely . . . it is time to have done with primitive speculation and superstition and look at life in rational terms."[1]

There are scientists who agree, predicting that the march of knowledge will ultimately trample belief in supernatural events. In 1937, German physicist Max Planck said, "The faith in miracles must yield ground, step by step, before the steady and firm advance of the forces of science, and its total defeat is indubitably a mere matter of time."[2]

Atheist Richard Dawkins, professor of public understanding of science at Oxford University and author of *The Selfish Gene*, believes that time is rapidly coming. "We're working on . . . a complete understanding of the universe and everything that is in it," he said in a television interview.[3]

That means *voilà!*—as with Penn and Teller's magically restored sash, there would be no need to appeal to the miraculous in order to explain away what previously had been shrouded in mystery.

But can a person be scientifically sophisticated and still believe in the possibility of miracles? "My faith can be summed up in this one paradox: I believe in science, and I believe in God," said nuclear physicist Hugh Siefken. "I plan to continue testifying to both."[4] He and many other scientists see no inherent conflict between their profession and their conclusion that a miracle-working God is responsible for creating and sustaining the universe.

Is that a form of professional denial? Can a person write off elves and fairies as being fanciful and yet at the same time embrace manna from heaven, the virgin birth, and the resurrection as being credible events of history? If miracles are direct violations of natural laws, then how can a reasonable person believe they could ever occur?

I knew that William Lane Craig was a rational man. And I was aware that he has used his considerable intellectual skills to defend the idea that God has intervened—and still does—in the world through miraculous acts. I called him and asked whether he'd be willing to let me question him on the topic.

"Sure," he said. "Come on down."

I jotted down a long list of challenges and booked a flight to Atlanta. On the plane, I mused that primitive people probably would have considered jet travel to be a miracle. How else could fifty tons of metal be kept aloft in apparent defiance of the law of gravity? Surely God's invisible hand must be beneath it.

People today know better. They understand aerodynamics and jet propulsion. But has our knowledge of science and technology really rendered all belief in miracles obsolete? Or would Craig be able to provide convincing evidence that a person can be sober-minded and discerning while at the same time maintaining the validity of the miraculous?

The Second Interview: William Lane Craig, PhD

My initial reaction to seeing Bill Craig was disbelief. His beard, which for twenty-three years had given him a serious and scholarly demeanor, was gone. My face must have registered my shock.

"I turned fifty," he explained, "so I celebrated by shaving it off."

Craig ushered me down a flight of stairs to his office, a well-organized room dominated by a dark wood desk and floor-to-ceiling bookshelves with neatly arranged rows of books and scholarly journals. I settled into a comfortable chair while Craig sat behind the desk, leaning back in a leather-clad office chair that protested with a loud squeak.

Craig has written extensively about miracles, especially the resurrection of Jesus. His books include *Reasonable Faith, Knowing the Truth about the Resurrection, The Historical Argument for the Resurrection of Jesus,* and *Assessing the New Testament Evidence for the Historicity of the Resurrection of Jesus,* and he contributed to *In Defense of Miracles, Does God Exist?, Jesus under Fire,* and *The Intellectuals Speak Out about God.*

He holds doctorates in philosophy from the University of Birmingham, England, and in theology from the University of Munich, and is currently a research professor of philosophy at the Talbot School of Theology. He is a member of nine professional societies, including the American Academy of Religion, Society of

Biblical Literature, and the American Philosophical Association, and he has written for *New Testament Studies, Journal for the Study of the New Testament, Journal of the American Scientific Affiliation, Gospel Perspectives, Philosophy,* and other scholarly publications.

Sans beard and wearing blue jeans, Craig looked a decade younger than his age, with piercing blue eyes, brown hair combed casually to the side, and a quick and enthusiastic laugh. He stroked his chin—subconsciously missing his beard perhaps—as he listened intently to my first question, which admittedly came with an edge of challenge.

"Okay, Dr. Craig, you're an intelligent and educated individual," I began. "Tell me: How can a modern and rational person still believe in babies being born from virgins, people walking on water, and cadavers emerging alive from tombs?"

Craig smiled. "It's funny you should ask specifically about the virgin birth," he replied, "because that was a major stumbling block to my becoming a Christian. I thought it was totally absurd."

"Really?" I said. "What happened?"

"When the Christian message was first shared with me as a teenager, I had already studied biology. I knew that for the virgin birth to be true, a Y chromosome had to be created out of nothing in Mary's ovum, because Mary didn't possess the genetic material to produce a male child. To me, this was utterly fantastic. It just didn't make sense."

"You're not alone," I observed. "Other skeptics have problems with it too. How did you proceed?"

Craig thought back for a moment. "Well, I sort of put that issue aside and became a Christian anyway, even though I didn't really believe in the virgin birth. But then after becoming a Christian, it occurred to me that if I really do believe in a God who created the universe, then for him to create a Y chromosome would be child's play!"

I told Craig that I found it interesting he could have become a Christian despite misgivings about a doctrine as significant as the virgin birth.

"I guess the authenticity of the person of Jesus and the truth of his message were so powerful that they simply overwhelmed any residual doubts I had," he replied.

I pressed him by asking, "Weren't you rushing headlong into something you didn't totally accept?"

"No, I think this can be a good procedure," he said. "You don't need to have all your questions answered to come to faith. You just have to say, 'The weight of the evidence seems to show this is true, so even though I don't have answers to all my questions, I'm going to believe and hope for answers in the long run.' That's what happened with me."

"Does a person have to suspend their critical judgment in order to believe in something as improbable as miracles?"

Craig sat upright in his chair and raised his index finger as if to punctuate his point. "Only if you believe that God does not exist!" he stressed. "Then I would agree—the miraculous would be absurd. But if there is a creator who designed and brought the universe into being, who sustains its existence moment by moment, who is responsible for the very natural laws that govern the physical world, then certainly it's rational to believe that the miraculous is possible."

Miracles versus Science

We were already getting into the interview but hadn't yet paused to define our terms. Before going any further, I knew it was important to settle on what *miracle* means.

"We throw around the word pretty haphazardly," I said. Harking back to my day thus far, I added, "For example, I might say, 'It was a miracle I made my flight to Atlanta,' or, 'It's a miracle I found your house.' Is that being too loose with the word?"

"Yes, I think it's a misuse to talk about these things as miracles," he said. "They're clearly natural events with natural consequences."

"Then how do you define the term?"

Craig spelled out his definition with precision. "In the proper sense," he said, "a miracle is an event that is not producible by the natural causes operative at the time and place the event occurs."

As he said it, I silently repeated the definition in order to cement it in my mind. I mulled it over for a few moments before continuing with what I considered to be the next logical question.

"But then isn't there a contradiction between science and miracles?" I asked. "Atheistic philosopher Michael Ruse said, 'Creationists believe the world started miraculously. But miracles lie outside of science, which by definition deals with the natural, the repeatable, that which is governed by law.'"[5]

"Notice that Ruse does not say miracles are *contradictory* to science," Craig pointed out. "He says miracles lie *outside* of science, and that's quite different. I think a Christian who believes in miracles could agree with him on that. He could say that miracles, properly speaking, lie outside the province of natural science—but that's not to say they contradict science."

I tried to digest the distinction. "Can you think of another example of something like that?" I asked.

Craig thought for a moment before answering. "Well, ethics, for instance, lies outside of the province of science," he replied. "Science doesn't make ethical judgments. So I wouldn't necessarily object to Ruse's statement. He's saying that the goal of science is to seek natural explanations, and therefore miracles lie outside of the scientific realm."

Before I could ask another question, Craig spoke up again. "I should add, though, that you can do a theistic form of science. For example, there's a whole movement of people like mathematician William Dembski and biochemist Michael Behe who infer by principled means that there is an Intelligent Designer of the universe and the biological world.[6] They aren't being arbitrary—from a rational and scientific perspective, they're concluding from the evidence that there must be an intelligent Creator."

"So," I said, "you're disagreeing with the great skeptic David Hume, who defined miracles as being violations of the laws of nature."

"Yes, absolutely. That's an improper understanding of miracles," he said. "You see, natural laws have implicit *ceteris paribus* conditions—this is Latin, meaning 'all other things being equal.' In other words, natural laws assume that no other natural or supernatural factors are interfering with the operation that the law describes."

"Can you give me an example of that?"

Craig's eyes swept the room in search of an illustration. He finally landed on one as near as his own body.

"Well, it's a law of nature that oxygen and potassium combust when they're combined," he explained. "But I have oxygen and potassium in my body, and yet I'm not bursting into flames. Does that mean it's a miracle and I'm violating the laws of nature? No, because the law merely states what happens under idealized conditions, assuming no other factors are interfering. In this case, however, there *are* other factors interfering with the combustion, and so it doesn't take place. That's not a violation of the law.

"Similarly, if there's a supernatural agent that is working in the natural world, then the idealized conditions described by the law are no longer in effect. The law isn't violated because the law has an implicit provision that nothing is messing around with the conditions."

I told Craig that his explanation reminded me of a conversation I had several years earlier with J. P. Moreland, the noted philosopher who wrote *Christianity and the Nature of Science*. He used an illustration of the law of gravity, which says that if you drop an object, it will fall to the earth. But, he said, if an apple falls from a tree and you reach out to catch it before it hits the ground, you're not violating or negating the law of gravity; you're merely intervening.

"Yes, that's my point with the *ceteris paribus* conditions," Craig said. "The law of gravity states what will happen under idealized conditions with no natural or supernatural factors intervening. Catching the apple doesn't overturn the law of gravity or require the formulation of a new law. It's merely the intervention of a person with free will who overrides the natural causes operative in that particular circumstance. And that, essentially, is what God does when he causes a miracle to occur."

That made sense to me. I knew, however, that some scientists would dismiss the miraculous as mere superstition. I decided to pursue this line of questioning further.

Real Acts of God

I asked Craig what he thought about physicist Max Planck's prediction that faith in miracles would inevitably yield ground to the advance of science and biologist Richard Dawkins's remark that scientists would someday understand the workings of the universe and thus vanquish the need for miraculous explanations. Craig's reaction surprised me.

"I think they're right," he declared.

I looked up from my notes, thinking he had perhaps misunderstood my question. "Excuse me?" I said.

"Really," he insisted, "I think they're correct—insofar as some superstitious people use miracles as an excuse for ignorance and sort of punt to God every time they can't explain something. I think it's a good thing that science will squeeze out that kind of simplistic thinking.

"But those aren't the miracles I've been talking about. I'm referring to events by which, in a principled way, we could legitimately infer that there was a supernatural agent intervening in the process. Those miracles—*real acts of God*—won't be squeezed out by the advance of science, because they're not based on an appeal to ignorance. They're substantiated by the weight of the scientific and historical evidence.

"Michael Behe does this in his book *Darwin's Black Box*. Behe explores 'irreducible complexity' in nature—organisms that could not have evolved step-by-step by a gradual Darwinian process of natural selection and genetic mutation. Now, he's not saying that this is merely scientifically inexplicable. He's giving a principled inference to an Intelligent Designer based on what the evidence shows. This is rational. His conclusions are based on solid scientific analysis."

Craig's discussion of evidence for miracles prompted me to ask about another point that was made by Hume, the eighteenth-century Scottish skeptic and history's most famous doubter of the miraculous. "Hume said the evidence for the uniformity of nature is so conclusive that any evidence for miracles would never be able to overcome it," I pointed out. "For instance, look at the resurrection. We have thousands of years of uniform evidence that dead people simply do not return from the dead. So Hume says no amount of evidence would be able to overcome that tremendous presumption."

Craig shook his head. "There's no contradiction between believing that people generally stay in their graves and that Jesus of Nazareth rose from the dead. In fact, Christians believe both of these. The opposite of the statement that Jesus rose from the dead is not that all other people remained in their graves; it's that Jesus of Nazareth remained in *his* grave.

"In order to argue against the evidence for the resurrection, you have to present evidence against the resurrection itself, not evidence that everybody else has always remained in their grave. So I think his argument is simply fallacious.

"Now, I would agree with Hume that a *natural* resurrection of Jesus from the dead, without any sort of divine intervention, is enormously improbable. But that's *not* the hypothesis. The hypothesis is that God raised Jesus from the dead. This doesn't say anything against the laws of nature, which say dead people don't come back to life *naturally*."

Extraordinary Evidence

While I could see Craig's point, I wanted to pursue this avenue further. "Some critics say the resurrection is an extraordinary event and therefore it requires extraordinary evidence," I said. "Doesn't that assertion have a certain amount of appeal?"

"Yes, that sounds like common sense," he replied. "But it's demonstrably false."

"How so?"

"Because this standard would prevent us from believing in all sorts of events we do rationally embrace. For example, you would not believe the report on the evening news that the numbers chosen in last night's lottery were 4, 2, 9, 7, 8, and 3, because that would be an event of extraordinary improbability. The odds against that are millions and millions to one, and therefore you should not believe it when the news anchor reports it. Yet we obviously believe we're rational in concluding it's true. How is that possible?

"Well, probability theorists say you must weigh the improbability of the event's occurring against the probability that the evidence would be just as it is if the event had not taken place."

Craig rattled off that statement so fast that my mind was having trouble assimilating it. "Whoa," I said, holding up my hand, "you're going to have to slow down and give me an example."

"Okay, look at it this way: if the evening news has a very high probability of being accurate, then it's highly improbable that they would inaccurately report the numbers chosen in the lottery. That counterbalances any improbability in the choosing of those numbers, so you're quite rational to believe in this highly improbable event.

"In the same way, any improbability that you might think resides in the resurrection of Jesus is counterbalanced by the improbability of the empty tomb, Jesus' resurrection appearances, and the sudden change in the first disciples taking place if there were no such event as the resurrection of Jesus. Do you see what I mean?"

"Yes," I said, seeing that the illustration made his point clear. As improbable as the resurrection may seem to skeptics, this has to be weighed against how improbable it would be to have all of the various historical evidence for its occurrence if it never actually took place.

"So," Craig concluded, "it becomes quite rational to believe in an event like the miraculous resurrection of Jesus. Besides, I look at it this way: If God really exists, then in what sense *is* it improbable that he would raise Jesus from the dead? I can't think of any."

"Have you seen skeptics who have become believers in Christianity because of the quality and quantity of the evidence for the resurrection?" I asked.

Craig's eyes got wide. "Oh, yes, certainly!" he said. "I recently met a fellow who became a Christian out of the so-called 'free thought' movement. He looked into the resurrection and concluded from the evidence that God raised Jesus from the dead. Of course, his free thought colleagues bitterly railed against him. He said, 'Why are they so hostile? I merely followed the principles of free thought, and this is where the evidence and reason led me!'"

I chuckled. "Are you saying some free thought folks aren't as free thinking as they would have people believe?"

"Frankly," he replied, "I think many skeptics act in a close-minded way."

As a former skeptic myself, I've noticed the same phenomenon. "Are you referring to the fact that some of them rule out even the possibility of miracles from the outset?" I asked.

"Precisely," Craig said. "Logicians have a term: 'inference to the best explanation.' This means you have a body of data to be explained, and then you have a pool of live options or various explanations for that data. You need to choose which explanation from that pool would, if true, best explain the observed data.

"Some skeptics, however, will not allow supernatural explanations even to be in the pool of live options. Consequently, if there is no natural explanation for an event, they're simply left with ignorance.

"That's prejudice. Apart from some proof of atheism, there's no warrant for excluding supernatural explanations from being a member of the pool of live options. If you do put them in that pool, you've got to be an open, honest investigator to see which is the best explanation of any given event."

The Miracles of Jesus

"Let's say you're an honest investigator," I said, picking up on his last thought. "What would you look for to convince you that something miraculous has occurred?"

"You would have a number of criteria. You would have to investigate to see if something cannot be accounted for in terms of the natural forces that were operable at that time and place. And you'd look for a religio-historical context."

I wanted to pursue this idea of context. Hume said that if historians uniformly agreed that the Queen of England died and then reappeared alive a month later, he would be inclined to accept any explanation other than God having performed a miracle. I asked Craig for his response to that.

"I would agree that a miracle without context is inherently ambiguous," Craig replied. "The context of a miracle can help us determine if it's from God or not. For instance, the queen's revivification would lack any religious context and would basically be a bald and unexplained anomaly.

"But that's not the case with Jesus. His supernatural feats took place in a context charged with religious significance because he performed his miracles and exorcisms as signs of the inbreaking of the kingdom of God into human history, and they served as an authentication of his message. And his resurrection came as the climax to his own unparalleled life and ministry and his radical claims to divine authority that had gotten him crucified. This is why the resurrection gives us pause, while the queen's return would only perplex us. Therefore, the religio-historical context is crucial in understanding miraculous events."

But I pressed further: "*Did* Jesus perform miracles? What convinces you that he did?"

"The fact is that most New Testament critics today admit he performed what we would call miracles. Granted, they may not all believe these were *genuine* miracles, but the idea of Jesus of Nazareth as a miracle worker and exorcist is part of the historical Jesus generally accepted by critics today."

With that, Craig swiveled his chair and withdrew a file from the shelf behind his desk. He flipped through some pages until he landed on the one he was after. "Let me read you a quote from Rudolf Bultmann, who is recognized as one of the most skeptical New Testament critics of this century":

> The Christian fellowship was convinced that Jesus had done miracles and they told many stories of miracles about him . . . Most of these stories contained in the gospels are legendary or are at least dressed up with legend. But, there can be no doubt that Jesus did such deeds, which were, in his and his contemporaries' understanding, miracles; that is to say, events that were the result of supernatural divine causality. Doubtless he healed the sick and cast out demons.[7]

Craig closed the file. "Even Bultmann says miracles and exorcisms belong to the historical Jesus. Now, in Bultmann's day these stories were considered legendary because of the supposed influence of Greco-Roman mythology on the gospels, but scholars today realize this influence was virtually nil. They now believe the role of Jesus as a miracle worker must be understood against the backdrop of first-century Palestinian Judaism, where it fits right in.

"In fact," he concluded, "the only reason to be skeptical that these were genuine miracles rather than psychosomatic healings would be philosophical—do you believe that such events can occur or not? The historicity of the events is not in doubt."

Miracles and Legends

The conclusions of these scholars were helpful, but I wanted more than that. "What is the specific evidence that Jesus performed miracles?" I asked.

"Part of it is that these events are found in all of the strata of the gospel sources. For example, the miracle of the feeding of the five thousand is found in all of the Gospels, so you have independent, multiple attestations to these events. There is no vestige of a non-miraculous Jesus of Nazareth in any of the sources; therefore, it's very likely that this belongs to the historical Jesus. Moreover, it fits right into the Jewish milieu. There were other Jewish exorcists and miracle workers who preceded Jesus."

That wasn't enough for me. "Just because several people said something extraordinary happened—like the feeding of the five thousand—doesn't necessarily mean it's true," I said.

"In one sense, it's a very individual question of what you will find convincing for yourself," he replied. "I think we can confidently say there isn't any reason to be doubtful about these narratives apart from philosophical reasons. In other words, if you believe God exists, then there's no good reason to be skeptical about these events.

"However, let me add this: regarding the central miracle of the New Testament—the resurrection—there is a very good case for concluding with confidence that, yes, this is really an event of history. You see, the evidence for the resurrection is much, much stronger than the evidence, say, that Jesus did a miracle by healing the blind man in John 9. You have a wealth of data concerning the empty tomb, the resurrection appearances, and the origin of the disciples' belief in the resurrection."

"Isn't it more likely that the accounts of Jesus' miracles actually were legends that developed years after his life?" I asked. "Atheist George Smith says, 'As one moves from the earlier to the later Gospels, some of the miracles become more exaggerated.'[8]

"He illustrates this legendary development by comparing Mark 1, which says *all* were brought to Jesus and *many* were healed; Matthew 8, which says *many* were brought to Jesus and *all* were healed; and Luke 4, which says *all* were brought and *all* were healed. As historian Archibald Robertson said, 'We are witnessing the progressive growth of a legend.'"[9]

Craig got a sour look on his face. "That argument is really quite fanciful," he said, "because the gospel writers don't use the word *all* or *many* in the way a police report would."

He pushed aside the Bultmann folder on his desk and reached for his Bible, opening it to the New Testament and running his finger down a page. Finding Mark 1:5, he read the verse aloud: "The whole Judean countryside and all the people of Jerusalem went out to him. Confessing their sins, they were baptized by him in the Jordan River."

"Okay, think about that," he said. "It says John the Baptist was baptizing all of Judea and Jerusalem. *Really? All* of Judea? *All* of Jerusalem?" Craig said, his voice rising in mock astonishment. "The *whole* province was emptied of people who went to the Jordan River and they were *all* baptized—all the infants, every elderly individual? Well, obviously not. This was not an expression that was meant to be read woodenly like a police report.

"Now, back to the accounts you mentioned earlier—what is the central point they're making? Clearly, that multitudes were going to Jesus for healings and exorcisms, and this is well-attested. The fact is that all these accounts are in absolute agreement that there were miracles performed by Jesus and that this involved lots of people."

He added one more point: "And it's important to remember that for the greatest miracle, the resurrection, we know from historical research that there was nowhere near enough time for legend to have developed and wiped out a solid core of historical truth."

The "Miracles" of Muhammad

Assuming there's historical evidence that Jesus did perform feats that eyewitnesses considered to be miraculous, what about miracles in other religions? To the critic Hume, miracles from different religions cancel each other out as being evidence for truth.

For instance, Islamic tradition says Muhammad ascended to heaven on a mule, that he healed the broken leg of a companion, that he fed large groups with little food, that he turned a tree branch into a steel sword, and that he was responsible for other supernatural accomplishments.

"If he and Jesus both performed similar miracles," I said to Craig, "then doesn't that water down the uniqueness of Jesus and negate miracles as being evidence of his truth?"

Craig furrowed his brow. "I think this is based on a misimpression of Islam," he said a bit tentatively. "Correct me if I'm wrong, but as I read the Qur'an, essentially there aren't any miracles, apart from the supposed miracle of the Qur'an itself."

"Granted," I replied. "Except for a few disputed passages, I think scholars generally interpret the Qur'an that way. But I said these miracles are reported in Islamic *tradition*, which is where they really proliferate."[10]

Craig searched his mind and then locked in on the issue. "Ah, yes, exactly—the miracles are mentioned in the so-called Hadith," he said. "And here's what's important: this Islamic tradition comes hundreds of years after Muhammad's life and therefore isn't comparable to the Gospels, which were written down within the first generation when the eyewitnesses were still alive.

"For example, in First Corinthians 15, the reports of Jesus' resurrection appearances go back to within the first five years after the event. Consequently, this is fresh data that could not have been the result of legendary development. It's simply not comparable to these legendary stories about Muhammad that accumulated many, many years later in Islamic tradition."

"Do you think it's significant that the Qur'an itself does not emphasize miracles by Muhammad in the way the Bible does about Jesus?"

"Perhaps in the sense that later the Hadith seemed to find it necessary to invent miracles for Muhammad. He never claimed any such things for himself. Basically, these stories illustrate how nonhistorical reports arise by legendary influences over centuries of time, in contrast to the Gospels, where miracle reports are part of the earliest strata of sources."

Still, I sensed a contradiction. If the immediacy of the reporting of miracles is important, then certainly the Book of Mormon passes that test. "There you have claims of the miraculous that are reported soon after they supposedly occurred, yet you wouldn't accept them as being true," I pointed out.

"In this case, what you have is just plain charlatanry by Joseph Smith, who created Mormonism," Craig replied. "It's interesting that Smith and his father, when they lived in New York, were obsessed with finding Captain Kidd's buried gold. Then what does Smith later claim he finds? Golden plates from the angel Moroni, and then they disappear and are supposedly taken to heaven and never seen again.

"What you have here is an elaborate hoax, compared to the Gospels, with the evident sincerity of the people in what they were reporting. The problem with Mormonism is basically one of credibility because of the unreliability of Joseph Smith and a blatant lack of corroboration. Unlike the Gospels, whose credibility has been greatly enhanced by archaeology, archaeological discoveries have repeatedly failed to substantiate the Book of Mormon."

The Personal Side of Miracles

My discussion with Craig had been stimulating so far, but it had remained exclusively on an intellectual plane. I wanted to get more personal, to probe beneath Craig's scholarly persona and relate the issue of miracles to his individual life. But I hesitated.

Through my years of acquaintance with Bill Craig, I had noticed some physical challenges he was facing. For instance, I could tell when we shook hands that his right hand was a bit gnarled. Out of politeness, I had never broached the subject with him. Now, as we explored this topic, his apparent ailment raised a troubling question I could no longer ignore: If God can perform miracles, why hasn't he healed someone who is as devoted to him as Bill Craig has been?

I began slowly. "Look, Bill," I said, "you believe God still does miracles, don't you?"

"I wouldn't deny that miracles can happen today," Craig said. "I would add, though, that there's no reason to expect them to be as frequent or evident as they were with Jesus. Miracles tend to cluster around great moments in salvation history, like the exodus or the ministry of Jesus, who saw his miracles as signs to the people of the inbreaking of the kingdom of God and his exorcisms as signs of his ability to destroy the powers of darkness."

"Then tell me this," I said gently. "If God loves you and he has the power to heal you, why doesn't he make your physical afflictions disappear?"

Craig didn't seem to be offended by the question. He shifted in his chair and then leaned forward, his voice changing from a professorial tone to one that was more personal and tender.

"Paul the apostle had what he called a thorn in his flesh that he asked God three times to remove," Craig began, "and God's answer was that his grace was sufficient and that his strength is made perfect in weakness. That passage has been a comfort to me in my own life."[11]

He glanced off to the side, perhaps deciding how much to say. When he looked back at me, the sharp, steely intensity of his blue eyes had softened to a vulnerable sincerity.

"I guess I don't discuss this very much publicly," he said, "but I have a congenital neuromuscular disease that causes progressive atrophy in the extremities. In my case it's fairly light. A lot of people with this syndrome have to wear metal braces on their legs. They're completely crippled. I've really been fortunate that mine hasn't been very bad."

"You've asked for a miracle?" I said.

He nodded. "As a young Christian I prayed that God would heal me. But he didn't."

Even though I could tell from his matter-of-fact tone that he wasn't seeking pity, my heart went out to him. "You're disappointed," I said, my words coming out more like an observation than a question.

A slight smile came to his face. "Lee, do you know what has amazed me?" he asked with an unmistakable sense of wonder. "As I look at my life, God has used this disease in so many remarkable ways to shape me and my personality. Because I couldn't do athletics, in order to succeed at something I was driven into academics. I really owe my existence as a scholar to my having this disease. It's what compelled me to the life of the mind.

"And it also affected me psychologically by giving me a tremendous drive to succeed. It caused me to have an achievement and goal orientation, which has helped me to do a lot in life. So I've really seen played out in a very personal way what Paul said—God's strength is made perfect in weakness."

"If you could have been healed, would you have wanted to be?"

He let out a laugh. "Well, *now* perhaps it would be nice, having learned the lessons!" he said.

Then he gave a more serious answer that echoed Peter Kreeft's earlier comments about suffering. "On the other hand, I've become quite accustomed to it. As I look back, I can honestly say I'm glad this was the way God directed my life. He can use even the bad things of life to bring about his ultimate purposes and ends.

"That doesn't mean those things aren't bad—they really *are* bad. But they're all within the sovereignty of God. Even good can come out of evil."

Faith in a God of Miracles

Bill Craig is not an ivory tower pontificator; he's a man whose everyday life embodies his Christian philosophy. Even when wrestling with the very real issue of his own affliction, he emerges with confirmation that his beliefs are well placed. Everything is undergirded by a supreme confidence in the rationality of Christianity, a religion whose linchpin is a miracle of unprecedented proportions.

"You titled one of your most popular books *Reasonable Faith*," I said, "but there are skeptics who would call that an oxymoron."

I reached into my briefcase and pulled out a book called *Critiques of God*, turning to a chapter titled "Religion and Reason." It was written by atheist Richard Robinson, a philosopher educated at Oxford and Cornell Universities. I read Craig a quote I had previously highlighted:

> Christian faith is not merely believing that there is a god. It is believing that there is a god no matter what the evidence on the question may be. "Have faith," in the Christian sense, means, "make yourself believe that there is a god without regard to evidence."[12]

Closing the book, I looked up at Craig and asked, "How do you see this interplay between faith and reason? Are the two really contradictory, as critics contend?"

Craig began with a definition. "Faith is trust in or commitment to what you think is true," he replied. "Why a person thinks Christianity is true may differ from individual to individual. For one person, it might be because God speaks to their heart and produces in them a conviction this is true. I certainly believe that's valid.

"To another person, though, it may be a more hardheaded intellectual exploration of the evidence that leads them to the same conclusion. But neither comes to faith until they make that act of trust or commitment to what they think is true. When you understand faith in these categories, you can see it's entirely compatible with reason."

When I asked Craig to elaborate, he thought for a moment and then offered an illustration from his own experience. He began, "I had corneal transplant surgery a while back," but as soon as the words left his mouth, he let out a laugh. One more medical problem did sound like "piling on" in light of our previous discussion about his health. Craig shrugged. "My wife says I'm a walking medical disaster area," he said with a chuckle, "but the healthiest person she knows!

"Anyway, before I was willing to let anyone operate on my eyes, Jan and I did a thorough search to find the best corneal surgeon in the country. We did research, looked at the evidence, contacted him, talked with him, and finally, after becoming convinced on the basis of the evidence he was the best, I placed my trust in him and let him operate on my eyes. My faith or trust in him was based on the good evidence I had in his qualifications and credibility.

"In the same way, with respect to belief in God or miracles, many people make that act of trust or commitment after they've become convinced by the evidence that Christianity is true. Not everybody takes that route, but there are certainly people who do. And that's a logical and rational approach that uses reason rather than negates it."

The subject of evidence opened the door to a fundamental issue that was begging to be explored. Time after time, Craig had referred to the fact that if God exists, then it's reasonable to believe that the miraculous is possible. And while that makes sense, to many people it hinges on a very big "if."

"What affirmative evidence convinces you that such a miracle-working being exists?" I asked. "Can you give me some solid reasons for believing in a divine Creator and the validity of Christianity?"

Craig was nodding all throughout my asking of the question. "In 1986, I heard a lecture in which Alvin Plantinga presented two dozen reasons for believing in God. He's the premiere Christian philosopher today, and it was a dazzling display of theistic arguments," Craig replied.[13]

I glanced at my watch. "How about zeroing in on five main arguments?" I suggested.

"Okay," he said, "I'll go through a conspiracy of arguments for God that reinforce and underline each other."[14]

Pushing up the sleeves of his shirt, Craig settled into his chair. As the author of *The Existence of God and the Beginning of the Universe* and coauthor of *Theism, Atheism, and Big Bang Cosmology*, Craig began his arguments exactly where one would expect.

Reason #1: God Makes Sense of the Universe's Origin

"Both philosophically and scientifically," Craig said, "I would argue that the universe and time itself had a beginning at some point in the finite past. But since something cannot just come out of nothing, there has to be a transcendent cause beyond space and time that brought the universe into being."

"And the universe came into being in what has been called the big bang?" I asked.

"Exactly. As Stephen Hawking said, 'Almost everyone now believes that the universe, and time itself, had a beginning at the "big bang."'[15] That's where the overwhelming scientific evidence points—to an event approximately fourteen billion years ago. Now, this poses a major problem for skeptics. As Anthony Kenny of Oxford University says, 'A proponent of the big bang theory, at least if he is an atheist, must believe that the . . . universe came from nothing and by nothing.'"[16]

Craig chuckled. "Of course, something coming from nothing doesn't make sense! Lee, you've been quoting the famous skeptic David Hume quite a bit in our interview. Well, even he said, 'But allow me to tell you that I never asserted so absurd a proposition as that anything might arise without a cause.'[17]

"Atheists recognize this. For example, one of contemporary philosophy's most prominent atheists, Kai Nielsen, once said, 'Suppose you suddenly hear a loud bang . . . and you ask me, "What made that bang?" and I reply, "Nothing, it just happened." You would not accept that.'[18]

"And he's absolutely correct. Yet think about it: If there must be a cause for a little bang, then doesn't it also make sense that there would be a cause for a big bang?"

It was a question that didn't seem to need a response. "So how would you summarize this initial argument?" I asked.

As he made each point, Craig grabbed a finger to count them off. "First, whatever begins to exist has a cause. Second, the universe began to exist. And, third, therefore, the universe has a cause. As the eminent scientist Sir Arthur Eddington wrote, 'The beginning seems to present insuperable difficulties unless we agree to look on it as frankly supernatural.'"[19]

I interrupted. "Okay, that points toward a creator, but does it tell us much about him?"

"Actually, yes it does," Craig replied. "We know this supernatural cause must be an uncaused, changeless, timeless, and immaterial being."

"What's the basis of your conclusions?"

"It must be uncaused because we know that there cannot be an infinite regress of causes. It must be timeless and therefore changeless, at least without the universe, because it was the creator of time. In addition, because it also created space, it must transcend space and therefore be immaterial rather than physical in nature."

There was an obvious question that had to be asked. "If everything must have a cause, then who or what caused God?" I said.

"Wait a second—I never said *everything* must have a cause," Craig replied. "The premise is that whatever *begins to exist* must have a cause. In other words, 'being' can't come from 'nonbeing.' Since God never began to exist, he doesn't require a cause. He never came into being."

I told him that sounded suspiciously like he was making a special exception for God.

"Atheists themselves used to be very comfortable in maintaining that the universe is eternal and uncaused," he replied. "The problem is that they can no longer hold that position because of modern evidence that the universe started with the big bang. So they can't legitimately object when I make the same claim about God—that he is eternal and he is uncaused."

Reason #2: God Makes Sense of the Universe's Complexity

"In the last thirty-five years," Craig said, "scientists have been stunned to discover that the big bang was not some chaotic, primordial event, but rather a highly ordered event that required an enormous amount of information. In fact, from the very moment of its inception, the universe had to be fine-tuned to an incomprehensible precision for the existence of life like ourselves. And that points in a very compelling way toward the existence of an Intelligent Designer."

"*Fine-tuned* is a subjective term," I pointed out. "It could mean a lot of things. What do you mean by it?"

"Let me put it this way," he said. "Scientifically speaking, it's far more probable for a life-*prohibiting* universe to exist than a life-*sustaining* one. Life is balanced on a razor's edge."

As an example, he cited Hawking's writings. "He has calculated," Craig said, "that if the rate of the universe's expansion one second after the big bang had been smaller by even one part in a hundred thousand million million, the universe would have collapsed into a fireball."[20]

In short order, Craig proceeded to go down a list of several other mind-boggling statistics to support his conclusion.[21] Among them:

- British physicist P. C. W. Davies has estimated the odds against the initial conditions being suitable for the formation of stars—a necessity for planets and thus life—to be a one followed by at least a thousand billion billion zeroes.[22]
- Davies also estimated that if the strength of gravity or of the weak force were changed by only one part in a ten followed by a hundred zeroes, life could never have developed.[23]
- There are about fifty constants and quantities—for example, the amount of usable energy in the universe, the difference in mass between protons and neutrons, the ratios of the fundamental forces of nature, and the proportion of matter to antimatter—that must be balanced to a mathematically infinitesimal degree for any life to be possible.[24]

"All of this," said Craig, "amply supports the conclusion that there's an intelligence behind creation. In fact, the alternate explanations just don't add up.

"For instance, one theory is called 'natural necessity,' which means there is some unknown 'theory of everything' that would explain the way the universe is. In other words, something in nature made it necessary that things would turn out this way.

"That concept falls apart, however, when we study it deeply. First, anyone who claims the universe must be life-permitting is making a radical claim that requires strong proof, but this alternative is merely an assertion. Second, there are other models of the universe that are different from ours, so it must be possible for the universe to have been different. And, third, even if the laws of nature are necessary, you still have to have initial conditions put in at the beginning on which these laws can operate."

Yet this wasn't the only possible alternative. I interrupted to raise a different scenario that sounded plausible on the surface. "What about the possibility that the fine-tuning of the universe is the result of pure chance?" I asked. "Maybe the whole thing is merely a big cosmic accident—a colossal roll of the dice, so to speak."

Craig sighed. "Lee, I'll tell you this: the precision is so utterly fantastic, so mathematically breathtaking, that it's just plain silly to think it could have been an accident. Especially since we're not just talking about simple odds but what theorists call 'specified probability,' which rules out chance beyond a reasonable doubt."

I wasn't ready to abandon the option of chance. "What if there were an infinite number of other universes existing apart from ours?" I asked. "Then the odds would be that one of them would have the right conditions for sustaining life—and that's the one in which we happen to find ourselves."

Craig had heard that theory before. "It's called the 'many worlds hypothesis,'" he said. "Hawking has talked about this concept. Here's the problem: these other theoretical universes are inaccessible to us and therefore there's no possible way to provide any evidence that this might be true. It's purely a concept, an idea, without scientific proof. The prominent British scientist and theologian John Polkinghorne has called it 'pseudo-science' and 'a metaphysical guess.'[25]

"And think about it: if this were true, it would make rational conduct of life impossible, because you could explain away any-thing—no matter how improbable—by postulating an infinite number of other universes."

I wasn't quite following that line of reasoning. "What do you mean by that?" I asked.

"For example, if you were dealing cards in a poker game and each time you dealt yourself four aces, you couldn't be accused of cheating, no matter how improbable the situation. You could merely point out that in an infinite ensemble of universes, there will occur a universe in which every time a person deals, he deals four aces to himself, and therefore—*lucky me!*—I just happen to be in that universe!

"Look—this is pure metaphysics. There's no real reason to believe such parallel worlds exist. The very fact that skeptics have to come up with such an outlandish theory is because the fine-tuning of the universe points powerfully toward an Intelligent Designer— and some people will hypothesize anything to avoid reaching that conclusion."

I knew that this astonishingly precise balance of the universe was one of the main factors in leading Harvard-educated Patrick Glynn, the associate director and scholar-in-residence at the George Washington University Institute for Communitarian Policy Studies, to abandon atheism and become a Christian. In his book *God: The Evidence*, he shoots holes in such other alternate theories as quantum mechanics and "baby universes," coming to this conclusion:

> Today, the concrete data point strongly in the direction of the God hypothesis . . . Those who wish to oppose it have no testable theory to marshal, only speculations about unseen uni-verses spun from fertile scientific imagination . . . Ironically, the picture of the universe bequeathed to us by the most advanced twentieth-century science is closer in spirit to the vision pre-sented in the Book of Genesis than anything offered by science since Copernicus.[26]

Reason #3: God Makes Sense of Objective Moral Values

Craig summarized his next point succinctly at the outset: "A third factor pointing toward God is the existence of objective moral values in the universe. If God does not exist, then objective moral values do not exist."

That, of course, raised the question of what he meant by "objective" values. Craig was quick to add both a definition and an illustration.

"Objective moral values are valid and binding independently of whether anyone believes in them or not," he explained. "For example, to label the Holocaust objectively wrong is to say it was wrong even though the Nazis thought it was right. And it would still be wrong even if the Nazis had won World War II and succeeded in brainwashing or exterminating everybody who disagreed with them. Now, if God does not exist, then moral values are not objective in this way."

I was shaking my head. "Wait a second," I interjected. "If you're saying that an atheist can't have moral values or live a basically ethical life, then I have a problem with that. I have a friend who doesn't believe in God, and he's as kind and caring an individual as many of the Christians I know."

"No, I'm not saying a person must believe in God in order to live a moral life. The question is, 'If God does not exist, do objective moral values exist?' And the answer is, 'No.'"

"Why not?"

"Because if there is no God, moral values are merely the products of sociobiological evolution. In fact, that's what many atheists think. According to philosopher Michael Ruse, 'Morality is a biological adaptation no less than are hands and feet and teeth,' and morality is 'just an aid to survival and reproduction . . . any deeper meaning is illusory.'[27]

"Or if there is no God, then morality is just a matter of personal taste, akin to statements like, 'Broccoli tastes good.' Well, it tastes good to some people but bad to others. There isn't any objective truth about that; it's a subjective matter of taste. And to say that killing innocent children is wrong would just be an expression of taste, saying, 'I don't like the killing of innocent children.'

"Like Ruse and atheist Bertrand Russell, I don't see any reason to think that in the absence of God, the morality evolved by *Homo sapiens* is objective. After all, if there is no God, then what's so special about human beings? They're just accidental by-products of nature that have only recently evolved on a tiny speck of dust lost somewhere in a mindless universe and are doomed to perish forever in a relatively short time.

"On the atheistic view, some actions, like rape, may not be socially advantageous, and therefore it has become taboo in the course of human development. But that doesn't prove that rape is really wrong. In fact, it's conceivable that rape could have evolved as something that's advantageous for the survival of the species. Thus, without God there is no absolute right and wrong that imposes itself on our conscience.

"However, we all know deep down that, in fact, objective moral values *do* exist. All we have to do to see that is to simply ask ourselves, 'Is torturing a child for fun really a morally neutral act?' I'm persuaded you'd say, 'No, that's not morally neutral; it's really wrong to do that.' And you'll say that in full cognizance of the Darwinian theory of evolution and all the rest.

"A good illustration of this is a fundraising letter sent out in 1991 by John Healey, the executive director of Amnesty International, in which he said, 'I am writing you today because I think you share my profound belief that there are indeed some moral absolutes. When it comes to torture, to government-sanctioned murder, to "disappearances" . . . these are outrages against all of us.'[28]

"Actions like rape and child abuse aren't just behaviors that happen to be socially unacceptable—they are clearly moral abominations. They are objectively wrong. And such things as love, equality, and self-sacrifice really are good in an objective sense. We all know these things deep down.

"And since these objective moral values cannot exist without God and they unquestionably do exist, it follows logically and inescapably that God exists."

Reason #4: God Makes Sense of the Resurrection

With this point, Craig said he was going to switch gears a bit. "We've been saying that if we have good reasons to believe in God, then we can believe in miracles," he said. "I've been giving reasons that point toward God's existence. But miracles themselves also can be part of the cumulative case for God. That's true, for instance, of the resurrection. If Jesus of Nazareth really did come back from the dead, then we have a divine miracle on our hands and, thus, evidence for the existence of God."

I asked Craig to recap why he believes the historical evidence points toward that conclusion. "But," I stressed, "don't assume that the New Testament is the inspired word of God." He agreed for the sake of his answer to consider the New Testament to be merely a collection of first-century Greek documents that can be subjected to analysis like any other ancient records.

"There are at least four facts about the fate of Jesus that are widely accepted by New Testament historians from a broad spectrum," Craig began. "The first is that after Jesus was crucified, he was buried by Joseph of Arimathea in a tomb. This is important because it means the location of the tomb was known to Jews, Christians, and Romans alike."

"What evidence do you have for this?" I asked.

"Jesus' burial is reported in extremely old information that Paul included in his first letter to the church in Corinth.[29] This information can be dated to within five years after Jesus' death, so it wasn't legendary. Further, the burial story is part of very old material that Mark used in writing his gospel, and his story lacks signs of legendary development. There are no traces of any competing burial story. What's more, it would be inexplicable for anyone to make up Joseph's involvement, since he was a member of the Sanhedrin that condemned Jesus.

"The second fact is that on the Sunday after the crucifixion, Jesus' tomb was found empty by a group of his women followers. This is substantiated by Paul's early report to the Corinthians, which implies the empty tomb, and by Mark's very old source material. So again we have early, independent attestation.

"And we have a lot more. For instance, the empty-tomb story lacks signs of legendary embellishment, and the earliest known Jewish response to the proclamation of Jesus' resurrection presupposes that his tomb was empty. In addition, it's reported that women discovered the tomb empty. Now, the testimony of women was considered so unreliable that they couldn't testify in Jewish courts. The only reason to include the highly embarrassing detail that women discovered the empty tomb is that the gospel writers were faithfully recording what really happened.

"The third fact is that on multiple occasions and under various circumstances, different individuals and groups of people experienced appearances of Jesus alive from the dead. This is almost universally acknowledged by New Testament scholars for several reasons.

"For example, the list of eyewitnesses to Jesus' resurrection, provided by Paul to the Corinthians, guarantees that such appearances occurred. Given the early date of the information and Paul's own acquaintance with the people involved, this cannot be dismissed as legendary.

"Also, the appearance narratives in the Gospels provide multiple, independent attestations of the appearances. Even the skeptical New Testament critic Gerd Lüdemann has concluded, 'It may be taken as historically certain that Peter and the disciples had experiences after Jesus' death in which Jesus appeared to them as the risen Christ.'[30]

"The fourth fact is that the original disciples suddenly and sincerely came to believe that Jesus was risen from the dead despite their predisposition to the contrary. Jewish beliefs precluded anyone's rising from the dead before the general resurrection at the end of the world. Even so, the original disciples suddenly came to believe so strongly that God had raised Jesus that they were willing to die for that belief. New Testament scholar Luke Johnson said, 'Some sort of powerful, transformative experience is required to generate the sort of movement earliest Christianity was.'"[31]

"Okay, then," I said, "what do you think is the best explanation for these four facts?"

"Frankly, there is absolutely no naturalistic explanation that fits," he replied. "All of the old theories like 'the disciples stole the body' or 'Jesus wasn't really dead' have been universally rejected by modern scholarship.

"Personally, I think the very best explanation is the same one provided by the eyewitnesses: that God raised Jesus from the dead. In fact, this hypothesis easily passes all six tests that historians use in determining what is the best explanation for a given body of historical facts."[32]

Reason #5: God Can Immediately Be Experienced

Craig said that this last point was not so much an argument for God's existence, "but rather it's the claim that you can know that God exists wholly apart from arguments by having an immediate experience of him. Philosophers call this a 'properly basic belief.'"

Craig looked straight at me. "Lee, let me illustrate this concept with a question," he said. "Can you prove that the external world exists?"

The question caught me off guard. I thought about it for a moment and could come up with no logical sequence of arguments that would incontrovertibly establish such a thing. "I'm not sure how I would go about doing that," I conceded.

"That's right," he replied. "Your belief in the reality of the external world is 'properly basic.' You can't prove that the external world exists. After all, you could be a brain in a vat being stimulated with electrodes by a mad scientist so that you just *think* you're seeing an external world. But you'd have to be crazy to think that. So this 'properly basic belief' in the external world is entirely rational. In other words, it's appropriately grounded in our experience.

"In the same way, in the context of an immediate experience of God, it's rational to believe in God in a properly basic way. And I've had such an experience. God invaded my life as a sixteen-year-old, and for more than thirty years I've walked with him day by day, year by year, as a living reality in my experience.

"In the absence of overwhelming arguments for atheism, it seems perfectly rational to go on believing in the reality of that experience. This is the way people in biblical days knew God. As John Hick wrote, 'To them God was not a proposition completing a syllogism or an idea adopted by the mind, but the experiential reality that gave significance to their lives.'"[33]

"But," I interjected, "what if an atheist says the same thing—that he has a 'properly basic belief' in the absence of God? Then you're deadlocked."

Replied Craig, "Philosopher William Alston says in that case, the Christian should do whatever is feasible to find common ground, like logic or empirical facts, to show in a noncircular way whose view is correct.[34]

"That's what I've tried to do in these other four arguments. I know God exists in a properly basic way, and I've tried to show he exists by appealing to the common facts of science, ethics, history, and philosophy. Taken together, they form a powerful case for God and Christianity."

A Knock on the Door

As I had been observing Craig while he rattled off his reasons for believing in God, I noticed he displayed a serene confidence in what he was saying. Before we finished, I wanted to get to the heart of what was producing that conviction.

"As you sit here right now, deep in your soul, do you know for a fact that Christianity is true?" I asked.

Without hesitating, he replied, "Yes, I do."

"Ultimately, how do you know for sure?"

"Ultimately, the way a Christian really knows that Christianity is true is through the self-authenticating witness of God's Spirit," he said. "The Holy Spirit whispers to our spirit that we belong to God.[35] That's one of his roles. Other evidence, though still valid, is basically confirmatory."

Craig thought for a moment and then asked, "You know Peter Grant, don't you?" I replied that, yes, I was a friend of the Atlanta pastor. "Well," Craig said, "he came up with a great illustration of how this works.

"Let's say you're going to the office to see if your boss is in. You see his car in the parking lot. You ask the secretary if he's in, and she says, 'Yes, I just spoke with him.' You see light from under his office door. You listen and hear his voice on the telephone. On the basis of all this evidence, you have good grounds for concluding that your boss is in his office.

"But you could do something quite different. You could go to the door and knock on it and meet the boss face-to-face. At that point, the evidence of the car in the parking lot, the secretary's testimony, the light under the door, the voice on the telephone—all of that would still be valid, but it would take a secondary role, because now you've met the boss face-to-face.

"And in the same way, when we've met God, so to speak, face-to-face, all the arguments and evidence for his existence—though still perfectly valid—take a secondary role. They now become confirmatory of what God himself has shown us in a supernatural way through the witness of the Holy Spirit in our hearts."

"And this immediate experience of God is available to anyone who seeks it?"

"Absolutely. The Bible says God is knocking on the door of our life, and if we open it, we will encounter him and experience him personally. He says in Revelation 3:20, 'Here I am! I stand at the door and knock. If anyone hears my voice and opens the door, I will come in and eat with that person, and they with me.'"

Craig gestured toward the tape recorder that had been capturing our conversation. "We've been talking a lot about miracles today," he said in conclusion. "It's no exaggeration to say that knowing God personally and seeing him change lives are the greatest miracles of all."

I reached over and clicked off the recorder. Because of my own experience with God after years of living in the mire of immorality as an atheist, I knew he was right.

Based on how God has transformed my life, my attitudes, my relationships, my motivations, my marriage, and my priorities through his very real ongoing presence in my life, I realized at that moment that miracles like manna from heaven, the virgin birth, and the resurrection—well, in the end, they're child's play for a God like that.

Deliberations
Questions for Reflection or Group Study

1. After reading this interview, do you believe that miracles are possible? What would convince you that something miraculous had occurred? Do you believe the evidence of history establishes that the miraculous resurrection of Jesus actually took place? Why or why not?

2. Which one of Craig's arguments for the existence of God was most persuasive to you? Why? Taken together, do these five points convince you that it's rational to believe in the existence of a miracle-working God? If not, how else would you account for these five categories of evidence?

3. Craig prayed for God to miraculously cure his medical condition, but he hasn't. What do you think of his reaction to that? Have you prayed for God to intervene with a miracle in your life? What happened? How has this affected your attitude toward God? In what way was Craig's response to his situation helpful or not helpful to you?

For Further Evidence
More Resources on This Topic

Geisler, Norman L. *Miracles and the Modern Mind: A Defense of Biblical Miracles.*
    Eugene, OR: Wipf and Stock, 2004.
Geivett, R. Douglas, and Gary R. Habermas, eds. *In Defense of Miracles:*
    A Comprehensive Case for God's Action in History. Downers Grove, IL: IVP
    Academic, 1997.
Keener, Craig. *Miracles: The Credibility of the New Testament Accounts.* 2 vols.
    Grand Rapids: Baker Academic, 2011.
————. *Miracles Today: The Supernatural Work of God in the Modern World.*
    Grand Rapids: Baker Academic, 2021.
Lewis, C. S. *Miracles.* 1947. Reprint, New York: HarperOne, 2015.
Metaxas, Eric. *Miracles: What They Are, Why They Happen, and How They Can*
    Change Your Life. New York: Penguin, 2015.
Moreland, J. P. *A Simple Guide to Experience Miracles: Instruction and Inspiration*
    for Living Supernaturally in Christ. Grand Rapids: Zondervan, 2021.
Strobel, Lee. *The Case for Miracles: A Journalist Investigates Evidence for the*
    Supernatural. Grand Rapids: Zondervan, 2018.

Evolution Explains Life, So God Isn't Needed

Charles Darwin didn't want to murder
God, as he once put it. But he did.
TIME MAGAZINE

[Evolutionary theory] is still, as it was in Darwin's time,
a highly speculative hypothesis entirely without direct factual
support and very far from that self-evident axiom some
of its more aggressive advocates would have us believe.

MICHAEL DENTON, MOLECULAR BIOLOGIST

Investigators were desperately searching for some piece of physical evidence to link suspect Ronald Keith Williamson to a brutal slaying that had shocked the tranquil community of Ada, Oklahoma, three years earlier.

They were having a difficult time building a solid case against Williamson, who vigorously denied strangling twenty-one-year-old Debra Sue Carter. So far their only evidence consisted of a witness who had seen Williamson talking with Carter earlier on the evening she was slain, an admission by Williamson that he once dreamed he had killed her, and the testimony of a jailhouse informant who claimed she had overheard him talking about the crime. Obviously, police needed more proof if they wanted to convict him.

97

Finally, detectives came up with the clincher. An expert took four hairs that had been found on the victim's body and elsewhere at the crime scene, examined them under a microscope, and concluded they were "a match" with samples taken from Williamson, according to a newspaper report. Their case bolstered by scientific evidence, investigators arrested Williamson and put him on trial.

It didn't take long for a jury to find the former minor-league baseball player guilty of the slaying and to dispatch him to death row. With the ghastly crime finally solved, the people of Ada breathed a collective sigh of relief. Justice had been done. The killer was going to pay with his life.

There was, however, one big problem: Williamson was telling the truth about his innocence. After he languished in prison for twelve years—nine of them awaiting execution—an analysis of DNA at the crime scene established that someone else had committed the murder. On April 15, 1999, Williamson was finally set free.[1]

But wait a second—what about the hair-comparison evidence that pointed toward Williamson's guilt? If his hair was found at the scene of the crime, didn't that implicate him in the slaying? The answer is disconcerting: hair evidence often purports to prove more than it actually does.

The newspaper report had glossed over some important nuances. The hair from the scene didn't really "match" Williamson's. A criminologist had merely concluded they were "consistent" with each other. In other words, their color, shape, and texture looked similar. Thus, the hairs from the crime scene could have come from Williamson—or perhaps they could have come from someone else.

Far from being as incriminating as fingerprints, hair analysis has been called "pseudoscience" by some legal analysts. Often jurors hear impressive-sounding testimony about what appears to be scientifically valid proof, and they conclude—incorrectly—that it establishes the defendant's guilt. Some prosecutors, in the heat of the courtroom battle, have even been known to mischaracterize or subtly overstate the value of hair analysis during their closing arguments.[2]

In the case of Williamson, a federal judge called the hair evidence "scientifically unreliable" and said it never should have been used against the defendant. Even more troubling, hair evidence had been used against eighteen death row prisoners who subsequently were declared innocent in the last quarter century.[3]

The case of Ronald Keith Williamson is an eye-opening example of justice gone awry. His unwarranted conviction demonstrates how easy it is for jurors to draw sweeping conclusions that aren't really justified by the actual scientific facts. And in a sense, Williamson's story paralleled my own investigation into one of the most potent bits of scientific evidence that is commonly used against the existence of God.

Darwin's Accomplishment

Although there was much that led up to it, I guess you could say I lost the last remnants of my faith in God during biology class in high school. So profound was the experience that I could take you back to the very seat I was sitting in when I first was taught that evolution explained the origin and development of life. The implications were clear: Charles Darwin's theory eliminated the need for a supernatural creator by demonstrating how naturalistic processes could account for the increasing complexity and diversity of living things.

My experience was not uncommon. Scholar Patrick Glynn has described how he took a similar path that ended up in atheism:

> I embraced skepticism at an early age, when I first learned of Darwin's theory of evolution in, of all places, Catholic grade school. It immediately occurred to me that either Darwin's theory was true or the creation story in the Book of Genesis was true. They could not both be true, and I stood up in class and told the poor nun as much. Thus began a long odyssey away from the devout religious belief and practice that had marked

my childhood toward an increasingly secular and rationalistic outlook.[4]

In the popular culture, the case for evolution is generally considered shut. "Darwinism remains one of the most successful scientific theories ever promulgated," *Time* magazine said in its recap of the second millennium.[5] To Charles Templeton, it's simply beyond dispute that "all life is the result of timeless evolutionary forces."[6]

Biologist Francisco Ayala said Darwin's "greatest accomplishment" was to show how the development of life is "the result of a natural process, natural selection, without any need to resort to a Creator."[7] Michael Denton, the Australian molecular biologist and physician, agreed that Darwinism "broke man's link with God" and consequently "set him adrift in the cosmos without purpose."[8] He added:

> As far as Christianity was concerned, the advent of the theory of evolution . . . was catastrophic . . . The decline in religious belief can probably be attributed more to the propagation and advocacy by the intellectual and scientific community of the Darwinian version of evolution than to any other single factor.[9]

As the textbook *Evolutionary Biology* declares, "By coupling undirected, purposeless variation to the blind, uncaring process of natural selection, Darwin made theological or spiritual explanations of the life processes superfluous."[10] British biologist Richard Dawkins was speaking for many when he said that Darwin "made it possible to be an intellectually fulfilled atheist."[11]

In fact, prominent evolutionist William Provine of Cornell University candidly conceded that if Darwinism is true, there are five inescapable implications: there's no evidence for God; there's no life after death; there's no absolute foundation for right and wrong; there's no ultimate meaning for life; and people don't really have free will.[12]

But is Darwinism true? I walked away from my formal education convinced it was. As my spiritual journey began taking me into the realm of science, however, I started to have an increasingly uneasy feeling. Like the hair-comparison evidence in the Williamson case, did the evidence for evolution purport to prove more than it actually does?

The more I investigated the issue, the more I saw how I had glossed over significant nuances in a rush to judgment, reminiscent of the Oklahoma murder trial. When I examined the matter thoroughly, I began to question whether the sweeping conclusions of Darwinists are really justified by the hard scientific facts. (A similar journey, incidentally, helped lead Patrick Glynn back to faith in God.)

This is not, I soon discovered, a case of religion versus science; rather, this is an issue of science versus science. More and more biologists, biochemists, and other researchers—not just Christians—have raised serious objections to evolutionary theory in recent years, claiming that its broad inferences are sometimes based on flimsy, incomplete, or flawed data.

In other words, what looks at first blush like an airtight scientific case for evolution begins to unravel upon closer examination. New discoveries during the past thirty years have prompted an increasing number of scientists to contradict Darwin by concluding that there was an Intelligent Designer behind the creation and development of life.

"The result of these cumulative efforts to investigate the cell—to investigate life at the molecular level—is a loud, clear, piercing cry of 'design!'" biochemist Michael Behe of Lehigh University said in his groundbreaking critique of Darwinism.[13] He went on to say:

> The conclusion of intelligent design flows naturally from the data itself—not from sacred books or sectarian beliefs . . . The reluctance of science to embrace the conclusion of intelligent design . . . has no justifiable foundation . . . Many people,

including many important and well-respected scientists, just don't *want* there to be anything beyond nature.[14]

That last sentence described me. I was more than happy to latch on to Darwinism as an excuse to jettison the idea of God so I could unabashedly pursue my own agenda in life without moral constraints.

Yet someone who knows me well once described me as being "a sucker for the truth." My training in journalism and law compels me to dig beneath opinion, speculation, and theories, all the way down until I hit the bedrock of solid facts. And try as I might, I couldn't turn my back on nagging inconsistencies that were undermining the foundation of Darwin's theory.

A Primordial Detective Story

Everyone concedes that evolution is true to some extent. Undeniably, there are variations within species of animals and plants, which explains why there are more than two hundred different varieties of dogs, cows can be bred for improved milk production, and bacteria can adapt and develop immunity to antibiotics. This is called "microevolution."

But Darwin's theory goes much further than that, claiming that life began millions of years ago with simple single-cell creatures and then developed through mutation and natural selection into the vast array of plant and animal life that populate the planet. Human beings came on the scene from the same common ancestor as the ape. Scientists call this more controversial theory "macroevolution."

Initially troubling to me was the paucity of fossil evidence for the transitions between various species of animals. Even Darwin conceded that the lack of these fossils was perhaps the most obvious and serious objection to his theory, although he confidently predicted that future discoveries would vindicate him.

Fast-forward to 1979. David Raup, the curator of the Field

Museum of Natural History in Chicago, Illinois, said, "We are now about one hundred and twenty years after Darwin and the knowledge of the fossil record has been greatly expanded. We now have a quarter of a million fossil species, but the situation hasn't changed much . . . We have even fewer examples of evolutionary transition than we had in Darwin's time."[15]

What the fossil record *does* show is that in rocks dating back some 570,000,000 years, there is the sudden appearance of nearly all the animal phyla, and they appear fully formed, "without a trace of the evolutionary ancestors that Darwinists require."[16] It's a phenomenon that points more readily toward a creator than Darwinism.

That isn't the only argument against evolution. In his book *On the Origin of Species*, Darwin also admitted, "If it could be demonstrated that any complex organ existed which could not possibly have been formed by numerous, successive, slight modifications, then my theory would absolutely break down."[17] Taking up that challenge, Michael Behe's award-winning book *Darwin's Black Box* showed how recent biochemical discoveries have found numerous examples of this very kind of "irreducible complexity."

I was particularly interested in a more fundamental issue, however. Biological evolution can only take place after there was some sort of living matter that could replicate itself and then grow in complexity through mutation and survival of the fittest. I wanted to go back even further and ask the cornerstone question of human existence: Where did life begin in the first place?

The origin of life has intrigued both theologians and scientists for centuries. "The most amazing thing to me is existence itself," said cosmologist Allan Sandage. "How is it that inanimate matter can organize itself to contemplate itself?"[18]

How, indeed? Darwin's theory presupposes that nonliving chemicals, if given the right amount of time and circumstances, could develop by themselves into living matter. Undeniably, that view has gained widespread popular acceptance through the years. But is there any scientific data to back up that belief? Or, like the hair-comparison evidence in the Oklahoma murder trial, is that analysis long on speculation but short on hard facts?

I knew that if scientists could convincingly demonstrate how life could emerge purely through natural chemical processes, it would cast considerable doubt on the need for God. On the other hand, if the evidence points in the other direction toward an Intelligent Designer, then Darwin's entire evolutionary house of cards would collapse.

This primordial detective story took me on a journey to Houston, Texas, where I rented a car and drove through the countryside and cattle ranches to the community of College Station, home of Texas A&M University. Down the block from the school, in a modest two-story frame house, I knocked on the door of one of the most influential experts on how life arose on primitive planet Earth.

The Third Interview: Walter L. Bradley, PhD

Walter Bradley caused a stir in 1984 when he coauthored the seminal book *The Mystery of Life's Origin*, which was a devastating analysis of theories about how living matter was created. Eyebrows were raised because its foreword was written by biologist Dean Kenyon of San Francisco State University, whose book *Biochemical Predestination* had previously argued that chemicals had an inherent ability to evolve into living cells under the right conditions. Calling Bradley's book "cogent, original, and compelling," Kenyon concluded, "The authors believe, and I now concur, that there is a fundamental flaw in all current theories of the chemical origins of life."[19]

Since then, Bradley has written and spoken widely on the topic of how life began. He has contributed to the books *Mere Creation* and *Three Views on Creation and Evolution*, while he and chemist Charles Thaxton wrote "Information and the Origin of Life" for the book *The Creation Hypothesis*. His more technical articles include coauthoring "A Statistical Examination of Self-Ordering of Amino Acids in Proteins," published in *Origins of Life and Evolution of Biospheres*, which reflects his personal research in the origin-of-life field.

Bradley received his doctorate in materials science from the University of Texas at Austin and was a professor of mechanical engineering at Texas A&M University for twenty-four years, serving as head of the department for four years. An expert on polymers and thermodynamics, both of which are critically important in the life-origin debate, Bradley has been director of the Polymer Technology Center at Texas A&M and has received research grants totaling four million dollars.

He has consulted with such corporations as Dow Chemical, 3M, BFGoodrich, General Dynamics, Boeing, and Shell Oil, and he has been an expert witness in about seventy-five legal cases. In addition, he is a fellow of the Discovery Institute's Center for the Renewal of Science and Culture and has been elected a fellow of the American Society for Materials and the American Scientific Affiliation.

The soft-spoken, self-effacing Bradley, who talks with an unhurried Texas drawl, is a strong family man. His two children and five grandchildren all live near each other in College Station, and they get together frequently. In fact, his wife, Ann; daughter, Sharon; and grandchildren Rachel, Daniel, and Elizabeth joined us for lunch at a local delicatessen after our interview.

As a scientist concerned about accuracy, Bradley answers questions in careful and complete sentences, making sure to acknowledge nuances and not to overstate his conclusions. He talks respectfully of the evolutionists he has debated through the years, including renowned chemistry professor Robert Shapiro of New York University, who called *The Mystery of Life's Origin* "an important contribution" that "brings together the major scientific arguments that demonstrate the inadequacy of current theories."[20]

Just three months after his retirement from Texas A&M, the fifty-six-year-old Bradley was relaxed and genial as we sat down at his dining room table. He was comfortably attired in a light blue sports shirt, blue jeans, and white socks with no shoes. It was clear from the outset that he had come prepared for our discussion. A pile of research papers was neatly stacked next to him. Ever the scientist, he wanted to be able to back up everything he said.

To lay some groundwork, I started our conversation by going back to Darwin himself. "His theory of evolution sought to explain how simple life-forms could develop over long periods of time into increasingly complex creatures," I said. "But that ignores the important issue of how life arose in the first place. What was Darwin's theory about that?"

Bradley picked up a book as he began to answer. "Well, he didn't really have a good idea of how life arose," Bradley said, slipping on his gold-rimmed reading glasses. "In 1871 he wrote a letter in which he did some speculation—it wasn't even a hypothesis, just some brainstorming." With that, Bradley read Darwin's words:

> It is often said that all the conditions for the first production of a living organism are now present which could ever have been present. But if (and oh! what a big if!) we could conceive in some warm little pond, with all sorts of ammonia and phosphoric salts, light, heat, electricity, etc. present, that a protein compound was chemically formed ready to undergo still more complex changes, at the present day such matter would be instantly devoured or absorbed, which would not have been the case before living creatures were formed.[21]

Closing the book, Bradley said, "So Darwin was the first one to theorize that life emerged from chemicals reacting in some 'warm little pond.'"

"He makes it sound pretty easy," I remarked.

"Darwin may have underestimated the problem because it was widely thought back then that life sort of naturally develops every place," he replied. "People thought maggots would spontaneously develop from decaying meat. But two hundred years before the publication of Darwin's *On the Origin of Species*, Francesco Redi demonstrated that meat kept away from flies never developed maggots.

Later, Louis Pasteur showed that air contains microorganisms that can multiply in water, giving the illusion of the spontaneous generation of life. He announced at the Sorbonne in Paris that 'never will the doctrine of spontaneous generation recover from the mortal blow of this simple experiment.'"[22]

Bradley let that thoroughly register with me before continuing. "But then in the 1920s, some scientists said they agreed with Pasteur that spontaneous genesis doesn't happen in a short time frame. But they theorized that if you had *billions* and *billions* of years—as the late astronomer Carl Sagan liked to say—then it might really happen after all."

"And that," I concluded, "is the basis for the idea that nonliving chemicals can combine into living cells if given enough time."

"That's exactly right," he said.

Building Blocks of Life

I told Bradley that in high school and college I was taught that the primitive earth was covered with pools of chemicals and had an atmosphere that was conducive to the formation of life. With energy supplied by lightning, chemicals in this "prebiotic soup"—over a period of billions of years—linked together and a simple life-form emerged. From there, evolution took over.

"Who conceptualized that scenario?" I asked.

"Russian biochemist Alexander Oparin proposed in 1924 that complex molecular arrangements and the functions of living matter evolved from simpler molecules that preexisted on the early earth," he said. "Then in 1928, British biologist J. B. S. Haldane theorized that ultraviolet light acting on the earth's primitive atmosphere caused sugars and amino acids to concentrate in the oceans, and then life eventually emerged from this primordial broth.

"Later, Nobel Prize winner Harold Urey suggested that earth's primitive atmosphere would have made it favorable for organic compounds to have emerged. Urey was the PhD advisor to Stanley

Miller at the University of Chicago, and it was Miller who decided to test this experimentally."

Miller's name rang a bell. I remember being taught in school about his landmark experiment in which he recreated the atmosphere of the primitive earth in a laboratory and shot electricity through it to simulate the effects of lightning. Before long, he found that amino acids—the building blocks of life—had been created. I can remember my biology teacher recounting the experiment with an infectious enthusiasm, suggesting it proved conclusively that life could have emerged from nonliving chemicals.

"This experiment was hailed as a major breakthrough at the time, wasn't it?" I asked.

"Oh, absolutely!" Bradley declared. "Carl Sagan called it the single most significant step in convincing many scientists that life is likely to be abundant in the cosmos.[23] Chemist William Day said the experiment showed that this first step in the creation of life was not a chance event, but it was inevitable.[24] Astronomer Harlow Shapley said Miller had proven that 'the appearance of life is essentially an automatic biochemical development that comes along naturally when physical conditions are right.'"[25]

That was certainly impressive. "Did that close the issue?" I asked.

"Hardly," replied Bradley. "For a while, evolutionists were euphoric. But there was a major problem with the experiment that has invalidated its results."

I had never been taught anything in school about the Miller experiment being fatally flawed. "What was the problem?" I asked.

"Miller and Oparin didn't have any real proof that the earth's early atmosphere was composed of ammonia, methane, and hydrogen, which Miller used in his experiment. They based their theory on physical chemistry. They wanted to get a chemical reaction that would be favorable, and so they proposed that the atmosphere was rich in those gases. Oparin was smart enough to know that if you start with inert gases like nitrogen and carbon dioxide, they won't react."

My eyes got wide. This was a devastating critique of Miller's experiment. "Are you saying that the deck was stacked in advance to get the results they wanted?" I asked, incredulity in my voice.

"Essentially, yes," he replied.

"What was the real environment of the early earth like?" I asked.

"From 1980 on, NASA scientists have shown that the primitive earth never had any methane, ammonia, or hydrogen to amount to anything," he said. "Instead, it was composed of water, carbon dioxide, and nitrogen—and you absolutely cannot get the same experimental results with that mixture. It just won't work. More recent experiments have confirmed this to be the case."

I slumped back in my chair, amazed at the implications of what Bradley had disclosed. My mind flashed back to my biology teacher, who seemed so utterly confident that Miller's experiment validated the chemical evolution of life. Certainly that was the thinking of his day. Now new discoveries have changed everything—and yet there are generations of former students still living under the impression that the origin-of-life issue has been resolved.

"So the scientific significance of Miller's experiment today—" I began, prompting Bradley to finish my sentence.

". . . is zilch," he said. "When textbooks present the Miller experiment, they should be honest enough to say it was interesting historically but not terribly relevant to how life actually developed."[26]

I let out a low whistle. The analogy of the Oklahoma murder trial was proving to be even more accurate than I had thought.

Assembling a Cell

Before we went any further, I thought it would be important to understand some fundamentals about living matter to determine whether it's reasonable to believe it could have been the product of unguided chemical reactions.

"Let's start by defining the difference between a living system and one that's not living," I said to Bradley.

"A living system must do at least three things: process energy, store information, and replicate," he said. "All living systems do that. Human beings do these three functions, although bacteria do them much more quickly and efficiently. Nonliving things don't do them."

Again thinking back to Darwin's day, I asked, "Did Darwin consider basic living matter—say, for instance, a one-cell organism—to be rather simple?"

"Yes, he undoubtedly would have," came his response. "Darwin probably didn't think it would be very difficult to create life from nonlife because the gap between the two didn't appear very great to him. In 1905, Ernst Haeckel described living cells as being merely 'homogeneous globules of plasm.'[27] In those days they didn't have any way of seeing the complexity that exists within the membrane of the cell. But the truth is that a one-cell organism is more complicated than anything we've been able to recreate through supercomputers.

"One person very creatively—but quite accurately—described a single-cell organism as a high-tech factory, complete with artificial languages and decoding systems, central memory banks that store and retrieve impressive amounts of information, precision control systems that regulate the automatic assembly of components, proof-reading and quality control mechanisms that safeguard against errors, assembly systems that use principles of prefabrication and modular construction, and a complete replication system that allows the organism to duplicate itself at bewildering speeds."

"That's extremely impressive," I said. "But maybe one-cell organisms are more complicated today due to the fact that they have developed and evolved through the eons. Maybe the first cells produced on the primitive earth were much more basic and therefore easier to create."

"Let's accept that theory," came Bradley's reply. "But even when we try to imagine what the minimal living cell would have been like, it's still not simple at all."

"What would go into building a living organism?" I asked—and then, before Bradley could open his mouth to reply, I quickly added, "And keep it basic."

"Okay," he said, clearing his throat. "Essentially, you start with amino acids. They come in eighty different types, but only twenty of them are found in living organisms. The trick, then, is to isolate only the correct amino acids. Then the right amino acids have to be linked together in the right sequence in order to produce protein molecules. Picture those plastic stick-together chains that kids play with—you have to put together the right amino acids in the right way to ultimately get biological function."

Imagining kids playing with plastic toys made the process seem—well, like child's play. "That doesn't sound very difficult," I said.

"It wouldn't be if you were applying your intelligence to the problem and purposefully selecting and assembling the amino acids one at a time. But remember, this is chemical evolution. It would be unguided by any outside help. And there are a lot of other complicating factors to consider."

"Such as what?"

"For instance, other molecules tend to react more readily with amino acids than amino acids react with each other. Now you have the problem of how to eliminate these extraneous molecules. Even in the Miller experiment, only 2 percent of the material he produced was composed of amino acids, so you'd have a lot of other chemical material that would gum up the process.

"Then there's another complication: there are an equal number of amino acids that are right- and left-handed, and only left-handed ones work in living matter. Now you've got to get only these select ones to link together in the right sequence. And you also need the correct kind of chemical bonds—namely, peptide bonds—in the correct places in order for the protein to be able to fold in a specific three-dimensional way. Otherwise, it won't function.

"It's sort of like a printer taking letters out of a basket and setting type the way they used to do it by hand. If you guide it with your intelligence, it's no problem. But if you just choose letters at random and put them together haphazardly—including upside down and backward—then what are the chances you'd get words, sentences, and paragraphs that would make sense? It's extremely unlikely.

"In the same way, perhaps one hundred amino acids have to be put together in just the right manner to make a protein molecule. And, remember, that's just the first step. Creating one protein molecule doesn't mean you've created life. Now you have to bring together a collection of protein molecules—maybe two hundred of them—with just the right functions to get a typical living cell."

Whew! Now I was beginning to see the enormity of the challenge. Even if Stanley Miller had been right about the ease with which amino acids could be produced in the primitive earth's atmosphere, nevertheless the process of putting them together into protein molecules and then assembling them into a functioning cell would be mind-boggling.

"In living systems," continued Bradley, "the guidance that's needed to assemble everything comes from DNA. Every cell of every plant and animal has to have a DNA molecule. Think of it as a little microprocessor that regulates everything. DNA works hand in glove with RNA to direct the correct sequencing of amino acids. It's able to do this through biochemical instructions—that is, information—that is encoded on the DNA."

That raised an obvious issue. "Where did the DNA come from?" I asked.

"The making of DNA and RNA would be an even greater problem than creating protein," he replied. "These are much more complex, and there are a host of practical problems. For instance, the synthesis of key building blocks for DNA and RNA has never been successfully done, except under highly implausible conditions without any resemblance to those of the early earth. Klaus Dose of the Institute for Biochemistry in Mainz, Germany, admitted that the difficulties in synthesizing DNA and RNA 'are at present beyond our imagination.'[28]

"Frankly, the origin of such a sophisticated system that is both rich in information and capable of reproducing itself has absolutely stymied origin-of-life scientists. As the Nobel Prize–winner Sir Francis Crick said, 'The origin of life appears to be almost a miracle, so many are the conditions which would have had to be satisfied to get it going.'"[29]

Even so, scientists have tried to come up with creative theories to try to explain how biopolymers (such as proteins) became assembled with only the right building blocks (amino acids) and only the correct isomers (left-handed amino acids) joined with only the correct peptide bonds in only the correct sequence. I decided to ask Bradley for his analysis of the most common hypotheses that scientists have proposed in recent years.

Theory #1: Random Chance

I had been taught in school that if chemicals had an ample amount of time to interact in the "warm little ponds" of early earth, eventually the improbable would become probable and life would emerge. Given Bradley's description of what would have to happen, however, I could see why this theory has lost support in recent years.

"Scientists once believed in the idea of random chance plus time yielding life, because they also believed in the steady-state theory of the universe," Bradley said. "This meant the universe was infinitely old, and who knows what could happen if you had an infinite amount of time? But with the discovery of background radiation in 1965, the big bang theory came to dominate in cosmology. The bad news for evolution was that this meant the universe was only about fourteen billion years old. More recent work has verified that the earth is probably less than five billion years old."

"Still," I interjected, "that's a long time. A lot can happen in five billion years."

"Actually, it's not as long as you think. The earth spent a long time cooling down to a temperature where it could support life. Based on the discovery of microfossils, scientists have now estimated that the time gap between the earth reaching the right temperature and the first emergence of life was only about four hundred million years. That's not much time for chemical evolution to take place. In fact, Cyril Ponnamperuma of the University of Maryland and Carl Woese of the University of Illinois have suggested that life may be as old as the earth and that its origin may have virtually coincided with the birth of the planet.[30]

"And not only was the time too short, but the mathematical odds of assembling a living organism are so astronomical that nobody still believes that random chance accounts for the origin of life. Even if you optimized the conditions, it wouldn't work. If you took all the carbon in the universe and put it on the face of the earth, allowed it to chemically react at the most rapid rate possible, and left it for a billion years, the odds of creating just one functional protein molecule would be one chance in a ten with sixty zeroes after it."

Those odds are so infinitesimal that the human mind can't comprehend them. "That makes winning the lottery look like a sure thing," I quipped.

"Absolutely. Michael Behe has said the probability of linking together just one hundred amino acids to create one protein molecule by chance would be the same as a blindfolded man finding one marked grain of sand somewhere in the vastness of the Sahara Desert—and doing it not just once, but three different times.[31] Sir Frederick Hoyle put it colorfully when he said that this scenario is about as likely as a tornado whirling through a junkyard and accidentally assembling a fully functional Boeing 747.

"In other words, the odds, for all practical purposes, are zero. That's why even though some people who aren't educated in this field still believe life emerged by chance, scientists simply don't believe it anymore."

Theory #2: Chemical Affinity

With random chance being soundly rejected as an explanation for the origin of life, scientists turned to another theory: that there must be some inherent attraction that would cause amino acids to spontaneously link up in the right sequence to create the protein molecules out of which living cells are made. This idea was popularized in a 1969 book coauthored by Dean Kenyon, which argued that the emergence of life actually might have been "biochemically predestined" because of these chemical bonding preferences.[32]

In fact, researchers studied the *Atlas of Protein Sequence and Structure* to determine whether certain amino acids preferentially positioned themselves next to a particular neighbor. They looked at ten proteins and performed a supporting experiment that seemed to suggest there was merit to this hypothesis.

"That sounds like a plausible explanation," I said to Bradley. "What's wrong with it?"

Although I didn't know it at the time, I was asking the scientist who was part of a team that refuted that hypothesis in 1986.

"We wrote a computer program to analyze not just ten proteins, but every one of the two hundred fifty proteins in the *Atlas*," Bradley replied. "The results demonstrated conclusively that the sequencing had nothing to do with chemical preferences. Consequently, that theory bit the dust.[33] Even Kenyon, one of its biggest proponents, has repudiated the idea."

Theory #3: Self-Ordering Tendencies

This theory comes with an intimidating title: "nonequilibrium thermodynamics." Basically, the concept says that under certain circumstances, if energy is passed through a system at a fairly high rate, the system becomes unstable and will actually rearrange itself into an alternate and somewhat more complicated form.

An example is water draining out of a bathtub. Initially, the water molecules merely drop at random down the drain. But toward the end, the exit becomes much more orderly as the molecules spontaneously form a vortex.

"Some scientists have suggested that this tendency for molecules to become more orderly could be an analogy for how nature spontaneously organizes itself under certain circumstances," I said to Bradley.

He was thoroughly familiar with this hypothesis. "The problem is that the level of organization you're talking about is quite low. Even Ilya Prigogine, the thermodynamicist who has speculated about this theory, admitted recently that 'there is still a gap between the most complex structures we can produce in nonequilibrium situations in chemistry, and the complexity we find in biology.'[34]

"He's right. Compare the vortex in a bathtub to the mind-boggling complexity I described in creating living matter, and you'll see it's an incredibly big gap."

Other scientists have brought up "equilibrium thermodynamics" as another possible solution. As an example, if water is cooled, it turns into ice. The molecules in ice are more orderly than the random molecules of water. Some have pointed to this as another way in which nature orders itself.

But Bradley discounted this theory for a similar reason. "Again," he said, "you have a very low level of information needed to create ice crystals compared to the high level of information required to order the amino acids to create protein molecules. That's why this theory hasn't caught on either."

Bradley said there's a significant difference between the "order" found in some nonliving things and the "specified complexity" of living cells.

"Ice crystals have a certain amount of order, but it's simple, repetitive, and has a low amount of information, sort of like filling a book with the words 'I love you, I love you, I love you' over and over again. In contrast, the kind of complexity we see in living matter has a high information content that specifies how to assemble amino acids in the right sequence, like a book being filled with meaningful sentences that communicate a story.

"Unquestionably, energy can create patterns of simple order. For instance, you could see ripples on the sand at a beach and know they were created by the action of waves. But if you saw the words

'John loves Mary' and a heart with an arrow drawn in the sand, you know that energy alone didn't create that. That's why the prominent information theorist H. P. Yockey has said, 'Attempts to relate the idea of order . . . with biological organization . . . must be regarded as a play on words which cannot stand careful scrutiny.'"[35]

Theory #4: Seeding from Space

Frustrated by the seemingly insurmountable obstacles to chemical evolution on earth, some scientists—including Crick, the co-discoverer of DNA—have proposed that the building blocks for life came from somewhere else in space. Sir Frederick Hoyle and N. C. Wickramasinghe have speculated that particles the size of living cells could reach earth without being incinerated by the atmosphere. While in space, a thin layer of graphite dust could protect them from the destructive rays of ultraviolet light.

This theory was bolstered by the discovery of amino acids in the famous Murchison meteorite that fell in Australia in 1969, as well as in another meteorite that plummeted into Antarctica some 3.8 billion years ago.[36]

Crick and Leslie Orgel have gone even further by suggesting that life spores may have been intentionally sent to earth by an advanced civilization, perhaps, some have speculated, with the intention of making earth a wilderness area, zoo, or cosmic dump.[37]

"All of that sounds pretty bizarre," I said to Bradley. "But then maybe it's not as bizarre as the idea that God created everything."

Bradley's face betrayed his distaste for this approach. "The fact that scientists come up with these kind of outlandish proposals shows that they just can't imagine any way that life could have naturally developed on earth, and they're right about that," he said. "I like the way Phillip Johnson put it: 'When a scientist of Crick's caliber feels he has to invoke undetectable spacemen, it is time to consider whether the field of prebiological evolution has come to a dead end.'[38]

"The biggest flaw in this theory is that it doesn't solve the origin-of-life problem," Bradley explained. "Think about this: if you say life emerged somewhere else, that just moves the problem to another location! The same obstacles exist."

While that was certainly true, I saw another possibility. "Maybe another planet would have an atmosphere of ammonia, methane, and hydrogen that would be more conducive to producing the building blocks of life," I suggested.

"Even if that were the case," he responded, "how did these amino acids and proteins get assembled into living matter? That's a problem of information—how to sequence the atoms in the right way—and that problem is independent of what the atmosphere is. Even if meteorites did deliver amino acids to earth, you still have the assembly problem.

"As Alexandre Dauvillier said in *The Photochemical Origin of Life*, this theory 'is a facile hypothesis, a subterfuge which seeks to avoid the fundamental problem of the origin of life.'[39] Even Stanley Miller has no use for the theory. He told *Discover* magazine, 'Organics from outer space—that's garbage, it really is.'"[40]

Bradley picked up a report on a July 1999 international conference of origin-of-life scientists and read an excerpt to me: "Before the end of the conference's second day, researchers had to agree that extraterrestrial delivery could *not* have supplied all the needed prebiotic molecules."[41] The report went on to say that evolutionist Robert Shapiro had studied the Murchison meteorite and "showed that side reactions would effectively prevent any prebiotic molecules in the meteorite from *ever* spontaneously forming life molecules."[42]

"Meanwhile," added Bradley, "Christopher Chyba, a planetary scientist from NASA, said that even though spacecraft have confirmed some organic compounds in comets out in space, 'at these velocities, at least ten to fifteen miles per second, the temperatures you reach on impact are so high that you end up frying just about anything.'[43] Besides, even if they made it to earth, you still have the problem of how they would have become assembled into living matter."

Theory #5: Vents in the Ocean

In 1977, scientists aboard the research submarine *Alvin*, half a mile below the surface of the Pacific west of Ecuador, discovered exotic hydrothermal vents on the sea floor. Tubeworms, clams, and bacteria, whose primary source of energy is sulfur compounds from the vents, were flourishing nearby. Since then, dozens of other vents have been found at various undersea locations.

This led Jack Corliss, a marine biologist now working at NASA's Goddard Space Flight Center, to suggest that these vents might have provided an environment where the beginning of life might have been nurtured.

"The thing about hot springs is that they provide a nice, safe, continuous process by which you can go from very simple molecules all the way to living cells and primitive bacteria," he told *Discover* magazine.[44]

Some popular periodicals, long on speculation but short on specifics, have promoted this concept. However, when science writer Peter Radetsky asked origin-of-life researcher Stanley Miller about it, he got undisguised hostility. "The vent hypothesis is a real loser. I don't understand why we even have to discuss it," an exasperated Miller told him.[45]

Bradley also was skeptical when I brought up this theory. "Granted, the vents might provide an unusual energy source that could prompt some chemicals to become reactive," he said. "But it never even addresses the assembly problem. This theory does nothing to solve the problem of how to put together the building blocks of life in the right sequence and with the right connections."

What's more, he said, experiments by Miller and Jeffrey Bada at the University of California at San Diego have suggested that the high temperatures of these superheated vents would destroy rather than create complex organic compounds.

Explained Bradley, "It's now thought that all of the water in the ocean is periodically recirculated through these vents. If you were finally getting some molecules that were beginning to get bigger and more complex, they would be so fragile that they would get destroyed by the heat when they were recirculated. That means the timescale for chemical evolution would be shrunk dramatically. The vents would make you go back and start over at pretty short intervals—and that would work against the development of life."

Theory #6: Life from Clay

Another hypothesis popularized by the media in recent years was Scottish chemist A. G. Cairns-Smith's suggestion that life somehow arose on clays whose crystalline structure had enough complexity to somehow encourage prebiotic chemicals to assemble together.[46]

"What about that approach?" I asked Bradley.

"In one sense, the clays might help, because molecules don't like to react in water, and the surface of the clay might give them a less-wet environment," Bradley replied.

"But how would the clay be able to impart the information needed to sequence the chemicals together in the right way? The best that crystalline clay can do is provide very, very low-grade sequencing information, and it's going to be very repetitive. It's like the book I talked about a minute ago that's filled with 'I love you, I love you, I love you' over and over again. Is it orderly? Yes. Does it have much information? No. That's what a crystal is—nothing more than redundant information. It's far, far short of the specified complexity that living matter needs.

"Even Cairns-Smith has recognized the problems with his idea. He admitted in 1991, 'No one has been able to coax clay into something resembling evolution in a laboratory; nor has anyone found anything resembling a clay-based organism in nature.'"[47]

The Most Reasonable Inference

Time after time, origin-of-life scientists have come up empty when they've tried to theorize how chemicals could evolve into living matter. Recently, some have used computer models to try to show how chemical reactions might have occurred on the primitive earth, but these scenarios only work if the computer is programmed to eliminate some of the insurmountable obstacles that chemicals would have actually faced in the real world.

When a scientist at the Santa Fe Institute, where some computer simulations have been conducted, commented, "If Darwin had a computer on his desk, who knows what he could have discovered," origin-of-life expert John Horgan wryly remarked, "What indeed: Charles Darwin might have discovered a great deal about computers and very little about nature."[48]

With so many theories evaporating under scrutiny, I asked Bradley for his personal assessment of the state of research into how life emerged.

"There isn't any doubt that science, for the moment at least, is at a dead end," he replied. "The optimism of the 1950s is gone. The mood at the 1999 international conference on origin of life was described as grim—full of frustration, pessimism, and desperation.[49] Nobody pretends that any alternative provides a reasonable path of how life went unguided from simple chemicals to proteins to basic life-forms."

Bradley reached over to a book and quickly located the quote he was after. "Klaus Dose, the biochemist who is considered to be one of the foremost experts in this area, summed up the situation pretty well," Bradley said, reading his words:

> More than thirty years of experimentation on the origin of life in the fields of chemical and molecular evolution have led to a better perception of the immensity of the problem of the origin of life on Earth rather than to its solution. At present all discussions on principle theories and experiments in the field either end in stalemate or in a confession of ignorance.[50]

Continued Bradley, "Robert Shapiro argues strongly that all current theories are bankrupt.[51] Francis Crick said out of frustration,

'Every time I write a paper on the origin of life, I swear I will never write another one, because there is too much speculation running after too few facts.'[52] Even Stanley Miller, some forty years after his famous experiment, said in a great understatement to *Scientific American*, 'The problem of the origin of life has turned out to be much more difficult than I, and most other people, envisioned.'"[53]

By coincidence, at about the same time as my interview with Bradley, Harvard University's outspoken evolutionist Stephen Jay Gould was asked to write an essay for *Time* magazine on whether scientists will ever figure out how life began. The result was a vague and equivocating piece that hemmed and hawed but never even came close to suggesting a single hypothesis for how life managed to emerge from nonlife.[54]

"What does one do with this scientific stalemate?" I asked Bradley.

"That depends a lot on one's metaphysics," he said. "Robert Shapiro, whom I highly respect, says there must be some physical laws we haven't discovered yet that will eventually show us how life arose naturally. But there's nothing in science that guarantees a natural explanation for how life began. Science is neutral in regard to the outcome. It's hard to imagine new natural laws, because they're going to have characteristics that are consistent with the existing ones."

"Then what," I said, "is your own best hypothesis?"

Bradley didn't answer immediately. He glanced over at the stack of research papers, lingering for a moment before he looked back at me. When our eyes met, he continued.

"If there isn't a natural explanation and there doesn't seem to be the potential of finding one, then I believe it's appropriate to look at a supernatural explanation. I think that's the most reasonable inference based on the evidence."

That seemed to be a big concession for someone trained in science. "You don't see a problem in saying that the best explanation seems to be an Intelligent Designer?"

"Absolutely not. I think people who believe that life emerged naturalistically need to have a great deal more faith than people who reasonably infer that there's an Intelligent Designer."

"What prevents more scientists from drawing that conclusion?"

"Many *have* reached that conclusion. But for some, their philosophy gets in the way. If they're persuaded ahead of time that there isn't a God, then no matter how compelling the evidence, they'll always say, 'Wait, and we'll find something better in the future.' But that's a metaphysical argument. Scientists aren't more objective than anybody else. They all come to questions like this with their preconceived ideas."

I quickly interjected, "Yes, but you came in with a preconceived idea that there *is* a God."

Bradley nodded. "Sure," he conceded. "And I've been pleasantly surprised, because a lower level of evidence probably would have satisfied me. But what I've found is absolutely overwhelming evidence that points toward an Intelligent Designer."

"So you think the facts point convincingly toward a creator?"

"*Convincingly* is too mild a term," he replied. "The evidence is compelling. 'Convincing' suggests it's a little more likely than not; 'compelling' says you have to really work hard not to get to that conclusion."

"But it sounds so . . . ," I said, stumbling a bit while searching for the right word, "*unscientific*," I finally said.

"On the contrary," Bradley replied, "it's very scientific. For the past hundred fifty years, scientists have used arguments based on analogies to things we do understand to formulate new hypotheses in emerging areas of scientific work. And that's what this is about."

Reasoning by Analogy

The analogical method was described in the nineteenth century by astronomer John F. W. Herschel, who wrote, "If the analogy of two phenomena be very close and striking, while, at the same time, the cause of one is very obvious, it becomes scarcely possible to refuse to admit the action of an analogous cause in the other, though not so obvious in itself."[55]

"How does this apply to the origin-of-life issue?" I asked Bradley.

"If the only time we see written information—whether it's a painting on a cave wall or a novel from Amazon—is when there's an intelligence behind it, then wouldn't that also be true of nature itself?" Bradley said in responding.

"In other words, what is encoded on the DNA inside every cell of every living creature is purely and simply written information. We use a twenty-six-letter alphabet in English; in DNA, there is a four-letter chemical alphabet, whose letters combine in various sequences to form words, sentences, and paragraphs. These comprise all the instructions needed to guide the functioning of the cell. They spell out in coded form the instructions for how a cell makes proteins. It works just the way alphabetical letter sequences do in our language.

"Now, when we see written language, we can infer, based on our experience, that it has an intelligent cause. And we can legitimately use analogical reasoning to conclude that the remarkable information sequences in DNA also had an intelligent cause. Therefore, this means life on earth came from a 'who' instead of a 'what.'"

Undeniably, it was a powerful and persuasive argument. Bradley seemed to reflect on it for a few moments before offering an illustration that would clinch his point.

"Did you see the movie *Contact*?"

"Sure," I said. "It was based on Carl Sagan's book."

"That's right," he replied. "In the movie, scientists are scanning the skies for signs of intelligent life in space. Their radio telescopes just receive static—random sounds from space. It's reasonable to assume there's no intelligence behind that. Then one day they begin receiving a transmission of prime numbers, which are numbers divisible only by themselves and one.

"The scientists reason that it's too improbable that there would be a natural cause behind a string of numbers like that. This wasn't merely unorganized static; it was information, a message with content. From that, they concluded there was an intelligent cause behind it. As Sagan himself once said, 'The receipt of a single message from space' would be enough to know there's an intelligence out there.[56] That's reasoning by analogy—we know that where there's intelligent communication, there's an intelligent cause."

Bradley's eyes bored in on me as he delivered his conclusion. "And if a single message from space is enough for us to conclude there's an intelligence behind it, then what about the vast amounts of information contained in the DNA of every living plant and animal?" he said, his voice rising in emphasis.

"Each cell in the human body contains more information than in all thirty volumes of the *Encyclopedia Britannica*. It's certainly reasonable to make the inference that this isn't the random product of unguided nature, but it's the unmistakable sign of an Intelligent Designer."

It was an argument without an answer. "Then," I said, "the origin of life is the Achilles' heel of evolution."

"That's right. As Phillip Johnson said, 'If Darwinists are to keep the Creator out of the picture, they have to provide a naturalistic explanation for the origin of life.'[57]

"Lee, they haven't been able to do it. Despite all their efforts, they haven't even come up with a single possibility that even remotely makes sense. And there's no prospect they will. In fact, everything is pointing the other way—in the unmistakable direction of God. Today it takes a great deal of faith to be an honest scientist who is an atheist."

"I Build Molecules"

By happenstance, over in nearby Houston, nanoscientist James Tour, a professor at Rice University's Department of Chemistry and Center for Nanoscale Science and Technology, had recently finished giving a speech.

With a doctorate in organic chemistry from Purdue University and postdoctoral work at Stanford University and the University of Wisconsin, Tour is on the cutting edge of research into the molecular world. He has written more than 140 technical research articles and holds seventeen United States patents.

"I build molecules for a living," he said in introducing himself. "I can't begin to tell you how difficult that job is."

The purpose of his talk was not to dazzle the audience with descriptions of his latest high-tech efforts to store enormous amounts of information on a microscopic scale, replacing silicon chips that are large and unwieldy by comparison. Instead, it was to describe something else he has found the deeper and deeper he has probed into the awe-inspiring wonders of the molecular level: the fingerprints of an Intelligent Designer.

"I stand in awe of God because of what he has done through his creation," he said. "Only a rookie who knows nothing about science would say science takes away from faith. If you really study science, it will bring you closer to God."[58]

How ironic, I thought. Once, a rudimentary understanding of evolutionary science had propelled me toward atheism; now, an increasing grasp of molecular science was cementing my confidence in God. Like the Oklahoma murder case, my initial verdict had been based on flawed evidence that yielded a flawed conclusion.

The idea that undirected processes could somehow be responsible for turning dead chemicals into all the complexity of living things is surely, as microbiologist Michael Denton observed, "no more nor less than the great cosmogenic myth" of our times.[59]

Time magazine was wrong—Darwin didn't murder God. There are simply too many powerful clues—especially in the astounding intricacy of unseen molecules and the uncanny chemical language encoded on the double helix of DNA—to establish that the Creator is alive and well.

Deliberations
Questions for Reflection or Group Study

1. Describe the education you received in evolution. In what ways did it affect your outlook toward God?
2. Before reading this interview with Walter Bradley, how specifically did you believe life arose on earth? Did the interview change your viewpoint? How and why?
3. Based on the evidence, do you believe it's reasonable to infer the existence of an Intelligent Designer? Why or why not? In light of the facts, do you believe it would take more faith to believe that life arose naturalistically or through an intelligent cause?

For Further Evidence
More Resources on This Topic

Behe, Michael. *Darwin's Black Box: The Biochemical Challenge to Evolution.* 2nd ed. New York: Free Press, 2006.

Collins, Francis S. *The Language of God: A Scientist Presents Evidence for Belief.* New York: Free Press, 2007.

Dembski, William A., and Sean McDowell. *Understanding Intelligent Design: Everything You Need to Know in Plain Language.* Eugene, OR: Harvest House, 2008.

Johnson, Phillip E. *Darwin on Trial.* 20th Anniversary ed. Downers Grove, IL: InterVarsity, 2010.

Lennox, John. *Can Science Explain Everything?* Charlotte, NC: Good Book, 2019.

———. *Cosmic Chemistry: Do God and Science Mix?* Oxford, UK: Lion Hudson, 2021.

Meyer, Stephen. *Return of the God Hypothesis: Three Scientific Discoveries That Reveal the Mind behind the Universe.* New York: HarperOne, 2021.

———. *Signature in the Cell: DNA and the Evidence for Intelligent Design.* New York: HarperOne, 2010.

Moreland, J. P. *Scientism and Secularism: Learning to Respond to a Dangerous Ideology.* Wheaton, IL: Crossway, 2018.

Rana, Fazale, and Hugh Ross. *Origins of Life: Biblical and Evolutionary Models Face Off.* Colorado Springs, CO: NavPress, 2014.

Strobel, Lee. *The Case for a Creator: A Journalist Investigates Scientific Evidence That Points toward God.* Grand Rapids: Zondervan, 2004.

Thaxton, Charles et al. *The Mystery of Life's Origin: The Continuing Controversy.* Seattle, WA: Discovery Institute, 2020.

God Isn't Worthy of Worship If He Kills Innocent Children

The Bible tells us to be like God, and then on page after page it describes God as a mass murderer.

ROBERT ANTON WILSON, AGNOSTIC MYSTIC

But you, Lord, are a compassionate and gracious God, slow to anger, abounding in love and faithfulness.

KING DAVID, PSALM 86:15

As I walked through the metal detectors and past the uniformed guards, I could sense an undercurrent of expectation at the White House. Despite efforts to project a business-as-usual facade, it was clear that something big was going on behind the scenes. The Monica Lewinsky scandal had been escalating, and pressure was building for President Bill Clinton to come clean before special prosecutor Kenneth Starr released his long-awaited report.

Clinton arrived half an hour late for breakfast, sitting down directly across from me. His face was drawn, his eyes tired and puffy. Concerned for his health, I asked him how he was feeling.

"I was up until 3:00 a.m.," he replied in a husky whisper.

The press corps noisily jockeyed for position at the rear of the room, cameras whirring, pencils and notebooks poised. Clinton stood and took a few steps to a lectern. A hush fell over the room. His usual glibness was gone.

"I may not be quite as easy with my words today as I have been in years past," he told the small gathering of religious leaders. "I was up rather late last night thinking and praying about what I ought to say today."

He pulled out his glasses so he could read what he had written on a piece of paper. What followed was his most emotional and dramatic statement since news of his affair had broken in the media.

"I don't think there is a fancy way to say that I have sinned," he said, his eyes moist and his face pained. "It is important to me that everybody who has been hurt knows that the sorrow I feel is genuine—first and most important, my family, also my friends, my staff, my Cabinet, Monica Lewinsky and her family, and the American people. I have asked all for their forgiveness. I have repented . . . I must have God's help to be the person that I want to be."

There he was, the most powerful individual in the world, saying he had "a broken spirit" over his grossly immoral conduct with the former intern. All of his economic initiatives, all of his foreign policy efforts and social programs, had faded into the background. Taking center stage was the stark and convicting issue of character.

Politicians are expected to fashion a positive public image, burnishing it to a lustrous shine through self-serving press releases and adroit spin-doctoring, but their real character often gets revealed through their private choices far from the spotlight. Certainly a person's behind-the-scenes moral decisions—their marital fidelity and fundamental honesty in their relationships—are relevant to how they will conduct the business of the people. After all, they unmask the true individual.

When I was an atheist, I thought Christians could teach politicians a few tricks about creating a positive public image. Christians would focus relentlessly on certain appealing aspects of God's character—his love, his grace, his forgiveness, his compassion, his mercy—but underplay or ignore the biblical passages that seem to reveal more troubling aspects of his character.

When attention is focused on the little-mentioned Old Testament stories of massacres and other broad-scale bloodshed, suddenly God is seen in a different light. Like Bill Clinton, whose carefully crafted public persona fell apart once credible stories of extramarital dalliances were documented, God's image as a loving and benevolent deity gets called into question by stories of seemingly cruel and vengeful behavior. Do these brutal accounts disclose the true character of God? And if they do, does he deserve to be worshiped?

Charles Templeton has his own opinion. "The God of the Old Testament is utterly unlike the God believed in by most practicing Christians," he said. "His justice is, by modern standards, outrageous . . . He is biased, querulous, vindictive, and jealous of his prerogatives."[1]

Atheist George Smith agrees. "The Old Testament God garnered an impressive list of atrocities," he said. "Jehovah himself was fond of directly exterminating large numbers of people, usually through pestilence or famine, and often for rather unusual offenses."[2] Smith likes to quote former president Thomas Jefferson as saying that the Old Testament accounts reveal God to be "cruel, vindictive, capricious and unjust."[3]

This issue is disturbing enough, but in addition there's an ancillary matter that demands to be explored. In evaluating the character of God, both critics and Christians cite the Bible as their source of information. But is it really a trustworthy book? Isn't the Bible chock-full of contradictions and inconsistencies that undermine its reliability? Haven't its references to history been called into question by modern archaeology? Isn't it more likely a collection of imaginative legends than an accurate description of the Creator of the universe?

These two issues—the character of God and the reliability of the book that purports to tell us about him—were major hurdles when I was a spiritual seeker. At the time, I immersed myself in books and articles to try to come to some well-reasoned conclusions. I wish I could have done then what I was about to do now: sit down to interview a scholar who is one of the most well-known and effective defenders of Christianity in the world.

The Fourth Interview: Norman L. Geisler, PhD

Norman Geisler can be a tenacious and intimidating debater when he's marshaling biblical references, archaeological findings, scientific discoveries, and historical events to refute someone bent on discrediting Christianity. His encyclopedic memory and rapid-fire delivery have overwhelmed many critics through the years.

But it was a soft-spoken and grandfatherly Geisler who invited me into his modest yet comfortable office at Southern Evangelical Seminary in Charlotte, North Carolina, where he is president of the school. Casually dressed in a multicolored sweater over a blue button-down shirt, he had an easy smile and a down-to-earth sense of humor. Even so, I soon found him focused with laser-beam intensity on the challenges I had come halfway across the country to raise with him.

Geisler, a prodigious and award-winning author, has written, coauthored, or edited more than fifty books, including such standards as *A General Introduction to the Bible, Inerrancy, Introduction to Philosophy, Philosophy of Religion, When Skeptics Ask, When Critics Ask,* and *When Cultists Ask.* One of his most recent volumes is the ambitious, 841-page *Baker Encyclopedia of Christian Apologetics,* which systematically discusses issues ranging from "absolute truth" to "Zen Buddhism."

Having studied at Wheaton College, the University of Detroit, Wayne State University, William Tyndale College, and Northwestern University, Geisler received his doctorate in philosophy from Loyola University in Chicago. He is the former chairman of philosophy of religion at Trinity Evangelical Divinity School in Deerfield,

Illinois, and professor of systematic theology at Dallas Theological Seminary. His memberships include the American Philosophical Society, the American Scientific Association, and the American Academy of Religion.

Geisler has traveled widely—through all fifty states and twenty-five countries on six continents—giving lectures on the evidence for Christianity and debating such well-known skeptics as humanist Paul Kurtz. Consequently, I knew there was little chance I would take him completely off guard by a question. However, I came armed with some of the most difficult issues of all.

As we sat across from each other in maroon leather chairs, I pulled out a piece of paper on which I had jotted the biting words of an esteemed American patriot whose criticism of Christianity is legendary.

"In 1794," I began, "Thomas Paine wrote in *The Age of Reason*, 'Whenever we read the obscene stories, the voluptuous debaucheries, the cruel and torturous executions, the unrelenting vindictiveness, with which more than half the Bible is filled, it would be more consistent that we called it the work of a demon, than the word of God.'"[4]

I looked up at Geisler to see if he was wincing at the sting of Paine's words. "That's a tough challenge," I said. "How would you respond to him if he were sitting here today?"

Geisler adjusted his gold-rimmed glasses and then remarked with a chuckle, "First of all, I'd say too bad he didn't have a Bible. When he wrote the first part of *The Age of Reason*, he didn't have one. But apart from that, I think he's confusing two things: what the Bible records and what the Bible approves."

"Give me some examples of the difference," I said.

"For instance, the Bible records Satan's lies and David's adultery, but it doesn't approve of them," he explained. "It's true that there are a lot of gross stories in the Bible. The book of Judges reports the raping of a woman, then cutting her in twelve pieces and sending one piece to each of the tribes of Israel.[5] But the Bible certainly doesn't approve of that. Secondly, I think that Paine is just factually wrong. The Bible doesn't have any cruel and torturous executions that God commanded."

I raised my hand to protest. "David was called a man after God's own heart, and yet the Bible says he tortured his enemies," I pointed out. "It says he 'put them under saws . . . and under axes of iron, and made them pass through the brick-kiln.'[6] That sounds cruel and torturous to me!"

"Not so fast," Geisler cautioned. "You're quoting from the King James Version, and it's open to misinterpretation there. The New International Version clarifies the original Hebrew language and says David 'brought out the people who were there, consigning them to labor with saws and with iron picks and axes, and he made them work at brickmaking.' That's labor—not torture—and it's quite humane compared to the cruelties his enemies had unleashed. Besides, this is another case where the Bible records something but doesn't necessarily condone it."

Touché, I thought to myself. Quickly regrouping, I pressed on. "That passage aside, there's still a lot of carnage in the Old Testament," I said. "Isn't there a big difference between the often-cruel God of the Old Testament and the loving God of the New Testament?"

Geisler smiled. "It's interesting you ask that," he replied, "because I just did a study of every time the Bible uses the word that the King James Version translates as 'mercy.' I found it occurs 261 times in the Bible—and 72 percent of them are in the Old Testament. That's a three-to-one ratio. Then I studied the word *love* and found it occurs 322 times in the Bible, about half in each Testament. So you have the same emphasis on love in both.

"Ironically," he added, "you could make a case that God is more judgmental in the New Testament than the Old. For example, the Old Testament talks very little about eternal punishment, but the New Testament does."

"There's no evolution in God's character then?"

"That's right. In fact, the Bible says, 'I the LORD do not change.'[7] In both Testaments you've got the identical, unchangeable God—the one who is so holy he cannot look upon sin, and yet the one whose loving, merciful, gracious, and compassionate heart wants to pour forgiveness on all people who repent."

Compassionate? I thought to myself. *Merciful?* The time had come to get to the crux of the character issue.

God's Orders to Kill

I looked intently into Geisler's eyes. My voice leaked sarcasm as I posed the most pointed objection to God's character. "You talk about compassion and mercy," I said, "but those qualities are hard to understand when we see God ordering genocide by telling the Israelites in Deuteronomy 7 to totally destroy the Canaanites and six other nations and to show them no mercy."

That got me started on a roll. "And that wasn't an isolated incident," I continued, picking up speed as I went. "God ordered the execution of every Egyptian firstborn; he flooded the world and killed untold thousands of people; he told the Israelites, 'Now go, attack the Amalekites and totally destroy all that belongs to them. Do not spare them; put to death men and women, children and infants, cattle and sheep, camels and donkeys.'[8] That sounds more like a violent and brutal God than a loving one. How can people be expected to worship him if he orders innocent children to be slaughtered?"

Despite the force of the question, Geisler retained a calm and reasoned tone. "This shows," he said, "that God's character is absolutely holy, and that he has to punish sin and rebellion. He's a righteous judge; that's undeniably part of who he is. But, secondly, his character is also merciful. Listen: if anyone wants to escape, he will let them."

Geisler paused. My questions clearly required a more extended explanation. "Lee, you've raised a whole bunch of good issues, and they deserve a thoughtful response," he said. "Do you mind if we go through those passages a little more carefully? Because if we do, I think we'll see the same pattern over and over."

I gestured for him to proceed. "Please," I said, "go through them. I really do want to understand."

"Let's start with the Amalekites," he began. "Listen, Lee, they were far from innocent. *Far* from it. These were not nice people. In fact, they were utterly and totally depraved. Their mission was to destroy Israel. In other words, to commit genocide. As if that weren't evil enough, think about what was hanging in the balance. The Israelites were the chosen people through whom God would bring salvation to the entire world through Jesus Christ."

"So you're saying they deserved to be destroyed?" I asked.

"The destruction of their nation was necessitated by the gravity of their sin," Geisler said. "Had some hard-core remnant survived, they might have resumed their aggression against the Israelites and God's plan. These were a persistent and vicious and warring people. To show you how reprehensible they were, they had been following the Israelites and had been cowardly slaughtering the most vulnerable among them—the weak, elderly, and disabled who were lagging behind.

"They wanted to wipe every last one of the Israelites off the face of the earth. God could have dealt with them through a natural disaster like a flood, but instead he used Israel as his instrument of judgment. He took action not only for the sake of the Israelites, but ultimately for the sake of everyone through history whose salvation would be provided by the Messiah who was to be born among them."

"But the children," I protested. "Why did innocent children need to be killed?"

"Let's keep in mind," he said, "that technically nobody is truly innocent. The Bible says in Psalm 51 that we're all born in sin, that is, with the propensity to rebel and commit wrongdoing. Also, we need to keep in mind God's sovereignty over life. An atheist once brought up this issue in a debate, and I responded by saying, 'God created life, and he has the right to take it. If you can create life, then you can have the right to take it. But if you can't create it, you don't have that right.' And the audience applauded.

"People assume that what's wrong for us is wrong for God. However, it's wrong for me to take your life, because I didn't make it and I don't own it. For example, it's wrong for me to go into your yard and pull up your bushes, cut them down, kill them, transplant them, move them around. I can do that in my yard, because I own the bushes in my yard.

"Well, God is sovereign over all of life, and he has the right to take it if he wishes. In fact, we tend to forget that God takes the life of every human being. It's called death. The only question is when and how, which we have to leave up to him."

What about the Children?

Intellectually, I could understand Geisler's answer up to this point. However, emotionally it didn't go far enough. I was still unsettled. "But the children . . ." I persisted.

Geisler, himself the father of six children and grandfather of nine, was sympathetic. "Socially and physically, the fate of children throughout history has always been with their parents, whether that's for good or for ill," he pointed out.

"But, Lee, you need to understand the situation among the Amalekites. In that thoroughly evil, violent, and depraved culture, there was no hope for those children. This nation was so polluted that it was like gangrene that was taking over a person's leg, and God had to amputate the leg or the gangrene would spread and there wouldn't be anything left. In a sense, God's action was an act of mercy."

"Mercy?" I asked. "How so?"

"According to the Bible, every child who dies before the age of accountability goes to heaven to spend eternity in the presence of God," he replied. "Now, if they had continued to live in that horrible society, past the age of accountability, they undoubtedly would have become corrupted and thereby lost forever."

"What makes you think children go to heaven when they die?" I asked.

"Isaiah 7:16 talks about an age before a child is morally accountable, before the child 'knows enough to reject the wrong and choose the right.' King David spoke of going to be with his son who died at birth. Jesus said, 'Let the little children come to me, and do not hinder them, for the kingdom of God belongs to such as these,' which indicates they will go to heaven.[9] There's a considerable amount of other scriptural support for this position as well."

I jumped on an apparent inconsistency. "If ultimately it was best for those children to die before the age of accountability because they would go to heaven, why can't the same be said about unborn children who are aborted today?" I asked. "If they're aborted, they're definitely going to heaven, but if they are born and grow up they might rebel against God and end up in hell. Isn't that a forceful argument in favor of abortion?"

Geisler's response came quickly. "No, that's a false analogy," he insisted. "First, God doesn't command anyone today to have an abortion; in fact, it's contrary to the teachings of the Bible. Remember, he's the only one who can decide to take a life, because he's the ultimate author of life. Secondly, today we don't have a culture that's as thoroughly corrupt as the Amalekite society. In that culture, there was no hope; today, there's hope."

"So," I said, "you don't think God was being unreasonable by ordering the destruction of the Amalekites?"

"You have to remember that these people were given plenty of opportunity to change their ways and to avoid all of this," he said. "In fact, if you take all of the Canaanites along with the Amalekites, they had four hundred years to repent. That's a very long time. Finally, after waiting centuries to give them an opportunity to abandon their path toward self-destruction, God's nature demanded that he deal with their willful evil. He certainly didn't act precipitously.

"Now, we have to keep in mind that those who wanted to get out of this situation had already done so; they had ample opportunity through the years. Surely the ones who wanted to be saved from destruction fled and were spared.

"In Joshua 6, where the Bible talks about the destruction of Jericho and the Canaanites, we've got the same pattern. This was a thoroughly evil culture, so much so that the Bible says it nauseated God. They were into brutality, cruelty, incest, bestiality, cultic prostitution, and even child sacrifice by fire. They were an aggressive culture that wanted to annihilate the Israelites.

"Again, we've got evil people who were destroyed but the righteous among them who were saved. For instance, Rahab, who protected the Israelite spies, was not judged with the other people. And look at what happened to the corrupt residents of the city of Nineveh. God was going to judge them because they deserved it, but they repented and God saved the whole bunch. So here's the point: *whoever has repented, God has been willing to save.* That's important to remember.

"You see, God's purpose in these instances was to destroy the corrupt nation because the national structure was inherently evil, not to destroy people if they were willing to repent. Many verses indicate that God's primary desire was to drive these evil people out of the land that they already knew had been promised for a long time to Israel. That way, Israel could come in and be relatively free from the outside corruption that could have destroyed it like a cancer. He wanted to create an environment where the Messiah could come for the benefit of millions of people through history."

"The pattern, then, was that people had plenty of warning?" I asked.

"Certainly," he said. "And consider this: most of the women and children would have fled in advance before the actual fighting began, leaving behind the warriors to face the Israelites. The fighters who remained would have been the most hardened, the ones who stubbornly refused to leave, the carriers of the corrupt culture. So it's really questionable how many women and children might actually have been involved anyway.

"Besides, under the rules of conduct God had given to the Israelites, whenever they went into an enemy city, they were to first make the people an offer of peace. The people had a choice: they could accept that offer, in which case they wouldn't be killed, or they could reject the offer at their own peril. That's appropriate and fair."

I had to admit that these insights shed new light on the situation, especially his comments about the ample warning that had been given and the likelihood that women and children had probably evacuated the area prior to any battle. And as troubling as these passages are, it helped to know that Israel would offer peace before engaging in a fight, and that the biblical pattern was that repentant people are given opportunities to avoid the judgment.

"God, then, was not being capricious?"

"He's not capricious, he's not arbitrary, he's not cruel. But, Lee, I have to tell you something: he is undeniably just. His nature demands that he deal with corrupt people who stubbornly and willfully persist in their evil. And isn't that what he should do? Isn't that what we want—for justice to be done? One of the key things to remember is that throughout history, for those who repent and turn to him, he's compassionate, merciful, gracious, and kind. In the end, we'll all see his fairness."

Still, there was another troubling episode—again, involving children—that seemed to challenge Geisler's opinion that God does not act capriciously. It involves one of the strangest episodes in the entire Bible.

Cosmic Overkill?

The prophet Elisha was walking down the road toward Bethel when he was confronted by some little children who teased him by making fun of his baldness. "Get out of here, baldy!" they taunted.

"Get out of here, baldy!" He reacted by cursing them in the name of God. Then, in a stunning act of retribution, two bears suddenly emerged from the woods and mauled forty-two of them.[10]

"Now, Dr. Geisler, you insisted that God is not capricious," I said. "But that sounds like an outrageous response to a minor and silly offense. Mauling forty-two innocent little children just because they poked fun of some bald guy is awfully severe."

Geisler was well-acquainted with the issue. "The presupposition of your question is wrong," Geisler replied. "These were not small, innocent children."

Having anticipated his response, I pulled out a photocopy of the passage and thrust it in his direction. "Yes, they were," I retorted. "Look right there," I said, pointing to the words. "It says 'little children.'"

Geisler glanced briefly at the page, immediately recognizing its source. "Unfortunately, the King James Version has a misleading translation there," he said. "Scholars have established that the original Hebrew is best translated 'young men.' The New International Version renders the word 'boys.' As best we can tell, this was a violent mob of dangerous teens, comparable to a modern street gang. The life of the prophet was in danger just because of the sheer number of them—if forty-two were mauled, who knows how many were threatening him in total?"

"Threatening him?" I asked. "Give me a break! They were just making fun of his baldness."

"When you understand the context, you'll see that this was much more serious than that," Geisler replied. "Commentators have noted that their taunts were intended to challenge Elisha's claim to be a prophet. Essentially, they were saying, 'If you're a man of God, why don't you go up to heaven like the prophet Elijah did?' Apparently, they were mocking the earlier work of God in taking Elijah to heaven. They were contemptuous in their disbelief over what God had done through both of these prophets.

"And their remarks about Elisha being bald were most likely

a reference to the fact that lepers in those days shaved their heads. So they were assailing Elisha—a man of dignity and authority as a prophet of God—as a detestable and despicable outcast. They were casting a slur not only on his character but on God's as well, since he was God's representative."

"Still," I said, "isn't that a rather minor offense?"

"Not in the context of those days," he said. "Elisha justifiably felt threatened by the gang. His life was in danger. They were, in effect, attacking him and God. This was a kind of preemptory strike to put fear in the hearts of anyone else who would do this, because this could be a dangerous precedent. If a menacing mob of teens got away with this and God didn't come to the defense of his prophet, just think of the negative effect that event would have on society. It could open the door to further attacks on prophets and consequently a disregard for the urgent message they were trying to bring from God.

"In fact, as one commentator said, 'Instead of demonstrating unleashed cruelty, the bear attack shows God trying repeatedly to bring his people back to himself through smaller judgments until the people's sin is too great and judgment must come full force . . . The disastrous fall of Samaria would have been avoided had the people repented after the bear attack.'"[11]

"Last of all," Geisler added, "I'd say once again that we have to consider the sovereignty of God. It wasn't Elisha who took their lives; it was the God who created them who let the bears loose. And if he created life, he has every right to take it away. The attack of this gang on the prophet revealed their true attitudes toward God, and it's always a perilous path that leads to destruction when we defiantly curse and stubbornly oppose God."

I folded the photocopy of the passage. "Then it's a misreading of the original text to see these as mere children," I said.

"That's right," he said. "The Hebrew that was used to describe them indicates they were most likely between the ages of twelve and thirty. In fact, one of the same Hebrew words is used elsewhere to describe men in the army.[12] As you can see, when everything is put into perspective, you get a much different picture than was originally supposed."

By now, Geisler's answers had deflated much of the case against God's character by bringing some balance and context to understanding his apparent intent in these controversial episodes. While these passages were still sticking points, seeing the other side did make it easier to give God the benefit of the doubt, especially in light of the preponderance of other evidence for his compassion and love.

There was also, however, a related matter about God's character that concerns many people these days: how he has dealt with animals. Why did he create a world where predators constantly stalk prey and where violent death is an integral part of life? And more fundamentally, doesn't that reveal something disturbing about his attitude?

The Pain of Animals

Charles Templeton raised the issue of suffering in the animal kingdom when he wrote the following in his book *Farewell to God*:

> The grim and inescapable reality is that all life is predicated on death. Every carnivorous creature must kill and devour other creatures . . . How could a loving and omnipotent God create such horrors? . . . Surely it would not be beyond the competence of an omniscient deity to create an animal world that could be sustained and perpetuated without suffering and death.[13]

"What about that?" I asked Geisler after reading Templeton's quote to him.

"He's got a lot of truth in there," Geisler replied.

That wasn't the response I was expecting. "You think so?" I asked.

"Yes," he said. "But unfortunately, it's like a glass of good water with a drop of arsenic in it. There's good water there, but it's poisoned."

"How so?"

"The good water is, yes, God can create those kind of animals. And the fact is, he did. The original paradise had those kind of animals, and the paradise to come—the paradise restored—is going to have those kind of animals. In fact, we're told that God originally created animals and human beings to be herbivorous."

With that, Geisler reached under his chair and removed a Bible. He opened it toward its beginning; his eyes scanned the page until he stopped near the end of the first chapter, and read:

> Then God said, "I give you every seed-bearing plant on the face of the whole earth and every tree that has fruit with seed in it. They will be yours for food. And to all the beasts of the earth and all the birds in the sky and all the creatures that move along the ground—everything that has the breath of life in it—I give every green plant for food." And it was so.[14]

Shutting the book, Geisler continued. "God did not appoint animals to be eaten in paradise, and animals weren't eating each other. The prophet Isaiah said someday God will 'create new heavens and a new earth' where 'the wolf and the lamb will feed together, and the lion will eat straw like the ox.'[15] In other words, there's not going to be the kind of killing that goes on now.

"In sum, everything that God created was good. What changed things was the fall. When God was told, in effect, to shove off, he partially did. Romans 8 says all creation was affected—that includes plant life, human beings, animals, everything. There were fundamental genetic changes; we see, for instance, how life spans rapidly decreased after the fall. God's plan was not designed to be this way; it's only this way because of sin. Ultimately, it will be remedied."

"But in instituting the animal sacrifice system in the Old Testament, wasn't God being cruel to animals?" I asked.

"The manner in which these animals were killed was quite humane. It was the most painless way to die. And there was no waste. They ate the meat and used the skin for clothing, so essentially they were growing and harvesting animals. This was not an attempt to eliminate a species. And of course, there was an important reason for the animal sacrifices—they pointed ahead toward the ultimate sacrifice of Jesus Christ, the Lamb of God, on the cross as payment for our sin."

"What about all the pain in the world as a result of animals hunting and killing other animals?" I asked. "The sum total of suffering that God allows in the world is absolutely enormous."

"I think that entire presupposition is wrong," he replied. "As C. S. Lewis said, there is no sum total of pain.[16] It's a misnomer. No one person or animal experiences the sum total of pain. In fact, no one person experiences at one time the sum total of pain of their lifetime. If you had thirty ounces of pain spread over thirty years, you only get an ounce a year and therefore only a fraction of an ounce a day.

"As far as animals are concerned, we have to remember that the Bible clearly forbids their abuse. Christians should oppose any mistreatment of animals. However, I would challenge the premise of the animal rights movement that animals have moral rights. They are not moral creatures. Now, moral people can do immoral things to animals, but the Bible says, 'The righteous care for the needs of their animals.'[17] They are to serve us and help us, and it's morally wrong to be cruel to them."

Can the Bible Be Trusted?

In assessing the character of God, Geisler was relying on the Bible. Having written a book on the inerrancy of Scripture, Geisler's opinion of it is well-known: he believes the Bible to be uniquely inspired by God and factual in all it teaches and touches on. Still, is there any rational reason to believe that the Bible really does accurately reveal the truth about God?

George Smith, the atheistic philosopher, thinks not. "The Bible shows no traces whatsoever of supernatural influence," he said. "Quite the contrary, it is obviously the product of superstitious men who, at times, were willing to deceive if it would further their doctrines."[18]

Templeton cavalierly dismisses most of the Bible as being "embellished folk tales," adding that it is "no longer possible for an informed man or woman to believe that . . . the Bible is either a reliable document . . . or, as the Christian church insists, the infallible Word of God."[19]

During my years as an atheist, I mocked the fantastical tales and blatant mythology that I believed disqualified the Bible from being a divinely inspired book—an opinion, incidentally, that quite conveniently relieved me from any need to follow its moral dictates. Although I had never thoroughly studied its contents, I was quick to reject the Bible in order to free myself to live the kind of corrupt lifestyle that was blatantly at odds with its tenets.

My time with Geisler was a rare opportunity to hear firsthand why he draws the opposite conclusion and so zealously defends the Bible as being trustworthy. I stood to stretch my legs, walking over to a bookshelf and casually scanning the titles. Then I turned and said, "Everything hinges on whether the Bible is true. What's your basis for believing it is?"

With characteristic confidence, Geisler replied, "There's more evidence that the Bible is a reliable source than there is for any other book from the ancient world."

To me, however, that seemed more of a conclusion than evidence. "You're going to have to give me some facts to back that up," I said, sitting back down on the edge of my seat in anticipation of Geisler's response.

"There's lots of evidence I could talk about," he began. "I could talk about the Bible's unity—sixty-six books written in different literary styles by perhaps forty different authors with diverse backgrounds over fifteen hundred years, and yet the Bible amazingly unfolds one continuous drama with one central message.

That points to the existence of the divine mind that the writers claimed inspired them.

"And there's the Bible's transforming power—from the beginning, it has renewed people; given them hope, courage, purpose, wisdom, guidance, and power; and formed an anchor for their lives. While early Islam was spread by the sword, early Christianity spread by the Spirit, even while Christians were being killed by Roman swords.

"I believe the most convincing evidence falls into two categories, however. First, there's archaeological confirmation of its reliability, and, second, there's miraculous confirmation of its divine authority."

Reason #1: Confirmation by Archaeology

Geisler started his discussion of the archaeological evidence by quoting the words of Jesus, who said: "I have spoken to you of earthly things and you do not believe; how then will you believe if I speak of heavenly things?"[20]

"Conversely," said Geisler, "if we can trust the Bible when it's telling us about straightforward earthly things that can be verified, then we can trust it in areas where we can't directly verify it in an empirical way."

"How, then, has the Bible been corroborated?" I asked. Having investigated some of the archaeological confirmation of the New Testament in my previous book, *The Case for Christ*, I was especially interested in archaeology and the Old Testament, and that's where I asked Geisler to begin.

"There have been thousands—not hundreds—of archaeological finds in the Middle East that support the picture presented in the biblical record. There was a discovery not long ago confirming King David. The patriarchs—the narratives about Abraham, Isaac, and Jacob—were once considered legendary, but as more has become known, these stories are increasingly corroborated. The destruction of Sodom and Gomorrah was thought to be mythological until evidence was uncovered that all five of the cities mentioned in Genesis were, in fact, situated just as the Old Testament said. As far as their destruction goes, archaeologist Clifford Wilson said there is 'permanent evidence of the great conflagration that took place in the long distant past.'[21]

"Furthermore," Geisler added, "various aspects of the Jewish captivity have been confirmed. Also, every reference in the Old Testament to an Assyrian king has been proven correct; an excavation during the 1960s confirmed that the Israelites could, indeed, have entered Jerusalem by way of a tunnel during David's reign; there is evidence the world did have a single language at one time, as the Bible says; the site of Solomon's temple is now being excavated; and on and on. Many times, archaeologists have been skeptical of the Old Testament, only to have new discoveries corroborate the biblical account."

"For example . . . ?" I asked.

"For instance, Samuel says that after Saul's death his armor was put in the temple of Ashtaroth, who was a Canaanite fertility goddess, at Beth Shan, while Chronicles reports that his head was put in the temple of a Philistine corn god named Dagon. Now, archaeologists thought that must have been an error and therefore the Bible was unreliable. They didn't think enemies would have had temples in the same place at the same time."

"What did the archaeologists find?" I asked.

"They confirmed through excavations that there were two temples at that site, one each for Dagon and Ashtaroth. They were separated by a hallway. As it turned out, the Philistines had apparently adopted Ashtaroth as one of their own goddesses. The Bible was right after all.

"That kind of phenomenon has happened again and again. The Bible makes about three dozen references to the Hittites, but critics used to charge that there was no evidence that such people ever existed. Now archaeologists digging in modern Turkey have discovered the records of the Hittites. As the great archaeologist William F. Albright declared, 'There can be no doubt that archaeology has confirmed the substantial historicity of the Old Testament tradition.'"[22]

I asked Geisler to continue by briefly summarizing why he believes that archaeology corroborates the New Testament.

"The noted Roman historian Colin J. Hemer in *The Book of Acts in the Setting of Hellenistic History* shows how archaeology has confirmed not dozens, but hundreds and hundreds of details from the biblical account of the early church," Geisler said. "Even small details have been corroborated, like which way the wind blows, how deep the water is a certain distance from shore, what kind of disease a particular island had, the names of local officials, and so forth.

"Now, Acts was authored by the historian Luke. Hemer gives more than a dozen reasons for why Acts had to have been written before AD 62, or about thirty years after Jesus' crucifixion. Even earlier, Luke wrote the gospel of Luke, which is substantially the same as the other biblical accounts of Jesus' life.

"So here you have an impeccable historian, who has been proven right in hundreds of details and never proven wrong, writing the whole history of Jesus and the early church. And it's written within one generation while eyewitnesses were still alive and could have disputed it if it were exaggerated or false. You don't have anything like that from any other religious book from the ancient world."[23]

"Is Hemer a lone voice on that?" I asked.

"Hardly," came the reply. "Prominent historian Sir William Ramsay started out as a skeptic, but after studying Acts, he concluded that 'in various details the narrative showed marvelous truth.'[24] The great Oxford University classical historian A. N. Sherwin-White said, 'For Acts the confirmation of historicity is overwhelming,' and that 'any attempt to reject its basic historicity must now appear absurd.'[25]

"Earlier, I mentioned archaeologist William Albright, who was a leader in the American School of Oriental Research for forty years. He started out as a liberal but became more and more conservative as he studied the archaeological record. He concluded that the radical New Testament critics are 'pre-archaeological' and their views are 'quite antiquated.'"[26]

I sat back in my leather chair as I reflected on Geisler's barrage of facts and quotes. The argument was strong: If archaeology shows that the Bible was accurate in what can be checked out, why would it be any less accurate in its other points? That only proves so much, however.

"Even if archaeology does confirm that the Bible is historically accurate, that doesn't mean it's divinely authoritative," I said.

"Correct," Geisler said crisply. "The only reason anyone should accept the Bible as divinely authoritative is because it has miraculous confirmation."

Reason #2: Evidence of Divine Origin

Geisler thumbed through his well-worn Bible, turning all the way to its opening sentence and then balancing the open book on his lap.

"It all goes back to whether the first verse of the Bible is true when it says, 'In the beginning God created the heavens and the earth,'" Geisler said. "I believe there's overwhelming scientific evidence that it is true—everything that has a beginning has a beginner; the universe had a beginning, therefore it had a beginner; the universe was tweaked and fine-tuned from the very moment of creation for the emergence of human life; and so on."

I interrupted to inform him that I had already interviewed Walter Bradley about the evidence pointing to a divine origin of the universe.

"Ah, good," he said. "What people often forget is that if this first verse is true, not only are miracles possible, but miracles are actual, because the biggest miracle has already happened—making something out of nothing. What's harder: for Jesus to take water and turn it into wine or to take a handful of nothing and make water? It's a lot harder to make water out of nothing than to make wine out of water.

"A skeptic once said to me, 'I don't believe the Bible because it has miracles.' I said, 'Name one.' He said, 'Turning water into wine. Do you believe that?' I said, 'Yeah, it happens all the time.' He said, 'What do you mean?' I said, 'Well, rain goes through the grapevine, up into the grape, and the grape turns into wine. All Jesus did was speed it up a little bit.'

"My point is, if you've got a God who can make something out of nothing, then he can make miracles. And then the only thing we have to look at is what book in the world has been miraculously confirmed. There's only one, and that's the Bible."

"Okay," I said. "Tell me how."

Geisler raised two fingers. "Two ways," he said. "First, the Bible is miraculously confirmed by the fulfillment of predictive prophecies, and, second, it's confirmed by the miracles performed by those who purported to be speaking for God."

Confirmation by Prophecies

Geisler began with a sweeping sentence: "The Bible is the only book in the world that has precise, specific predictions that were made hundreds of years in advance and that were literally fulfilled."

Gesturing toward one of the books packed into his shelves, he continued by saying, "According to Barton Payne's *Encyclopedia of Biblical Prophecy*, there are 191 predictions in the Old Testament about the coming of Christ, including his ancestry, the city in which he would be born, that he would be born of a virgin, precisely the time in history when he would die, and so on.

"In fact, Psalm 22:16 says his hands and feet would be pierced; verse 14 says his bones would be out of joint; verse 18 talks about the casting of lots for his garments; and Zechariah 12:10 says he would be pierced, as Jesus was with a lance. That's obviously a picture of his crucifixion—however, it was written before crucifixion was even implemented as a method of execution by the Romans. The Jews stoned people to death back then.

"And, of course, Isaiah 53:2–12 has perhaps the most amazing predictions about Christ in the entire Old Testament. This passage foretells twelve aspects of his passion that were all fulfilled—he would be rejected, be a man of sorrows, live a life of suffering, be despised by others, carry our sorrow, be smitten and afflicted by God, be pierced for our transgressions, be wounded for our sins, would suffer like a lamb, would die with the wicked, would be sinless, and would pray for others."

I spoke up. "Wait a second," I said. "If you talk to a rabbi, he'll tell you that this passage refers symbolically to Israel, not to the Messiah."

Geisler shook his head. "In Old Testament times, the Jewish rabbis *did* consider this to be a prophecy concerning the Messiah. That's the opinion that's really relevant," he said.

"Only later, after Christians pointed out this was obviously referring to Jesus, did they begin saying it was really about the suffering Jewish nation. But clearly that's wrong. Isaiah customarily refers to the Jewish people in the first-person plural, like 'our' or 'we,' but he always refers to the Messiah in the third-person singular, like 'he' and 'him'—and that's what he did in Isaiah 53. Plus, anyone who reads it for themselves will readily see it's referring to Jesus. Maybe that's why it's usually skipped over in synagogues these days.

"So here you have incredible predictions that were literally fulfilled in the life of one man, even though he had no control over most of them. For instance, he couldn't have arranged his ancestry, the timing of his birth, and so on. These prophecies were written two hundred to four hundred years in advance. No other book in the world has this. The Bible is the only book that's supernaturally confirmed this way."

I pondered this. "But Old Testament prophets weren't the only ones in history who have made predictions that have amazingly come true. For instance, Nostradamus, the physician and astrologer who lived in the 1500s, is famous for having made forecasts about the future. Didn't he predict the rise of Hitler and Nazi Germany?"

I said, more as a statement than a question. "If he can do that, what's so special about the predictive prophecies of the Bible?"

"The problem with Nostradamus and so many other so-called psychics is that their predictions are often very enigmatic, ambiguous, and inaccurate," Geisler retorted.

"But what about the Hitler prediction?" I demanded. "That's pretty specific."

"Actually, it wasn't specific at all," he replied.

Geisler stood up and strolled over to his bookshelf, pulling down one of his books and rummaging through it until he located what he was after. Then he read the words of Nostradamus's prediction:

> Followers of sects, great troubles are in store for the Messenger. A beast upon the theater prepares the scenical play. The inventor of that wicked feat will be famous. By sects the world will be confused and divided . . . Beasts mad with hunger will swim across rivers. Most of the army will be against the Lower Danube [*Hister sera*]. The great one shall be dragged in an iron cage when the child brother [*de Germain*] will observe nothing.[27]

Continued Geisler, "Obviously, this is not a reference to Adolf Hitler. The word isn't 'Hitler' but 'Hister,' and it's clearly not a person but a place. The Latin phrase *de Germain* should be interpreted as 'brother' or 'near relative,' not Germany. He doesn't cite any dates or even a general time frame. Besides, what does he mean by 'beasts' and 'iron cage'? It's so confusing that the entire prophecy is meaningless.

"The pattern is that Nostradamus's predictions are very ambiguous and could fit a great variety of events. His followers are inconsistent in how they interpret what he said. And some of his prophecies have been shown to be false. In fact, not a single prediction of Nostradamus has ever been proven genuine."

"I'll concede that many psychics, like Nostradamus, are vague in their predictions," I said. "But you have to admit that the same is true of some of the biblical prophecies."

"Granted, not all biblical prophecy is sharp," Geisler replied. "However, many prophecies are very specific. How much more detailed can you get than accurately predicting when Jesus would die, as Daniel 9:24–26 did? When you do the math, you find that this passage pinpoints when Jesus would enter human history. And what about predictions of his birthplace or how he would suffer and die? The specificity is astounding—and they have invariably proven to be true."

I countered with a contemporary example of a psychic whose predictions often were quite detailed. "In 1956, Jeane Dixon predicted a Democrat would win the 1960 presidential election and be assassinated in office. That was fulfilled in John F. Kennedy—and that's a pretty specific prophecy."

Geisler wasn't impressed. "She also predicted the 1960 election would be dominated by labor, which it wasn't. She later hedged her bets by saying Richard Nixon would win, so there was a 100 percent chance of one of those predictions coming true. As far as the assassination, three of the ten presidents in the twentieth century had died in office and two others were critically ill at the end of their terms. The odds against her weren't too bad.

"Besides, unlike the biblical prophets, she made numerous predictions that turned out to be false—that Red China would plunge the world into war over Quemoy and Matsu in 1958, that World War III would begin in 1954, that Castro would be banished from Cuba in 1970. My favorite is that she predicted Jacqueline Kennedy would not remarry—and the very next day, she wed Aristotle Onassis!" he said with a chuckle.

"A study of the prophecies made by psychics in 1975, including Dixon's, showed they were only accurate 6 percent of the time. That's pitiful! You probably could just guess and get a better record than that. Besides, you'll find that Dixon, Nostradamus, and other psychics commonly deal with occult practices—she used a crystal ball, for example—and that could account for some of what they predicted."

As someone skeptical of psychics, I didn't want to get pushed further into a position of trying to defend them. And Geisler's point had been made: they are completely different from biblical prophets. I decided to advance to a more potent criticism of biblical prophecy, which is the allegation that Christians wrench them out of context and claim they predicted the coming of Jesus when actually they were dealing with another issue. One example popped into my mind.

"Do you mind?" I asked as I reached over and took Geisler's Bible. I turned to Matthew 2:14–15, which says: "So [Joseph] got up, took the child and his mother during the night and left for Egypt, where he stayed until the death of Herod. And so was fulfilled what the Lord had said through the prophet: 'Out of Egypt I called my son.'"

That's a reference to Hosea 11:1. I turned to that verse and read it to Geisler: "When Israel was a child, I loved him, and out of Egypt I called my son." Closing the book and handing it back to Geisler, I said, "Now, obviously that passage is about the children of Israel coming out of Egypt in the exodus. It's not about the Messiah. Isn't that yanking a prophecy out of context?"

"That's a good question," Geisler remarked. "You have to understand, however, that not all prophecies are predictive."

"Meaning what?" I asked.

"It's true that the New Testament did apply certain Old Testament passages to Jesus that were not directly predictive of him. Many scholars see these references as being typologically fulfilled in Christ, without being directly predictive."

"Meaning?"

"In other words, some truth in the passage can appropriately be applied to Christ even though it was not specifically predictive of him. Other scholars say there's a generic meaning in certain Old Testament passages that apply to both Israel and Christ, both of whom were called God's 'son.' This is sometimes called a double-reference view of prophecy.

"I can see the merit of both views. But again, these passages were not directly predictive, and I don't use them that way. There are certainly, however, a sufficient number of examples of prophecies that are clearly predictive to establish the divine authority of the Bible. Mathematics has shown there's absolutely no way they could have been fulfilled by mere chance."

Confirmation by Miracles

Advancing to the other reason for the Bible's divine authority, Geisler said there's one sure way to determine whether a prophet is truly a spokesperson for God or a charlatan trying to deceive the masses: Can they produce clear-cut miracles? All three great monotheistic religions—Christianity, Judaism, and Islam—recognize the validity of miracles as a means of confirming a message from God. Even famed skeptic Bertrand Russell conceded that miracles would authenticate a truth claim.[28]

"In the Bible—which, remember, we've seen is historically reliable—we have prophets who were challenged but who then performed miracles to establish their credentials," Geisler said.

"For example, Moses said in Exodus 4:1, 'What if they do not believe me or listen to me and say, "The LORD did not appear to you"?' How does God respond? By telling Moses to throw his staff to the ground; instantly, it turned into a snake. He told Moses to pick it up by its tail; it turned back into a staff. Then God said in verse 5, 'This is so that they may believe that the LORD, the God of their fathers—the God of Abraham, the God of Isaac and the God of Jacob—has appeared to you.'

"The same thing for Elijah on Mount Carmel—he was challenged, and God sent down fire from heaven to confirm he was a true prophet.[29] As for Jesus, he actually came out and said, 'Do not believe me unless I do the works of my Father.'[30] And then he did them. Even Nicodemus conceded this when he said to Jesus, 'Rabbi, we know that you are a teacher who has come from God. For no one could perform the signs you are doing if God were not with him.'[31]

"This never happened to Muhammad. In fact, Muhammad

actually believed Jesus was a prophet who performed miracles, including raising the dead. Muslims also believe Moses and Elijah performed miracles. That's very interesting, because in the Qur'an when unbelievers challenged Muhammad to perform a miracle, he refused. He merely said they should read a chapter in the Qur'an."[32]

"He did?" I interjected.

"Absolutely. And yet Muhammad himself said, 'God hath certainly power to send down a sign.'[33] He even said, 'They [will] say: "Why is not a sign sent down to him from his Lord?"'[34] Unlike Jesus, miracles were not a sign of Muhammad's ministry. It wasn't until a hundred fifty or two hundred years after his life that his followers invented miracles and ascribed them to him.

"But when John the Baptist raised the question of whether Jesus was the Messiah, Jesus was able to respond confidently to John's disciples, 'Go back and report to John what you have seen and heard: The blind receive sight, the lame walk, those who have leprosy are cleansed, the deaf hear, the dead are raised, and the good news is proclaimed to the poor.'"[35]

Geisler stopped for a moment while I considered what he was saying. Then he summed up his arguments: "When you add this up—the historical reliability of the Bible as authenticated by archaeology, the miraculous fulfillment of clear predictive prophecies, and the performance of documented miracles—you get a supernaturally confirmed book unlike any other in history."

I wanted to clarify something. "What you're not saying is, 'I believe the Bible is divinely inspired because it says it is.'"

"That's right. That's a circular argument. No, the argument goes like this: the Bible *claims* to be the Word of God and the Bible *proves* to be the Word of God."

That would seem to be a pretty good case—*if* the Bible didn't have so many apparent contradictions within it. But how can the Bible really be trustworthy if it can't keep its own story straight? How can it be considered divinely inspired if it makes statements that simply cannot be reconciled with each other?

Coping with Contradictions

When I asked about alleged contradictions in the Bible, Geisler leaned back in his chair and smiled. It was an issue he had spent a lifetime studying.

"I've made a hobby of collecting alleged discrepancies, inaccuracies, and conflicting statements in the Bible," he said. "I have a list of about eight hundred of them. A few years ago I coauthored a book called *When Critics Ask*, which devotes nearly six hundred pages to setting the record straight.[36] All I can tell you is that in my experience, when critics raise these objections, they invariably violate one of seventeen principles for interpreting Scripture."

"What are those?" I asked.

"For example, assuming the unexplained is unexplainable. I'm sure some sharp critic could say to me, 'What about this issue?' and even though I've done a forty-year study of these things, I wouldn't be able to answer him. What does that prove—that the Bible has an error or Geisler is ignorant? I'd give the benefit of the doubt to the Bible, because of the eight hundred allegations I've studied, I haven't found one single error in the Bible, but I've found a lot of errors by the critics."

I cocked my head. "Is that really reasonable, though, to give the Bible the benefit of the doubt?"

"Yes, it is," he insisted. "When a scientist comes upon an anomaly in nature, does he give up science? When our space probe found braided rings around Jupiter, this was contrary to all scientific explanations. So do you remember when all the NASA scientists resigned because they couldn't explain it?"

I laughed. "Of course not," I said.

"Exactly. They didn't give up. They said, 'Ah, there must be an explanation,' and they continued to study. I approach the Bible the same way. It has proven over and over to be accurate, even when I initially thought it wasn't. Why shouldn't I give it the benefit of the doubt now? We need to approach the Bible the way an American is treated in court: presumed innocent until proven guilty.

"Critics do the opposite. They denied the Hittites of the Old Testament ever existed. Now archaeologists have found the Hittite library. Critics say, 'Well, I guess the Bible was right in that verse, but I don't accept the rest.' Wait a minute—when it has been proven to be accurate over and over again in hundreds of details, the burden of proof is on the critic, not on the Bible."

I asked Geisler to briefly describe some of the other principles for resolving apparent conflicts in Scripture.

"For example," he said, "failing to understand the context of the passage. This is the most common mistake critics make. Taking words out of context, you can even cause the Bible to prove there's no God. After all, Psalm 14:1 comes right out and says it: 'There is no God.' But, of course, in context it says, 'The fool says in his heart, "There is no God."' Therefore, context is critically important, and most often critics are guilty of wrenching verses out of context to create an alleged discrepancy when there isn't one.

"Another mistake is assuming a partial report is a false report. Matthew reports that Peter said to Jesus, 'You are the Messiah, the Son of the living God.' Mark said, 'You are the Messiah.' Luke said, 'God's Messiah.'[37] Critics say, 'See? Error!' I say, 'Where's the error?' Matthew didn't say, 'You *aren't* the Messiah' and Mark said, 'You are.' Matthew gave more. That's not an error; those are complementary.

"Other mistakes include neglecting to interpret difficult passages in light of clear ones; basing a teaching on an obscure passage; forgetting that the Bible uses nontechnical, everyday language; failing to remember the Bible uses different literary devices; and forgetting that the Bible is a human book with human characteristics."

"Humans make mistakes," I said. "If it's a human book, aren't errors inevitable?"

"Except for, say, the Ten Commandments, the Bible wasn't

dictated," Geisler replied. "The writers weren't secretaries to the Holy Spirit. Sometimes they used human sources or used different literary styles or wrote from different perspectives or emphasized different interests or revealed human thought patterns and emotions. There's no problem with that. But like Christ, the Bible is totally human, yet without error."

"However," I interjected, "people bring up alleged contradictions all the time."

"Like what, for example?" he responded. "What are the most common you hear?"

I thought for a moment. "Matthew says there was one angel at Jesus' tomb; John says there were two. The gospels say Judas hung himself; Acts says his bowels gushed out."

"You're right; those are frequently cited," he replied. "But they're easily reconciled. Concerning the angels, have you ever noticed that whenever you have two of anything, you also have one? It never fails. Matthew didn't say there was *only* one. John was providing more detail by saying there were two.

"As for Judas's suicide, you hang yourself in a tree or over the edge of a cliff. It was against the law to touch a dead body in those days. So somebody came along later, found his body, cut the rope, and the bloated body fell onto the rocks. What happens? The bowels gush out, just as the Bible says. They're not contradictory, they're complementary."

All in all, I had to admit that Geisler was on track. I remember as an atheist peppering ill-prepared Christians with a flurry of apparent biblical contradictions and discrepancies. They would get flustered and embarrassed because they couldn't answer them, and I'd walk away feeling smug and self-satisfied.

But just because they weren't able to answer them didn't mean there weren't answers. As with the troubling passages about the Canaanites and Elisha, the more I delved into the historical evidence and subjected the issues to scrutiny, the more they tended to fade away as objections.

Why Is It Hard to Believe?

It was almost time for lunch, and I was getting hungry. "Do you want to get a bite to eat?" I asked Geisler.

"Sure," he said. "There's a little sandwich place down the road."

I glanced through my notes. I thought I had covered everything I wanted to discuss, but then I noticed a quotation I had brought along with me. It was a sentiment that reflected the frustration of a lot of people: Why does God make it so difficult to believe in him? I didn't want to end the interview without asking Geisler about it.

"One more thing before we go," I said as I read him the colorful words of a frustrated spiritual seeker:

> So if I want to avoid hell, I presumably have to believe that a snake talked to Eve, that a virgin got pregnant from God, that a whale swallowed a prophet, that the Red Sea was parted, and all sorts of other crazy things. Well, if God wants me so bad . . . why does He make believing in Him so . . . impossible? . . . It seems to me that an all-powerful God could do a much better job of convincing people of His existence than any evangelist ever does . . . Just write it in the sky, nice and big: "Here's your proof, Ed. Believe in Me or go to hell! Sincerely, the Almighty."[38]

Looking up at Geisler, I said, "What would you say to him?"

Geisler was a bit bemused. "My answer would be that God *did* do something like that," he replied. "Psalm 19:1 says, 'The heavens declare the glory of God; the skies proclaim the work of his hands.' In fact, it's written across the heavens so vividly that more and more scientists who search the stars are becoming Christians.

"The great cosmologist Allan Sandage, who won astronomy's version of the Nobel Prize, concluded that God is 'the explanation for the miracle of existence.'[39] Sir Fred Hoyle, who devised the steady state theory of the universe to avoid the existence of God, eventually became a believer in an Intelligent Designer of the universe.

"The astrophysicist Hugh Ross, who got his doctorate in astronomy from the University of Toronto and did research on quasars and galaxies, said scientific and historical evidence 'deeply rooted my confidence in the veracity of the Bible.'[40] Robert Jastrow, a confessed agnostic and director of the Mount Wilson Observatory and founder of the Goddard Space Institute, concluded the big bang points toward God.[41] And I like what mathematical physicist Robert Griffiths said: 'If we need an atheist for a debate, I go to the philosophy department. The physics department isn't much use.'[42] The evidence, Lee, is so clear."

Not to a skeptic like Bertrand Russell, I noted. "He said if he someday stands before God and is asked why he never put his faith in him, he'll say he hadn't been given enough evidence," I reminded him.

Geisler, one of whose hobbies is collecting quotes from atheists and agnostics, pointed out something else Russell said. "He was asked in a *Look* magazine interview, 'Under what condition would you believe in God?' and he essentially said, 'Well, if I heard a voice from heaven and it predicted a series of things and they came to pass, then I guess I'd have to believe there's some kind of supernatural being.'"[43]

In light of our discussion about the miraculous fulfillment of predictive prophecies in the Bible, the irony in Russell's statement was obvious.

"I'd say, 'Mr. Russell, there *has* been a voice from heaven. It has predicted many things, and we've seen them undeniably come to pass,'" Geisler declared.

"Then you don't think God is making it hard for people to believe?"

"On the contrary, the evidence is there if people will be willing to see it. It's not for a lack of evidence that people turn from God; it's from their pride or their will. God isn't going to force anyone into the fold. Love never works coercively. It only works persuasively. And there's plenty of persuasive evidence there."

I felt an obligation to disclose the identity of the person I quoted as asking why God makes it so difficult to believe. I told Geisler his name is Edward Boyd, and he made that remark to his son, Christian philosopher Gregory Boyd, as they exchanged a series of letters in which they debated the evidence for Christianity. In 1992, after personally weighing the evidence, the formerly skeptical Edward Boyd decided to become a follower of Jesus.[44]

Geisler smiled at the story, and then he turned personal, even poetic, as he closed by discussing his personal faith.

"For me, I say the same thing that the apostle Peter said: 'Lord, to whom shall we go? You have the words of eternal life.'[45] He's the only one who not only claimed to be God but proved to be God. When I compare this to all other claimants of all other religions, it's like the poet who said 'the night has a thousand eyes, and the day but one; yet the light of the bright world dies with the dying sun.'"[46]

Geisler's voice softened but kept its intensity. "At the midnight of human ignorance, there are a lot of lights in the sky. Noontime, there's only one. And that's Jesus Christ, the light of the world. Based on the evidence for who he was, there really aren't any competitors.

"So I cast my lot with him—not the one who claimed wisdom, Confucius; or the one who claimed enlightenment, Buddha; or the one who claimed to be a prophet, Muhammad, but with the one who claimed to be God in human flesh. The one who declared, 'Before Abraham was born, I am!'[47]—and proved it."

Deliberations
Questions for Reflection or Group Study

1. Evaluate how well you believe Geisler succeeded in dealing with the troublesome issues of how God dealt with the Amalekites, the Canaanites, and the mob that threatened the prophet Elisha. What was the strongest part of his explanation? Is the issue of God's character a sticking point in your spiritual journey? Why or why not?

2. Do Geisler's guidelines for interpreting Scripture make sense to

you? Which ones have you seen violated by critics? Do you agree that it's reasonable to give the Bible the benefit of the doubt on grounds that it has already proven reliable in numerous instances? Why or why not?

3. What's your reaction to the quotation by former skeptic Edward Boyd? Do you believe God has made it difficult for us to believe in him? What's your biggest impediment to faith? What specific steps could you take to overcome that obstacle?

4. Have you been stumped by an apparent discrepancy or contradiction in the Bible? If so, how would you go about researching an answer? Try posing your question as succinctly as you can, and then take advantage of internet and library resources, including the books listed below, and see if there's an explanation that will satisfy you.

For Further Evidence
More Resources on This Topic

Copan, Paul. *Is God a Moral Monster? Making Sense of the Old Testament God.* Grand Rapids: Baker, 2011.

———. *Is God a Vindictive Bully?* Grand Rapids: Baker Academic, forthcoming.

Copan, Paul, and Matthew Flannagan. *Did God Really Command Genocide? Coming to Terms with the Justice of God.* Grand Rapids: Baker, 2014.

Cowan, Steven, and Terry L. Wilder. *In Defense of the Bible: A Comprehensive Apologetic for the Authority of Scripture.* Nashville, TN: Broadman & Holman, 2013.

Geisler, Norman, and Ronald Brooks. *When Skeptics Ask: A Handbook on Christian Evidences.* Grand Rapids: Baker, 2013.

Geisler, Norman, and Thomas Howe. *The Big Book of Bible Difficulties: Clear and Concise Answers from Genesis to Revelation.* Grand Rapids: Baker, 2008.

Jones, Clay. *Why Does God Allow Evil? Compelling Answers for Life's Toughest Questions.* Eugene, OR: Harvest House, 2017.

Köstenberger, Andreas J., Darrell L. Bock, and Josh Chatraw. *Truth in a Culture of Doubt: Engaging Skeptical Challenges to the Bible.* Nashville, TN: B&H Academic, 2014.

It's Offensive to Claim Jesus
Is the Only Way to God

I am absolutely against any religion that says that one faith
is superior to another. I don't see how that is anything
different than spiritual racism. It's a way of saying that we
are closer to God than you, and that's what leads to hatred.

RABBI SHMULEY BOTEACH

Moses could mediate on the law; Muhammad could brandish
a sword; Buddha could give personal counsel; Confucius
could offer wise sayings; but none of these men was qualified
to offer an atonement for the sins of the world . . . Christ
alone is worthy of unlimited devotion and service.

THEOLOGIAN R. C. SPROUL

Walter Chaplinsky had strong opinions about religion and wasn't shy about expressing them. In 1940 he caused a ruckus in Rochester, New Hampshire, by loudly denouncing organized religion as being a racket and condemning several Christian denominations by name. The result: he found himself arrested and convicted under a state law making it a crime to speak "any offensive, derisive or annoying word to any person who is lawfully in any street or other public place."[1]

Believing that his free speech rights were being violated,

Chaplinsky appealed his case all the way to the United States Supreme Court. However, in 1942 the justices unanimously affirmed his conviction, saying that "fighting words" like the ones he shouted fall outside the protection of the First Amendment.[2] Thirty years later, the high court clarified its definition of "fighting words" by calling them "personally abusive epithets" that are "inherently likely to provoke violent action."[3]

The phrase "fighting words" arouses a visceral response in people, making their guts churn and their hands ball into fists. This offensive language strikes deep inside by attacking their most cherished beliefs, virtually taunting them to lash out in retaliation. To some people, such are the outrageous words of Jesus Christ: "I am the way and the truth and the life. No one comes to the Father except through me."[4]

Many people consider it arrogant, narrow-minded, and bigoted for Christians to contend that the only path to God must go through Jesus of Nazareth. In a day of religious pluralism and tolerance, this exclusivity claim is politically incorrect, a verbal slap in the face of other belief systems. Pluralist Rosemary Radford Ruether labeled it "absurd religious chauvinism,"[5] while one Jewish rabbi called it a "spiritual dictatorship" that fosters the kind of smug and superior attitude that can lead to hatred and violence toward people who believe differently.[6]

Certainly an approach like the one expressed by Indian philosopher Swami Vivekananda is much more acceptable today: "We [Hindus] accept all religions to be true," he told the World's Parliament of Religions in 1893. The real sin, he said, is to call someone else a sinner.[7]

That kind of open-mindedness and liberality fits well with our current culture of relativism, where no "fact" is considered universally true at all times, at all places, for all people, and in all cultures. Indeed, a majority of Americans now deny there's any such thing as absolute truth.

When I was an atheist, I bristled at assertions by Christians that they held a monopoly on the only correct approach to religion.

"Who do they think they are?" I'd grouse. "Who are they to judge everyone else? Where's the love of Jesus in that?"

Charles Templeton called it "insufferable presumption"[8] for the Bible to claim that besides Jesus there is "no other name under heaven . . . by which we must be saved."[9] Templeton added:

> Christians are a small minority in the world. Approximately four out of every five people on the face of the earth believe in gods other than the Christian God. The more than five billion people who live on earth revere or worship more than three hundred gods. If one includes the animist or tribal religions, the number rises to more than three thousand. *Are we to believe that only Christians are right?*[10]

In short, the exclusivity claim of Jesus is one of the biggest obstacles to spiritual seekers today. Even a young Paul Copan, who was raised in a pastor's home, pondered the implications of this doctrine when it came to those who never hear the gospel. While an undergraduate student, his many questions prompted him to write a letter to noted Christian apologist Norman Geisler, whom I interviewed for the last chapter. Geisler responded by assuring Copan that whatever God does, he will never be unjust, nor will he shortchange anyone. That pivotal point proved helpful to Copan as he processed the issue.

Now, many years later, Copan himself is a highly credentialed scholar and professor of philosophy in Florida, which is where I traveled one spring day to meet with him in his book-choked office just a stone's throw from the ocean.[11]

The Fifth Interview: Paul Copan, PhD

With two master's degrees from Trinity Evangelical Divinity School and a doctorate in philosophy of religion from Marquette University, Copan is the Pledger Family Chair of Philosophy and Ethics at

Palm Beach Atlantic University. He also has been a visiting scholar at Oxford University and served as president of the Evangelical Philosophical Society for six years.

Copan and his wife, Jacqueline, are parents of six children. Though he has a mild-mannered and soft-spoken personality, the bespectacled Copan doesn't shy away from tackling controversial topics. For example, his books *Is God a Moral Monster?* and *Did God Really Command Genocide?*, as well as his forthcoming *Is God a Vindictive Bully?*, wrestle with nettlesome Old Testament texts, while his book *Loving Wisdom: Christian Philosophy of Religion* explores the subject of hell and the problem of evil, among other weighty topics. He deals extensively with religious pluralism in several of the forty books he has written or edited, which range from popular level (*True for You, but Not for Me*) to the scholarly (*The Routledge Companion to Philosophy of Religion*).[12]

We settled into facing chairs in Copan's modest office, which happens to be next to the office of his older brother, Vic, who earned his doctorate at the University of Vienna and is a professor of ministry and biblical studies.

I have to admit that my first question came out more biting than I intended. "Frankly," I said, "isn't it unmitigated arrogance for Christians to say that Jesus is the only way to God? Why do they think they're justified in asserting that they're right and everybody else in the world is wrong?"

Copan didn't flinch. "Arrogance has to do with tone and attitude, not with truth," he said calmly.

I gestured for him to elaborate.

"How is asserting the truth arrogant?" he asked. "When you take a multiple-choice test, Lee, do you circle every answer just to be tolerant toward all possibilities?"

I chuckled. "Well, no."

"Of course not. You choose the answer that's true. You see, a statement is true if it matches up with reality. If I say the earth is round and you say it's flat, I'm not being arrogant for claiming my view is true. By its very nature, truth excludes something—namely, error or falsehood. And if Jesus is correct when he says, 'The one who has seen me has seen the Father,'[13] then this 'narrow way' of Jesus will spare us from going down many wrong pathways or taking a broad road that leads to destruction."[14]

He paused to let his comments sink in and then added, "By the way, what's wrong with the claim that Jesus is the only way to God? Oprah Winfrey says there are 'millions of ways' to what we call God.[15] Some say there are so many different religions that there couldn't be just one way. Or maybe since a lot of sincere people believe there are many ways to be saved, God should give them salvation. Notice what's happening there—we're simply switching authoritative truth claims. What's the justification for making these claims? *Says who?*"

He leaned forward. "If we have to decide between the religious authority of Jesus or Oprah," he said, throwing up his arms, "well . . . then I'll go with Jesus every time!"

Relevance of the Resurrection

Copan emphasized that Christians didn't make up the idea that Jesus is the only way to God; rather, they are merely trying to faithfully relay what he said about himself. "And remember," Copan added, "Jesus didn't just claim to be the Son of God, but he backed up that assertion by his bodily resurrection from the dead." He pointed at me and added with a smile, "You've written enough books about that to convince just about any open-minded person."[16]

"Does that mean there's no truth to be found in any other religion?" I asked.

"No, I'm not saying that," he replied. "Worldviews often overlap in their claims. They'll stress compassion, for example—or sacrificial love. We're not going to disagree with those. I think it's more helpful to say that the Christian faith is true and that where other belief systems disagree with it, they would, at that specific point, be in error. But there's a lot of overlap. We see this in Acts, where the apostle Paul is making connections with people who disagree with him. He's building bridges to them based on what we hold in common. So rather than claiming, 'Every other worldview is 100 percent wrong,' it's better to say, 'There are some mutually held beliefs we can pick up on and use as bridges to connect people to the One who actually embodies these truths.'"

He continued. "Keep in mind that not only has God revealed himself in a specific way through Scripture, but he's also revealed himself more generally through creation, reason, conscience, common sense, and human experience. That means we should expect an overlap of some accepted truths across various worldviews."

Anybody can make claims, of course. But how can we determine which worldview is accurate? "On what basis can we know that Christianity's claims are actually true?" I asked.

"Unlike many religious traditions, the Christian faith opens itself up to falsification," he said. "In 1 Corinthians 15, Paul affirms repeatedly that if Christ did not bodily rise from the dead, then the Christian faith is finished. We should just eat, drink, and be merry, since we're still in our sins and there's no hope of salvation. But on the other hand, if Jesus rose victorious from the grave, then this vindicates his claim that he's the unique Son of God."

"You agree, then, that the evidence for the resurrection is persuasive?"

"Absolutely, yes. It makes excellent historical sense. The empty tomb is affirmed by both friend and foe alike;[17] there are many eyewitnesses of Jesus' postmortem appearances;[18] there's the conversion of Jesus' half brother, James, who didn't believe in Jesus during his earthly ministry;[19] and there's the conversion of Saul of Tarsus, who was a persecutor of the church.[20] In fact, in a short period of time, Saul went from killing Christians to saying in 1 Corinthians 8:6 that Jesus is Lord and Creator of all things.

"Not only that," Copan added, "but Jesus claimed to stand in the place of God, saying and doing those things that belonged only to God.[21] His followers—who were monotheistic Jews—were persuaded against their deeply held traditional beliefs that he was telling the truth.[22] So when Christians are accused of arrogance for saying Jesus is the only way to salvation, their response should be, '*I'm* not making this up—*Jesus* said it first!' And not only did he say it, but his claim is made all the more plausible by his bodily resurrection from the dead."

Exclusivity of Other Worldviews

I asked, "Is Christianity the only religion that makes a claim of exclusivity?"

Copan put up his hand to slow me down. "Wait a second," he said. "Let's admit something. The term *religion* is hopelessly vague and confusing."

"How so?"

"According to scholar Martin Marty, there are at least seventeen different definitions of religion—and scholars will never agree on any one of them.[23] Ninian Smart, founder of the first religious studies department in Britain, recommended we abandon all attempts to define religion."[24]

"Doesn't religion merely connote belief in an Almighty?" I asked.

"Not really. Buddhists, for instance, deny God's existence."

"What would be a better term to use instead of religion?"

"I think *worldview* or *philosophy of life* would be more helpful," he said. "Like traditional religions, a worldview involves comprehensive commitments of central importance that people consider incapable of immediate or casual abandonment.[25] It's inescapable for humans to have a philosophy of life. To have a worldview is to take a stance on fundamental questions, such as 'What is really real?' or, 'What are human beings?' or, 'Do right and wrong exist?'"

He added, "Though we may think of a worldview as merely a cluster or web of interrelated beliefs, assumptions, and values, at the root of each worldview is a heart commitment and a volitional stance."

"You'd agree that proponents of all worldviews should be able to defend their truth claims in the marketplace of ideas," I said.

"Yes, that's right," Copan replied. "And a key question should be, 'Which worldview does the evidence support?' The fact that worldviews present contradictory truth claims means these truth claims can't all be true at the same time. For instance, what's the nature of the human problem—is it sin, ignorance, or desire? What's the solution to that problem—is it grace and forgiveness, enlightenment, or eradication of desire? What's the nature of the afterlife—is it reincarnation, union with a personal God, or extinction? And there are other crucial details that matter too."

"Such as?"

"Islam denies that Jesus was crucified, but the Bible and other historical sources make it clear that he really did die on a cross. Buddhism's Dalai Lama, who is often viewed as 'open' and 'pluralistic,' plainly acknowledges conflict when it comes to Buddhism and Christianity. For example, he said that Buddhists don't accept the concept of a creator, while Christians base their philosophy on it.[26] So the Dalai Lama accepts the binary nature of truth—namely, that it excludes falsehood or error. He even goes so far as to assert that his version of Buddhism—Tibetan Buddhism—is the highest and complete form of Buddhism,[27] and that indeed 'only Buddhism can accomplish' what's necessary for liberation.[28] So he's actually making an exclusive claim of his own."

Copan went on. "One orthodox Jewish rabbi claims to be 'absolutely against any religion that says that one faith is superior to another'—something he calls spiritual racism, which leads to hatred.[29] Presumably, though, he believes his own version of religion is superior to that of those who disagree with him. He believes he has a virtue that those religious 'superiorists' don't. And isn't orthodox Judaism itself uncompromisingly monotheistic? If God exists, then those who believe in God are closer to the truth intellectually than the Buddhist who rejects God's existence."

"What about pluralists?" I asked, referring to those who believe all religions provide paths to salvation or liberation.

"Logically, it's just as exclusivistic as Christianity or any other traditional worldview."

"Explain why you say that."

"Pluralists believe they are right and that traditional religionists are misguided. Though they often accuse Christians of being arrogant for believing Jesus is the only way, pluralism takes its own authoritative stance, just as any traditional religion does—and those who disagree with the pluralist would be in error."

I asked, "What about those who argue that you're just using 'Western logic'?"

Copan sighed. "Yes, I've heard that before."

"What's your response?"

"The late Alan Watts, who popularized Eastern philosophies for Western audiences, rejected the either-or of 'Western logic' in favor of a both-and 'Eastern logic.'[30] The problem, though, is that in doing so he ended up assuming the inescapable 'either-or' logic that is fundamental to all thought. In other words," Copan said, suppressing a chuckle, "it's *either* Western *or* Eastern logic—not both!"

Touché, I mused. "So," I asked, "what's the bottom line?"

"We simply can't escape exclusivism—or the laws of logic. Truth claims, by their very nature, are exclusive—and every worldview makes them."

The Arrogance of Christianity

When I was an atheist, I encountered more than a few obnoxious Christians whose condescending attitude toward me smacked of elitism. Frankly, it deterred me from wanting to look into the faith. I sensed I wasn't alone in this reaction.

"Do you believe that the smug way some Christians make the exclusivity claim has driven a certain number of people away from considering Christianity?" I asked.

"Probably, yes. People may be turned off from the Christian faith for this and a host of other reasons—although, as Christians themselves should know, we should be the last people on earth to feel smug."

"What do you mean?"

"The apostle Paul asks, 'What do you have that you did not receive?'[31] Our faith is a gift from God, not something we've earned or merited through our talent or achievements. Just as we have freely received God's grace, we should seek to humbly pass it on by showing grace to others. Paul asked, 'Where, then, is boasting? It is excluded.'[32] We could paraphrase that to say, 'Where, then, is smugness? It is ruled out.'"

"Then again," I observed, "even if Christians did act in a haughty way, that wouldn't negate the historical and scientific evidence undergirding the faith."

"Exactly right. You'll find smug and hypocritical people in all faith traditions and worldviews. But as we've noted, personal hypocrisy doesn't disprove the truth of a position. The existence of counterfeit money doesn't negate the reality of authentic currency. In fact, Jesus predicted that people would say all kinds of false, immoral, or hypocritical things in his or the Father's name[33]—and that he will call them to account.[34] Clearly, he didn't consider this hypocrisy as justification to ignore him."

"Just as Jesus claimed to be God, others have made the same assertion about themselves throughout history," I said. "Why believe Jesus and not them?"

"Of course, in the monistic Hindu Advaita Vedanta philosophical tradition, *you* are actually viewed as divine. The soul—*atman*—is *Brahman*, or God. Ultimately, all that exists is a pure, divine consciousness without any differentiation. In the pantheistic tradition of the Hindu philosopher Ramanuja, all things are divine, including you and me. This, of course, carries over into the more contemporary New Age movement. One of its proponents, the actress Shirley MacLaine, said, 'Maybe the tragedy of the human race was that we had forgotten that we were each Divine.'[35] So who needs a way to God when you *are* God?"

"Why should we trust Jesus? Other than the resurrection, what are his divine credentials?" I asked.

"Well, yes, the resurrection is the crucial foundation on which the Christian faith rests. On top of that, though, Jesus performed public miracles to back up his claim to being divine. It's interesting that his opponents never disputed that he did these miracles—they just got mad because sometimes he did them on the Sabbath.[36] The Scriptures say that the Jews picked up stones to kill him, but Jesus asked, 'I have shown you many good works from the Father. For which of these do you stone me?' The Jews answered that it wasn't for the good works that they were trying to kill him, but it was 'for blasphemy, because you, a mere man, claim to be God.'[37]

"But there's more," Copan continued. "In a monotheistic culture, Jesus' followers were well aware of the dangers of worshiping someone who wasn't God—that they would forfeit any right standing with God in the afterlife. But they worshiped Jesus anyway and ascribed deity to him.[38] It's hard for us to comprehend how bold this was for them to do. This went against a lifetime of training and tradition. They believed their eternal destinies were at stake. And yet they concluded that Jesus was, indeed, the Son of God, especially after he rose triumphantly from the grave."

A Sincere and Moral Life

I glanced through my notes, which were scrawled on a yellow legal pad, and then looked back up at Copan. "Wouldn't you admit," I said, "that if you had grown up in Thailand, you'd be a Buddhist? Doesn't the place where you're born and raised have a disproportionate impact on what faith you will later adopt? So how can God hold you responsible for the path you take?"

Copan slipped off his glasses and put them on the table between us. "This is sometimes called the 'geographical objection,'" he replied. "Statistically, it's true. But what does that actually prove? Very little. If a person was born in Nazi Germany, he would likely become part of the Hitler Youth. Does that mean Nazism is just as valid of a political system as democracy? Of course not."

He slipped his glasses back on. "Besides, the pluralist must wrestle with the same issue. If the pluralist had been born in Madagascar or medieval France, she wouldn't have been a pluralist. And what if a person is born into a pluralistic culture? The chances are she would have been a pluralist. So if the geographical objection is really so decisive, then we should reject pluralism itself.

"Again," he said, "the fundamental question is, 'What is true? What comports with reality?' Let's say a person grows up in a pluralistic culture but explores various worldviews and concludes Christianity has remarkable intellectual and existential credentials, including a sound historical foundation, rational coherence, and a rich tradition of philosophical rigor. And what if this person finds the arguments for pluralism cannot be sustained? For example, what if she realizes that pluralism's dismissal of the resurrection of Jesus is wholly flawed and appears to be an attempt to prop up the appeal of pluralism? Logically, shouldn't that individual abandon the pluralism she had grown up with and adopt a Christian position? Shouldn't that be applauded rather than condemned?"

I spoke up. "But in the end, a lot of people will say that regardless of which faith you follow, the most important thing is that you're sincere and live a moral life."

Copan's eyes got wide. "By whose authority is sincerity or morality crowned king over all other considerations?" he asked. "Who is the proper authority to make this sweeping claim? If God desires a relationship with human beings, sincerity or morality—however important—is insufficient. Where does truth fit in? What if someone is sincerely wrong or misguided? Sincerity is a necessary condition for salvation, but it isn't sufficient."

I interrupted. "But what about living a moral life?"

"Can you name anyone who has lived a life without any moral failings?"

"No," I conceded. "Including me."

"Living a generally moral life, as valuable as this is, doesn't go far enough. How moral is good enough for God? God's grace is needed to bridge that moral gap between our own miserable performance and the ideal of which we have all fallen short. We need God's grace to overcome the guilt we experience and which no good deeds can wash away. The sufficiency of Christ puts an end to our moral striving without denying our need to live lives that are pleasing in God's sight."

Praying in the Puja Room

I decided to take a more pragmatic approach by saying, "Many people of other faiths say their beliefs work for them. They're happy in their faith. Shouldn't that be enough?"

"Our first commitment ought to be aligning our lives with reality—living in the light of truth," responded Copan. "Plato talked about people living by a 'noble lie,' but who wants to live a deceived life? We ought to reject as many false beliefs as possible and instead embrace true beliefs. If Jesus did rise from the dead, then this is the life-shaping reality by which we should live our lives. As one theologian put it, those who appear free from anxiety and think they have it all together 'may be only a well-adjusted sinner who is dangerously maladjusted to God; and it is infinitely better to be a neurotic saint than a healthy-minded sinner.'"[39]

"And yet," I interjected, "many people around the world seem happy in their particular worldview."

"Not everyone. Not when you delve beneath the surface," came his reply. "Some people live in fear of evil spirits; they dread the prospect of death; they don't know what to do with their guilt and shame; they feel trapped in the seemingly endless karmic cycle of birth, death, and rebirth."

With that, Copan told the story of Krister Sairsingh, who received his doctorate in religion from Harvard after growing up in a Hindu home in Trinidad. Despite being a zealous defender of Hinduism, he lived a life of terror and dread. He knew he would have to pay for his failings and self-centeredness in his next life. When a Christian friend told him about Jesus, Sairsingh thought it was arrogant to believe there was anything unique about him—until Sairsingh read the Gospels himself and was astounded to see that Jesus had the power to forgive sins and thus break the bondage of karma.

Sairsingh prayed for God to reveal his truth to him. Over time, as Sairsingh began to be transformed by Christ, even his mother, a prominent Hindu, saw how his fears were dissipating and being replaced by joy. She would prostrate herself on the floor of the puja room, in the presence of the images of various Hindu gods, and cry out for truth. "Within three weeks," recalled Sairsingh, "she too had become convinced by the teachings of Jesus."[40]

Copan paused after relating the story. "What's the lesson?" he asked. "Maybe there's an outward appearance of happiness on the surface, but who knows what really lies beneath? The apostle Paul once seemed 'happy' as a zealous Jew who persecuted the church in the name of the God of Israel, but he later considered all the things he had valued and in which he took pride to be garbage for the sake of knowing Jesus Christ.[41]

"And what do we tell people who are profoundly unhappy in their worldview?" Copan asked. "What if they feel hopeless and despairing? Would adopting pluralism really give them what their soul deeply needs? It's precisely the message of the gospel that brings confident hope, relief from despair, and the guarantee of our deepest longings being ultimately met in the new heaven and the new earth."

Gandhi versus Son of Sam

Nevertheless, I sensed an uncomfortable implication of the Christian message. I said to Copan, "Many people say Gandhi lived a more virtuous life than most Christians, even though he wasn't a follower of Jesus. But the serial killer David Berkowitz, the so-called Son of Sam, murdered several innocent people and says he has become a Christian. Christians would say Berkowitz is going to heaven but Gandhi isn't." I looked Copan straight in the eye. "Where's the equity in that?"

Copan was nodding as I spoke, seeming to acknowledge the weight of the question. "Without a doubt, there's much to commend about Gandhi—and yet he did have his blind spots," he began. "The author of India's constitution strongly urged him to condemn Hinduism's caste system as the source of pernicious evils in Indian society, but Gandhi didn't. Gandhi advised German Jews to commit 'collective suicide' to arouse the indignation of the world against Nazism, and he told the British not to resist the invasion of Nazis and their occupation of mere buildings and land.[42] But set all that aside; I bring this up only to stress that all people are a mixed bag to one degree or another.

"Let me go back to what I said earlier," he continued. "We *all* need redemption, no matter how 'good' we are, because none of us are morally perfect. The late Russian writer Aleksandr Solzhenitsyn, who experienced the harshness and ruthlessness of Soviet labor camps, said that 'the line separating good and evil passes . . . through all human hearts,' and that 'even in the best of all hearts, there remains . . . an un-uprooted small corner of evil.'[43]

"So there's a moral gap between each of us and the moral ideal. Many traditional religions and even secular worldviews teach a kind of self-salvation, or self-improvement, but we've already failed and fallen short. As John Calvin said, 'Surely there is no one who is not sunken in infinite filth.'"[44]

Copan brought up the criminal on the cross, who called out to Jesus for mercy and received compassion in return.[45] "Even non-Christians are touched by this story of a last-minute conversion," said Copan. "Since we all need God's grace, we shouldn't assume that his grace is too limited to forgive the worst kind of sins."

Jesus' atoning death, added Copan, pays the penalty for all people who have sinned, whether Gandhi or the Son of Sam. "The question is who wants to humble themselves and receive that free gift in repentance and faith," he said. "That's up to each individual in response to God's initiating grace."

Copan looked down at some papers. "I think of the story of the former atheist Francis Spufford, who no doubt was a decent chap before his conversion. He acknowledged that atheism didn't nourish his soul during difficult times. But it wasn't a philosophical process that led him out of disbelief. He said, 'I had made a mess of things in my life, and I needed mercy, and to my astonishment, mercy was there. An experience of mercy, rather than an idea of it.'"[46]

Copan's eyes met mine. "Compassion and mercy are there for all who seek it," he said. "Remember the story of Krister Sairsingh and his mother, both adamant Hindus who called out for truth and found it in Jesus. They knocked and he answered.[47] Jesus will rain his grace on all who reach out to him, but he will not impose himself on those who refuse him."

What about Those Who Haven't Heard?

Serial killer David Berkowitz is fortunate. He lives in a country where there are plenty of Christians who can freely talk about their faith. Someone came to Berkowitz's prison and told him about Christ's offer of forgiveness, and he says he confessed his offenses and put his trust in Jesus for forgiveness and eternal life.

But that raises thorny questions. What about people who live in places where Christianity is outlawed or squelched? Or where the gospel simply doesn't circulate yet? Isn't it fundamentally unfair to condemn people who never heard the name of Jesus and merely followed the faith traditions of their culture?

"This issue is called the problem of the contingently lost," Copan told me. "And, yes, it's one of the stickiest topics to address.

But there are explanations that can satisfy those who are sincerely curious about it."

"How do you begin?"

"By making it clear that God doesn't condemn people just because they haven't heard the name of Jesus," he said.

I nodded as I took notes. After all, this point is clear in Scripture. The Bible teaches that everyone has a moral standard written on their heart by God, and everyone violates that standard, for which we deserve punishment.[48] And the Bible says everyone has sufficient information from observing creation to know that God exists, but people suppress that and reject God anyway.[49]

But both the Old and New Testaments tell us that those who wholeheartedly seek God will find him;[50] in fact, the Holy Spirit is seeking us first, making it possible for us to seek him. This suggests that people who respond to the understanding they have and who earnestly seek after the one true God will find an opportunity, in some way, to receive the eternal life that God graciously provides through Christ.

"God isn't willing that any should perish,[51] and he works toward the salvation of all,"[52] Copan told me. "The only thing that prevents the salvation of everyone is the human will and sinfulness that resist the initiating grace of God in people's lives."

Copan said that theologians have proposed several ways of understanding the fate of those who never hear about the salvation available through Jesus. "For example," he said, "some Christians believe that certain persons may have a chance after death to hear the gospel clearly presented and to decide about Jesus in a fully informed manner."[53]

An objection popped into my mind. "Wouldn't Hebrews 9:27 preclude that?" I asked, referring to the verse that says, "People are destined to die once, and after that to face judgment."

Copan raised his index finger to stop me. "Notice that the verse doesn't say judgment is *immediately* the next thing a person faces after death," he pointed out. "The next verse says that 'Christ was sacrificed once to take away the sins of many; and he will appear a second time.' Those two events don't follow each other immediately either. There's a long time between them."

My eyes narrowed as I thought through the implications. "Who would get this postmortem opportunity of redemption?"

"Not people who steadfastly resisted God during their lifetime," he replied. "But perhaps other people who never heard the gospel or who were taught a twisted or distorted gospel or who couldn't understand the gospel because they were mentally disabled or died as a child. And for those who were given this postmortem opportunity, it wouldn't be available indefinitely. They would make their choice and then live with the consequences forever."

While the idea of a postmortem chance at salvation seemed radical, I couldn't immediately identify a way that Scripture would clearly preclude it. Even the Reformer Martin Luther wrote in a 1522 letter, "God forbid that I should limit the time of acquiring faith to the present life. In the depth of the Divine mercy, there may be opportunity to win it in the future."[54]

This was certainly a topic that warranted further investigation.[55] As Copan said to me, "If God commands each person without exception to repent,[56] then it would make sense that he would give each person sufficient grace to fulfill that command—despite their earthly incapacities, ignorance, or unwittingly inaccurate views of the gospel."

In the meantime, though, Copan cautioned that any postmortem opportunity for redemption is speculative, and therefore Christians shouldn't use it as a reason to slack off from fulfilling their mandate to clearly present the gospel to everyone they possibly can. "Love compels us to help bring people to a confident hope in Christ and his salvation," he said.[57]

Other theologians, such as followers of the sixteenth-century Spanish Jesuit Luis de Molina, theorize differently about those who never heard the gospel. They argue that God, in his omniscience, knows how individuals would respond to the gospel if they were to hear it. And God could place those receptive persons in a position to hear and freely respond to the good news. Those who would desire to hear the gospel have the opportunity to do so. In addition, God gives ample access to salvation for all persons through his general revelation such that no one is born at the 'wrong' place or time.

When I brought that up, Copan replied by saying, "That's another well-argued approach. This kind of philosophizing has value, though we must take care that our models and theorizing both conform to Scripture and are rationally coherent. Frankly, God hasn't explicitly told us how he will deal with people who don't hear the gospel, but we do know something with crystal clarity."

"What's that?"

"That God will never do anything unjust. He will be scrupulously fair. Genesis 18:25 says, 'Will not the Judge of all the earth do right?' We can trust that he is good and loving, and consequently whatever he does will be consistent with those attributes. If something is truly unjust, God will not do it."

He paused and then said with emphasis, "We can rest easy in that."

Good but Not Safe

If the evidence of history points to the divinity of Jesus of Nazareth, then why do so many people reject him? If he is the source and embodiment of the answers to life's deepest questions and opens the path to heaven for all who follow him, then what's the reason a lot of people turn their back on his gospel?

Copan pondered the question for a moment before saying, "If Jesus is the cosmic authority, then this reality comes with certain entailments."

"Such as?"

"Taking up one's cross and following him. In other words, death to self. And being willing to let go of economic security and social standing. Remember that Jesus promised his followers,

'In this world you will have trouble.'[58] Even the late historian Larry Hurtado wondered why anyone would become a Christian in the Roman Empire. It would only bring opprobrium—disgrace, shame, ignominy. Their social standing would sink."[59]

"What about today?"

"Not many years ago, it would have enhanced a person's social standing in America if they were seen as a churchgoer; these days, there's not the same benefit. On top of that, some people are opting for an easier form of faith that capitulates to cultural pressures both morally and theologically.[60] They see this as the path of least resistance. It's simpler and less demanding in the short run to follow this trend.

"On the other hand, the authentic Christian life involves important commitments of time, finances, and emotional energy— reading Scripture, praying, meeting together with believers, undertaking church discipline, sharing our faith, giving and participating in missions. Jesus spoke about a narrow road that leads to life and that those who lose their lives for his sake will find life.[61] Let's face it—the cost of discipleship is difficult. But the cost of non-discipleship is even greater."

"You've talked about the rise of religious pluralism as well," I said. "How do you define this worldview?"

"The late John Hick, probably the most prominent pluralist in our generation, laid out a description. Yes, he said, there are real differences between religions. Yet religions are culturally conditioned attempts to get at the ultimate reality. For Hick, religions are true in one sense: they aim at the ultimate reality. But they're false in another sense: they suffer from cultural limitations. Also, all of the world's religions are equally capable of bringing salvation or liberation. And the producing of morally upright and selfless 'saints' in various traditions—from Buddha and Gandhi to Jesus and the Dalai Lama—is evidence that salvation or liberation is being achieved."[62]

"The tenets of pluralism," I commented, "fit in well with our current culture."

"Yes, this philosophy expresses the spirit of the age, which rejects as intolerant any one particular pathway of salvation," Copan said. "In the end, the pluralist doesn't care what your truth claims are—as long as they don't conflict with *their* analysis of religion. If they do, watch out. The pluralist may claim to be tolerant, but they will dismantle and undermine any worldview that contradicts their own."

"And what about Jesus?" I asked.

"Their Jesus isn't the Jesus of the Gospels. The biblical Jesus personally confronts us and makes demands on us. In contrast, pluralism downplays the authority of Jesus and presents us with a generic ultimate reality. The pluralist's Jesus was no more than a mere human being who was highly God-conscious and who spread love to those he met. He wasn't the second person of the Trinity.

"Pluralism, then, takes the sting out of Jesus," Copan concluded. "It domesticates him. C. S. Lewis said that the Jesus figure of Narnia—Aslan—is 'good' but 'he isn't safe.'[63] Pluralism makes Jesus safe. It tames him. This is quite appealing to those who want to evade the implications of his lordship."

In the end, it was clear to me that this was neither the Jesus of the Bible nor the Jesus I had come to know years ago. It's not the Jesus who had the supernatural power to revolutionize my life, my character, my morality, my values, my relationships, my priorities—my entire being. If I could have made up my own idea of Jesus, he would have more closely reflected the pluralist version of him. He would have let me do whatever I wanted to do, whenever I wanted to do it.

But the real Jesus, the one who walked the earth and did miraculous works in history, the one who rose from the dead, the one who proved he's the only way to heaven, *that* Jesus loved me too much to let me continue to carve my own path of self-interest and fleeting pleasures. And he's the one who graciously leads the way down the path of truth—the only path that leads to eternity with God.

I slipped my legal pad into my briefcase. We stood to shake

hands. I was grateful for Copan's incisive analysis, clearheaded wisdom, and biblical expertise.

"Thank you," I said, "for using your intellect to cut through all the emotion of this issue."

Deliberations
Questions for Reflection or Group Study

1. What was your emotional reaction the first time you heard the claim that Jesus is the only path to God? Has your viewpoint shifted since reading this interview with Paul Copan? If so, how?

2. How important is the resurrection of Jesus to his claim of being the one and only Son of God? If you were to defend the historicity of Jesus' resurrection from the dead, what points would you make? What are the implications for you on a personal level if the resurrection is an actual historical event?

3. Have you considered any other world religion? If so, what did you find attractive about it? What problems did you discover related to it? What aspects of Christianity attract you and which ones challenge you?

4. Paul Copan stressed that God is good, loving, and just—and therefore we can trust that he will be fair to those who never heard the gospel during their lifetime. How encouraging is that to you? How do you assess the speculations discussed in this chapter for how God might deal with those who never hear the name of Jesus?

5. The Bible says about God, "You will seek me and find me when you seek me with all your heart." What three practical suggestions would you give to a friend who wants to know how they can seek God that way? Have you taken those steps yourself? What have been the results so far?

For Further Evidence
More Resources on This Topic

Beckwith, Francis J., and Gregory Koukl. *Relativism: Feet Firmly Planted in Mid-Air*. Grand Rapids: Baker, 1998.

Bowman, Robert M., Jr., and J. Ed Komoszewski. *Putting Jesus in His Place: The Case for the Deity of Christ*. Grand Rapids: Kregel, 2007.

Childers, Alisa. *Another Gospel? A Lifelong Christian Seeks Truth in Response to Progressive Christianity*. Carol Stream, IL: Tyndale Momentum, 2020.

Copan, Paul. *Loving Wisdom: A Guide to Philosophy and Christian Faith*, 2nd ed. Grand Rapids: Eerdmans, 2020.

Copan, Paul. *True for You, but Not for Me: Overcoming Objections to Christian Faith*, 2nd ed. Minneapolis: Bethany House, 2009.

McDermott, Gerald R. *God's Rivals: Why Has God Allowed Different Religions?* Downers Grove, IL: IVP Academic, 2007.

Murray, Abdu. *Saving Truth: Finding Meaning and Clarity in a Post-Truth World*. Grand Rapids: Zondervan, 2018.

Nash, Ronald. *Is Jesus the Only Savior?* Grand Rapids: Zondervan, 1994.

Netland, Harold. *Christianity and Religious Diversity: Clarifying Christian Commitments in a Globalizing Age*. Grand Rapids: Baker Academic, 2015.

Samples, Kenneth Richard. *God among Sages: Why Jesus Is Not Just Another Religious Leader*. Grand Rapids: Baker, 2017.

Strobel, Lee. *In Defense of Jesus: Investigating Attacks on the Identity of Christ*. Grand Rapids: Zondervan, 2007.

A Loving God Would Never Torture People in Hell

There is one very serious defect to my mind in Christ's moral character, and that is that he believed in hell. I do not myself feel that any person who is really profoundly humane can believe in everlasting punishment.

BERTRAND RUSSELL, ATHEIST

Hell is God's great compliment to the reality of human freedom and the dignity of human choice.

G. K. CHESTERTON, CHRISTIAN

Judge Cortland Mathers was in a quandary. Standing before him was a defendant who was guilty of playing a minor role in a drug case. She was a thirty-one-year-old impoverished mother with a young family. She was remorseful over her crime. In the judge's opinion, she deserved a second chance. Justice would be served by giving her probation.

But there was a problem: if Mathers found her guilty of the charge against her, he would have no choice under Massachusetts law but to sentence her to six years in the penitentiary. He knew that prison would scar her forever. More than likely, it would destroy her fragile family and leave her embittered, angry, unemployed, and destined for more trouble.

This is a system called "mandatory sentencing," which removes the discretion of judges in disposing of certain kinds of cases. The positive side is that judges are prevented from being too lenient. But the negative consequence is that in some instances the automatic sentence can be too harsh—like in this case, where the defendant stood to serve more time behind bars than most armed robbers.

Mathers was never known to shrink back from sentencing criminals to long prison terms if the circumstances warranted it. But in this case, he considered the mandatory sentence—with no possibility of early release—to be an "absolute miscarriage of justice."

And so Mathers made his choice: "Disobey the law in order to be just." He declared her guilty of a lesser offense that did not carry a preset prison term and sentenced her to five years of probation with required counseling.

"If a judge is not capable of doing that, then he shouldn't be on the bench," Mathers told the *Boston Globe* in its investigation of mandatory sentencing. "A judge either is an automaton, rubber-stamping these sentences, or is driven by a sense of justice."[1]

I was thinking about that case as my plane was descending toward Los Angeles International Airport on a sultry September morning. *How ironic*, I mused, *that a law designed to enforce justice threatened to thwart it instead*. I could understand the sense of fairness that prompted Mathers to sidestep one-size-fits-all sentencing and instead to impose a punishment that would more appropriately fit the crime.

For a long time as a spiritual seeker, I found my sense of justice outraged by the Christian teaching about hell, which I considered far more unjust than a mandatory prison term would have been in the case before Cortland Mathers. The doctrine seemed like cosmic overkill to me, an automatic and unappealable sentence to an eternity of torture and torment. It's mandatory sentencing taken to the extreme: everyone gets the same consequences, regardless of their circumstances. Step out of line with God—even a little bit, even inadvertently—and you're slapped with an endless prison sentence in a place that makes Leavenworth look like Disneyland.

Where's the justice in that? Where's the proportionality between crime and punishment? What kind of a God enjoys seeing his creatures writhe forever—without hope, beyond redemption—in a torture chamber every bit as ghastly and barbaric as a Nazi concentration camp? Wasn't atheist B. C. Johnson right when he charged that "the idea of hell is morally absurd"?[2]

Those are tough and emotionally charged questions. I needed answers from a tough-minded authority, someone who wouldn't flinch from honest challenges. I glanced out the plane's window as suburban Los Angeles passed beneath, shimmering in the bright sunlight. I was anxious for my one-on-one encounter with a well-respected philosopher who has wrestled extensively with this troubling doctrine of eternal damnation.

The Sixth Interview: J. P. Moreland, PhD

It didn't take long to get my rental car and drive to J. P. Moreland's house, which is located not far from the Talbot School of Theology, where he is a professor in the master's program in philosophy and ethics.

Moreland's book *Beyond Death: Exploring the Evidence for Immortality* showed that he had done a lot of thorough thinking and personal soul-searching about the doctrine of hell. He and coauthor Gary Habermas also delved into the nature of the soul, near-death experiences, reincarnation, and the theology of heaven.

I also selected Moreland because of his broad background. He is educated in science (with a chemistry degree from the University of Missouri), possesses a thorough knowledge of theology (he has a master's degree from Dallas Theological Seminary), and is a highly regarded philosopher (having earned his doctorate at the University of Southern California).

He has produced more than a dozen books, including *Scaling* the Secular City, Christianity and the Nature of Science, Does God Exist? (a debate with Kai Nielsen), *The Creation Hypothesis, Body and Soul, Love Your God with All Your Mind,* and the award-winning *Jesus under Fire.* All of that, and he's just fifty-one.

Moreland, dressed casually in a short-sleeved shirt, shorts, and deck shoes without socks, greeted me in the driveway of his ranch-style house. I shook his hand and offered my condolences. I knew he had traveled to San Diego the previous night and watched as his beloved Kansas City Chiefs were humiliated by the lowly Chargers. He was still wearing a baseball-style hat with his team's name emblazoned on the front.

Inside, after exchanging a few pleasantries, I slumped down on his living room couch and sighed. The subject of hell was big, heavy, controversial, a flash point for spiritual skeptics. I searched my mind for a starting point.

I finally decided just to be honest. "I'm not sure where to begin," I confessed. "How should we even approach the topic of hell?"

Moreland thought for a moment and then leaned back in his green padded chair. "Maybe," he offered, "we should distinguish between liking or disliking something and judging whether it's right to do."

"What do you mean?"

"Many times, something we like isn't the right thing to do," he explained. "Some people say adultery is pleasurable, but most people would agree it's wrong. And often doing the right thing isn't pleasurable. Telling someone a hard truth that they need to hear, or firing someone who isn't doing a good job, can be very unpleasant."

"And," I interjected, "hell evokes a visceral response. People react strongly against the mere idea of it."

"That's right. They tend to evaluate whether it's appropriate based on their feelings or emotional offense to it."

"How do we get beyond that?"

"I think people should try to set aside their feelings," he said. "The basis of their evaluation should be whether hell is a morally just or morally right state of affairs, not whether they like or dislike the concept."

Moreland paused before continuing. "And it's important to understand that if the God of Christianity is real, he hates hell and hates people going there," he added. "The Bible is very clear: God says he takes no pleasure in the death of the wicked."[3]

Maybe so, but they still end up spending their eternity in a place of absolute horror and abject despair. I thought back to my interview with Charles Templeton, the evangelist-turned-skeptic. Admittedly, he has strong emotions concerning hell, but they seemed to be legitimately fueled by righteous indignation and moral outrage.

Frankly, I was a bit wary of completely divorcing the discussion of hell from our emotional response to it—after all, they seemed hopelessly intertwined.

Tackling Templeton's Challenge

Although I understood Moreland's point that the morality or immorality of hell is independent of our feelings toward the issue, I decided my best tactic would be to confront Moreland head-on with Templeton's objections—emotion and all.

I cleared my throat and sat upright, turning to face Moreland more squarely. "Look, Dr. Moreland," I began, my voice notching up in intensity, "I interviewed Charles Templeton about this matter and he was very adamant. He told me, 'I couldn't hold someone's hand to a fire for a moment. Not an instant! How could a loving God, just because you don't obey him and do what he wants, torture you forever—not allowing you to die, but to continue in that pain for eternity?'"

Then I spit out Templeton's last words with the same tone of disgust he had used in talking to me: "'There is no *criminal* who would do this!'"

The challenge almost seemed to reverberate in his living room. Tension quickly mounted. Then, sounding more accusatory than inquisitive, I capped the question by demanding, "Dr. Moreland, what in the world do you say to that?"

So much for his idea of getting beyond feelings.

Now, you have to understand something about J. P. Moreland: he's a philosopher. He's a thinker. He's coolly rational. Nothing seems to rattle his cage. And despite my charged tone, which almost seemed to imply he was personally responsible for the creation of hell, Moreland took no offense. Instead, his mind quickly cut to the core of the issue.

"The key to answering Templeton is in his wording," Moreland began. "He has loaded his question to the point where it's like asking, 'When did you stop beating your wife?' No matter how you reply, you're doomed from the outset if you accept his wording."

"So his premise is wrong," I said. "How so?"

"Well, for one thing, hell is not a torture chamber."

My eyebrows shot up. Certainly that would be news to many generations of Sunday school children who have been frightened into nightmares by gruesome descriptions of the everlasting infliction of fiery agony in Hades.

"It's not?" I asked.

Moreland shook his head. "God doesn't torture people in hell, so he's flat wrong about that," he continued. "Templeton also makes it sound like God is a spoiled child who says to people, 'Look, if you're not willing to obey my arbitrary rules, then I'm going to sentence you for it. You need to know that *my* rules are *my* rules, and if I don't get my way, then I'm going to make you pay.' Well, of course, if God is just a child with arbitrary rules, then it would be capricious for him to sentence people. But that's not at all what is going on here.

"God is the most generous, loving, wonderful, attractive being in the cosmos. He has made us with free will and he has made us for a purpose: to relate lovingly to him and to others. We are not accidents, we're not modified monkeys, we're not random mistakes. And if we fail over and over again to live for the purpose for which we were made—a purpose, by the way, that would allow us to flourish more than living any other way—then God will have absolutely no choice but to give us what we've asked for all along in our lives, which is separation from him."

"And that is hell . . ."

"Yes, that's hell. One more point: it's wrong to think God is simply a loving being, especially if you mean 'loving' in the sense that most Americans use that word today. Yes, God is a compassionate being, but he's also a just, moral, and pure being. So God's decisions are not based on modern American sentimentalism. This is one of the reasons why people have never had a difficult time with the idea of hell until modern times. People today tend to care only for the softer virtues like love and tenderness, while they've forgotten the hard virtues of holiness, righteousness, and justice.

"So in the wording of his question, Templeton has given us a spiteful being who has imposed these unfair, arbitrary rules and who ultimately stomps his foot and says, 'If I don't get my way, I'm going to torture you forever.'"

Moreland's intense blue-gray eyes locked with mine. "Nothing," he stressed, "could be farther from the truth."

God's Fallback Position

"Okay, then," I said as I settled deeper into the couch, "here's your chance to set the record straight. Let's lay some groundwork by getting our definitions in order. You said hell is not a torture chamber. Then what is it?"

"The essence of hell is relational," he replied. "Christianity says people are the most valuable things in the entire creation. If people matter, then personal relationships matter, and hell is largely relational.

"In the Bible, hell is separation or banishment from the most beautiful being in the world—God himself. It is exclusion from anything that matters, from all value, not only from God but also from those who have come to know and love him."

I was confused about something. "Is hell a punishment for having broken God's standards?" I asked. "Or is it the natural consequence of people living a life where they say, 'I don't care if I'm separated from God, I want to do things my way,' and then they are given their desire for all eternity by being separated from God forever?"

"It's both," he said. "Make no mistake: hell *is* punishment—but it's not a punish*ing*. It's not torture. The punishment of hell is separation from God, bringing shame, anguish, and regret. And because we will have both body and soul in the resurrected state, the misery experienced can be both mental and physical. But the pain that's suffered will be due to the sorrow from the final, ultimate, unending banishment from God, his kingdom, and the good life for which we were created in the first place. People in hell will deeply grieve all they've lost.

"Hell is the final sentence that says you refused regularly to live for the purpose for which you were made, and the only alternative is to sentence you away for all eternity. So it *is* punishment. But it's also the natural consequence of a life that has been lived in a certain direction."

"According to Genesis, when God created everything, he declared it was good," I pointed out. "Obviously, God created hell. But how could he possibly think that hell is good? Doesn't that call his character into question?"

"Actually," replied Moreland, "hell was not part of the original creation. Hell is God's fallback position. Hell is something God was forced to make because people chose to rebel against him and turn against what was best for them and the purpose for which they were created.

"You know, when people founded the United States, they didn't start out by creating jails. They would have much rather had a society without jails. But they were forced to create them because people would not cooperate. The same is true for hell."

"Is hell a physical place?"

"Yes and no. When people die, their soul leaves their body and they're no longer physical. The Bible says when people who are ultimately headed for hell die before Christ's return, they're separated from the presence of God but they're not in a physical place because they're not physical. In that sense, hell is probably not a location, but it's a real part of the universe. It's like you go through a door into another kind of existence."

"Sounds like a near-death experience," I chuckled.

"Well, I think near-death experiences have demonstrated beyond a reasonable doubt that when people die, they're still able to be conscious," Moreland replied.

Then he continued. "At the final judgment, our body will be raised and our soul will be reunited with it. At that point, I do think there will be a part of the universe where people will be cut off from the primary place where the activity of God and his people will be manifested. So at that point it does make sense to talk about hell being a place—but it will not be a torture chamber or anything like that."

Flames, Worms, and Gnashing Teeth

There was that "torture chamber" imagery again. "No wonder that's a popular vision of hell," I said. "When I was about ten years old, I was taken to Sunday school, where the teacher lit a candle and said, 'Do you know how much it hurts to burn your finger? Well, imagine your whole body being in fire forever and ever. That's what hell is.'"

Moreland nodded as if he had heard that kind of story before.

"Now, some kids got scared," I added. "I just got resentful that this guy was trying to manipulate me. I think lots of people have had this sort of experience. You have to admit that when it comes to talking about hell, the Bible certainly does have a tendency to refer to flames."

"That's true," Moreland replied, "but the flames are a figure of speech."

I put up my hand. "Okay, wait a minute," I protested. "I thought you were a conservative scholar. Are you going to try to soften the idea of hell to make it more palatable?"

"Absolutely not," came his reply. "I just want to be biblically accurate. We know that the reference to flames is figurative because if you try to take it literally, it makes no sense. For example, hell is described as a place of utter darkness and yet there are flames too. How can that be? Flames would light things up.

"In addition, we're told Christ is going to return surrounded by flames and that he's going to have a big sword coming out of his mouth. But nobody thinks Christ won't be able to say anything because he'll be choking on a sword. The figure of the sword stands for the word of God in judgment. The flames stand for Christ coming in judgment. In Hebrews 12:29, God is called a consuming fire. Yet nobody thinks God is a cosmic Bunsen burner. Using the flame imagery is a way of saying he's a God of judgment."

"What about hell being a place where worms constantly eat people's flesh?" I asked.

"In Jesus' day, thousands of animals were sacrificed every week in the temple, and there was a sewage system for the blood and fat to flow outside, where it gathered in a pool. There were worms constantly ingesting that. It was a very ugly place," Moreland said. "When Jesus was teaching, he used this metaphor as a way of saying hell is worse than that disgusting place outside the city."

"There's also the phrase 'gnashing of teeth' to describe those in hell," I said. "Doesn't that refer to people reacting to the pain of torture?"

"More precisely, this is meant to describe a state of anger or realization of great loss," Moreland said. "It's an expression of rage at realizing that one has made a huge mistake. If you've ever been around people who are self-absorbed, self-centered, and highly narcissistic, they get angry when they don't get their way. I believe the gnashing of teeth is an expression of the type of personality of people who will belong in hell."

"No flames, no worms, no gnashing of teeth from torture—maybe hell isn't as bad as we thought," I said in an effort to inject a little levity.

Moreland responded quickly. "It would be a mistake to think that way," he said firmly. "Any figure of speech has a literal point. What is figurative is the burning flame; what is literal is that this is a place of utter heartbreak. It is a loss of everything, and it's meant to stand for the fact that hell is the worst possible situation that could ever happen to a person."

"You mentioned people in hell who are self-absorbed and narcissistic, who've rejected God all their life," I said. "Is it possible that, for these kind of people, heaven would be hell?"

"Let me put it this way," he said. "Have you ever been around somebody who was unbelievably good-looking, extremely attractive, and a lot smarter than you are? When you're in a social situation, people want to listen to them, not you. Suppose you don't care for that person, but you're kept in a room with them twenty-four hours a day for thirty years. That would be an unbelievably difficult experience.

"Now, multiply those qualities ten thousand times, and that's a little bit of what God is like. He is real, real smart. He's very attractive. He's a lot more morally pure than we are. And if people do not fall passionately in love with him, then to force them to have to be around him forever—doing the kinds of things that people who love him would want to do—would be utterly uncomfortable.

"You have to understand that people's character is not formed by decisions all at once, but by thousands of little choices they make every day without even knowing about it. Each day, we're preparing ourselves for either being with God and his people and valuing the things he values, or choosing not to engage with those things. So, yes, hell is primarily a place for people who would not want to go to heaven."

"You're saying people consciously choose hell?"

"No, I don't mean they consciously reject heaven and choose to go to hell instead. But they *do* choose not to care about the kinds of values that will be present in heaven every day."

I said, "So, in effect, by the way we live our lives we're either preparing ourselves for being in God's presence and enjoying him for eternity, or we're preparing ourselves for an existence where we try to make ourselves the center of the universe and have no interest in being with God or the people who love him."

Moreland nodded. "That's absolutely right. So hell is not simply a sentence. It *is* that, but it's also the end of a path that is chosen, to some degree, in this life right here and now, day by day."

Even so, there are aspects of hell that seem to violate our sense of justice. At least, I've felt that in the past. I took advantage of a pause in our conversation to reach into my briefcase and retrieve a list of them that I had written on the airplane.

"How about if I ask for your reply to each of these issues," I said to Moreland. "My goal isn't to get into an argument with you. I just want you to spell out your perspective, and then at the end I'll weigh whether I think you're giving adequate responses and if, in total, the doctrine of hell stands up to scrutiny."

"Sounds fair," he replied.

I glanced at the list and decided to begin with one of the most emotion-charged objections of all.

Objection #1: How Can God Send Children to Hell?

People recoil at the thought of children languishing in hell. In fact, some atheists like to taunt Christians by dredging up writings by nineteenth-century evangelists who used horrific language to describe the ghastly experiences of children in hell. For example, a British priest nicknamed "the children's apostle" wrote these gruesome words:

> A little child is in this red-hot oven. Hear how it screams to
> come out! See how it turns and twists itself about in the fire! It
> beats its head against the roof of the oven. It stamps its little feet

on the floor. You can see on the face of this little child what you see on the faces of all in hell—despair, desperate and horrible.[4]

"The idea of children in hell—well, it's too much," I said to Moreland. "How can there be a loving God if children are subjected to hell?" I was interested in seeing whether Moreland's response would be consistent with scholar Norman Geisler's earlier assessment of this issue.

"Remember," Moreland cautioned in light of the quote about the child in the oven, "the biblical language about fire and flames is figurative."

"Yes, okay, but still—will there be children in hell?"

Moreland, who is the father of two daughters, leaned forward as he spoke. "You must understand that in the afterlife, our personalities reflect an adult situation anyway, so we can say for sure that there will be no children in hell," he began.

"And certainly there will be no one in hell who, if they had a chance to grow up to be adults, would have chosen to go to heaven. No one will go to hell simply because all they needed was a little more time and they died prematurely."

Moreland reached over to a table and retrieved his leather-clad Bible. "Besides, in the Bible children are universally viewed as figures of speech for salvation. In all of the texts where children are used in regard to the afterlife, they're used as pictures of being saved. There's no case where children are ever used as figures of damnation."

He flipped through the Old Testament until he settled on 2 Samuel. "Here's a good example," he said. "The child that King David conceived in an adulterous relationship with Bathsheba died, and David says in Second Samuel 12:23, 'I will go to him, but he will not return to me.'

"David was expressing the truth that his child will be in heaven and that he would join him someday. So that is another piece of evidence that children will not be in hell."

Objection #2: Why Does Everyone Suffer the Same in Hell?

As I was formulating my next question, I rose from the couch and wandered toward the front window, pausing in a pool of sunlight dancing on the carpet. The Massachusetts case involving Judge Mathers was lurking in the back of my mind.

"Our sense of justice demands that evil people be held accountable for the way they've harmed others," I said. "And in that sense, hell might be an appropriate sanction for some. However, it violates our sense of fairness that Adolf Hitler would bear the same eternal punishment as someone who lived a pretty good life by our standards but who made the decision not to follow God."

Moreland was listening intently. "It seems unjust that everyone is subjected to the same consequences," he said. "Is that what you're saying?"

"Yes, that's right. Doesn't that bother you?"

Moreland turned in his Bible to the New Testament. "Actually," he said, "everyone doesn't experience hell in the same way. The Bible teaches that there are different degrees of suffering and punishment."

He came to Matthew 11, and his index finger searched until it settled on verses 20–24, which he read aloud:

> Then Jesus began to denounce the towns in which most of his miracles had been performed, because they did not repent. "Woe to you, Chorazin! Woe to you, Bethsaida! For if the miracles that were performed in you had been performed in Tyre and Sidon, they would have repented long ago in sackcloth and ashes. But I tell you, it will be more bearable for Tyre and Sidon on the day of judgment than for you. And you, Capernaum, will you be lifted to the heavens? No, you will go down to Hades. For if the miracles that were performed in you had been performed in Sodom, it would have remained to this day. But I tell you that it will be more bearable for Sodom on the day of judgment than for you."

Moreland closed the book. "Jesus is saying that people will be sentenced in accordance with their deeds," he said.

"No one-size-fits-all?" I asked. "Justice will be adjusted according to each individual?"

"Exactly. There will be degrees of separation, isolation, and emptiness in hell. I think this is significant because it emphasizes that God's justice is proportional. There is not exactly the same justice for everyone who refuses the mercy of God.

"Remember, if God really does let people shape their own character by the thousands of choices they make, he is also going to allow them to suffer the natural consequences of the character they've chosen to have. And those who are in worse shape personally will experience a greater degree of isolation and emptiness."

Objection #3: Why Are People Punished Infinitely for Finite Crimes?

How can any wrongs we've committed in this life merit *eternal* punishment? Isn't it unfair to say that a *finite* life of sin warrants *infinite* punishment? Where's the justice in that?

"Wouldn't a loving God make the punishment fit the crime by not making hell last forever?" I asked as I sat back down on the edge of the couch. "How can we do anything in this life that would warrant eternal torture?"

"Remember, it's not torture," Moreland pointed out. "The wording is critical. It's not eternal conscious torture; it's eternal conscious suffering due to being sentenced away from God."

"Okay," I said, "but that doesn't answer the question."

"No, it doesn't. But let me try. First, we all know that the degree to which a person warrants punishment is not a function of the length of time it took to commit a crime. For example, a murder can take ten seconds to commit; stealing somebody's *Encyclopedia Britannica* could take half a day if it took a long time to break into the house. My point is that the degree of someone's just punishment is not a function of how long it took to commit the deed; rather, it's a function of how severe the deed itself was.

"And that leads to the second point. What is the most heinous thing a person can do in this life? Most people, because they don't think much about God, will say it's harming animals or destroying the environment or hurting another person. And, no question, all of those are horrible. But they pale in light of the worst thing a person can do, which is to mock and dishonor and refuse to love the person we owe absolutely everything to, who is our Creator, God himself.

"You have to understand that God is infinitely greater in his goodness, holiness, kindness, and justice than anyone else. To think a person could go through their whole life constantly ignoring him, constantly mocking him by the way they choose to live without him, saying, 'I couldn't care less about what you put me here to do. I couldn't care less about your values or your Son's death for me. I'm going to ignore all of that'—*that's* the ultimate sin. And the only punishment worthy of that is the ultimate punishment, which is everlasting separation from God.

"As Alan Gomes has pointed out, the nature of the *object* against which the sin is committed, as well as the nature of the sin itself, must be taken into account when determining the degree of heinousness."[5]

Moreland's answer made me think of the incident where a lawyer asked Jesus what the greatest law is. Jesus told him, "'Love the Lord your God with all your heart and with all your soul and with all your strength and with all your mind'; and, 'Love your neighbor as yourself.'"[6]

In the United States, the most serious crime—murder—is punishable by its most severe sanction, which is being separated from society for life in prison. And there did seem to be a certain logic in saying that defiantly violating God's ultimate law should bring the ultimate sanction, which is being separated from God and his people for eternity.

Objection #4: Couldn't God Force Everyone to Go to Heaven?

"Let me go back to a point you made at the outset," I said to Moreland. "You said God is grieved by the necessity of hell."

"Yes, that's right."

"Then why can't he simply force everyone to go to heaven? That would seem to be a simple solution."

"Because that," replied Moreland, "would be immoral."

"Immoral?" I said in surprise. "More immoral than hell?"

"Yes, immoral. Follow me on this: there's a difference between *intrinsic* value and *instrumental* value. Something has intrinsic value if it's valuable and good in and of itself; something has instrumental value if it's valuable as a means to an end. For example, saving lives is intrinsically good. Driving on the right side of the street is an instrumental value; it's just good because it helps keep order. If society decided that everyone should drive on the left side, that would be okay. The goal is to preserve order and save lives.

"Now, when you treat people as instrumentally valuable, or only as a means to an end, you're dehumanizing them, and that's wrong. You're treating people as things when you treat them merely as a means to an end. You only respect people when you treat them as having intrinsic value."

"And how does this relate to forcing people to go to heaven?" I asked.

"If you were to force people to do something against their free choice, you would be dehumanizing them. You would be saying that the good of what you want to do is more valuable than respecting their choices, and so you're treating people as a means to an end by requiring them to do something they don't want. That's what it would be like if God forced everyone to go to heaven.

"If God has given people free will, Lee, then there's no guarantee that everybody's going to choose to cooperate with him. The option of forcing everyone to go to heaven is immoral, because it's dehumanizing; it strips people of the dignity of making their own decision; it denies them their freedom of choice; and it treats them as a means to an end.

"God can't make people's character for them, and people who do evil or cultivate false beliefs start a slide away from God that ultimately ends in hell. God respects human freedom. In fact, it would be unloving—a sort of divine rape—to force people to accept heaven and God if they didn't really want them. When God allows people to say no to him, he actually respects and dignifies them."

Objection #5: Why Doesn't God Just Snuff People Out?

Another aspect of hell that's especially troubling to people is that its duration is eternal. But what if hell didn't last forever? What if God annihilated people—that is, snuffed them out of existence—instead of forcing them to be consciously separated from him forever and ever?

"Surely," I said to Moreland, "that would be more humane than an eternity of regret and remorse."

"Believe it or not, everlasting separation from God is morally superior to annihilation," he replied. "Why would God be morally justified in annihilating somebody? The only way that's a good thing would be the end result, which would be to keep people from experiencing the conscious separation from God forever. Well, then you're treating people as a means to an end.

"It's like forcing people to go to heaven. What you're saying is, 'The thing that really matters is that people no longer suffer consciously, so I'm going to snuff this person out of existence in order to achieve that end.' Do you see? That's treating the person as a means to an end.

"What hell does is recognize that people have intrinsic value. If God loves intrinsic value, then he has to be a sustainer of persons, because that means he is a sustainer of intrinsic value. He refuses to snuff out a creature who was made in his own image. So in the final analysis, hell is the only morally legitimate option.

"God doesn't like it, but he quarantines them. This honors

their freedom of choice. He just will not override that. In fact, God considers people so intrinsically valuable that he sent his Son, Jesus Christ, to suffer and die so that they can, if they choose, spend eternity in heaven with him."

But some theologians claim that annihilation is taught by the Scriptures. They say the Bible teaches that while the punish*ment* of hell is eternal, the punish*ing* isn't eternal.

Annihilationists like to cite Psalm 37, which says the wicked "will be no more" and "will go up in smoke," and "all sinners will be destroyed."[7] And they point to Psalm 145:20, where David said, "The LORD watches over all who love him, but all the wicked he will destroy." And Isaiah 1:28: "Rebels and sinners will both be broken and those who forsake the LORD will perish." They also contend that the metaphors used by Jesus are evidence of annihilationism: the wicked will be "tied in bundles to be burned," the bad fish will be thrown away, and the harmful plants will be uprooted.[8]

I asked Moreland, "Doesn't this mean that annihilationism is consistent with Scripture and therefore a reasonable way to harmonize God's fairness with the doctrine of hell?"

Moreland stood firm. "No, it's not the biblical teaching," he insisted. "Whenever you're trying to understand what an author is teaching, you begin with clear passages that were intended by the author to speak on the question and then move to unclear passages that may not be intended to teach on the subject.

"Let me illustrate this. There are passages in the Bible that say Jesus Christ died for everyone. There's also Galatians 2:20, where the apostle Paul says that Christ 'gave himself for me.' Now, am I to assume from that passage that Christ only died for Paul? No, but why not? Because there are clear passages that teach that Christ died for everybody, so when we come to Paul's statement, we say that it's obvious he didn't mean Jesus died only for Paul, because we interpret the unclear in light of the clear.

"Now, how about these passages concerning hell? The Old Testament has clear passages on hell being everlasting. Daniel 12:2

says that at the end of the age, the just are raised to everlasting life, the unjust to everlasting punishment.[9] The identical Hebrew word for *everlasting* is used in both instances. If we're going to say that people are annihilated in hell, we should say they're annihilated in heaven. You can't have your cake and eat it too. And that passage is clearly meant to be teaching on this question.

"In the New Testament, in Matthew 25, Jesus offers a clear teaching where he's intending to address the question of the eternal state of heaven and hell, and he uses the same word *everlasting* to refer to both.

"So we go from these clear passages to the ambiguous teaching about being 'cut off.' All that talk about being destroyed and being cut off in the Old Testament is usually meant to mean people being cut off from Israel and the land. Most of those passages have little or nothing to do with everlasting life; they have to do with being cut off in this life to the promises Abraham gave to the people in the land."

But, I pointed out, the annihilationists also cite the biblical language of fire as evidence that people are destroyed rather than languish forever in hell. As well-respected British pastor John R. W. Stott put it, "The fire itself is termed 'eternal' and 'unquenchable,' but it would be very odd if what is thrown into it proves indestructible. Our expectation would be the opposite: it would be consumed forever, not tormented forever."[10]

Moreland, however, was adamant. "The flame language is figurative," he said. "In Revelation, we are told that hell and death are cast into the lake of fire. Now, hell is not something that can burn. It's a realm. That's like saying heaven could be burned. Heaven is not the kind of thing that burns. And how can you burn death? Death isn't something you can set a torch to and ignite.

"So it's obvious that the lake of fire is meant to stand for judgment. When it says an end is placed to hell, the word *hell* is meant to refer to the temporary state of those between their death and the final resurrection. At that point, they're given their bodies again and they will be located away from God. Death is put to an end because there's not going to be any more death. So the flame language of the lake of fire is clearly meant to be a figure of speech for judgment, not a literal burning."

Objection #6: How Can Hell Exist Alongside of Heaven?

"If heaven is supposed to be a place without tears, then how can there be an eternal hell existing at the same time?" I asked. "Wouldn't those in heaven mourn for those who are suffering forever in hell?"

"First of all, I think people in heaven will realize that hell is a way of honoring people as being intrinsically valuable creatures made in God's image," Moreland said.

"Second, a person's ability to enjoy something often comes from growing older and gaining a more mature perspective. When my children were young, one child was not able to enjoy a gift if the other child got a present she thought was a little bit better. When they got older, they were able to enjoy their present, irrespective of the other person's. In fact, if they were worrying about what the other person got, they would be allowing the other person to control them.

"C. S. Lewis said hell doesn't have veto power over heaven.[11] He meant that people in heaven will not be denied the privilege of enjoying their life just because they're consciously aware of hell. If they couldn't, then hell would have veto power over heaven.

"You have to remember that the soul is big enough to have an unperturbed sense of joy, well-being, love, and happiness, while at the same time having a sense of grief and sadness for others. Those are not inconsistent states in a person's life, and it is a mark of a person's character and maturity that they're able to have those states at the same time."

Objection #7: Why Didn't God Create Only Those He Knew Would Follow Him?

"If God knows the future, why did he create people he knew would never turn to him and would therefore end up in hell?"

I asked. "Couldn't he have created only those he knew would follow him and simply not created those he knew would reject him? That option would seem to be much more humane than hell."

"It depends on God's goal," said Moreland. "If God had chosen to create just a handful of four, six, or seven people, maybe he could have only created those people who would go to heaven. The problem is that once God starts to create more people, it becomes more difficult to just create the people who would choose him and not create the people who wouldn't."

"Why is that?"

"Because one of the reasons God put us here is to give us a chance to affect other people."

Moreland thought for a moment before coming up with an analogy. "Do you recall the *Back to the Future* movies?" he asked. "Remember how they went back in time and changed one small detail, and then when they returned to the future, the entire town was completely changed? I think there's an element of truth to that.

"The simple fact of the matter is that we are impacted by observing other people. Suppose, for example, that when I was a little boy, God gave my parents the choice to move to Illinois instead of staying in Missouri. Let's say there was a Christian neighbor who was a hypocrite, and I observed this man and chose because of his life to say no to the gospel the rest of my life. Now suppose that people at work looked at how obnoxious I was, and five people become followers of Christ because of my bad example of what a non-Christian life looks like. Well, if we go to Illinois, we get one person lost—me—but five people are redeemed.

"On the other hand, suppose God chooses not to give the offer of a new job to my dad and we stay in Missouri. I might have a track coach who is a Christian and who pours his life into me, and I end up choosing to follow God because of that. But because my Christian life is not really what it ought to be, five people are influenced away from Christ.

"Do you see? It's a *Back to the Future* scenario. When God

chooses to create somebody, they have an impact on other people's choices, and it might be that they have an impact on their decisions to trust Christ or not.

"There is another part of this, which has to do with how the soul is created. There's a view that the soul comes into existence at conception and is in some way passed on by the parents. In other words, soulish potentialities are contained in the parents' egg and sperm. It's called traducianism. This means my parents created my soul in the act of reproduction. Consequently, I could not have had different parents. That means, then, that the only way God could make me is if my entire ancestral lineage had preceded me, because different grandparents mean different parents and thus different materials for the soul.

"And here's the implication of traducianism for our question: God has to weigh completely different ancestral chains in their entirety. He can't just weigh individual people. So it may be that God allows some chains to come about, with some individuals in them who reject Christ—say, my great-great-grandfather—but that allow for others to be born who do trust Christ. In other words, God would be balancing alternative chains and not just alternative people.

"When God is making these judgments, his purpose is not to keep as many people out of hell as possible. His goal is to get as many people into heaven as possible.

"And it may be, sadly enough, that he's going to have to allow some more people who will choose to go to hell to be created in order to get a larger number of people who choose to go to heaven."

Objection #8: Why Doesn't God Give People a Second Chance?

The Bible says explicitly that people are destined to die once and then to face judgment.[12] Yet if God is really loving, why wouldn't he give people a second chance after death to make the decision to follow him and go to heaven?

"If people tasted hell, wouldn't that give them a strong motivation to change their minds?" I asked.

"This question assumes God didn't do everything he could do before people died, and I reject that," Moreland said. "God does everything he can to give people a chance, and there will be not a single person who will be able to say to God, 'If you had just not allowed me to die prematurely, if you'd have given me another twelve months, I know I would have made that decision.'

"The Bible tells us God is delaying the return of Christ to the earth to give everybody all the time he possibly can so they will come to him.[13] If all a person needed was a little bit more time to come to Christ, then God would extend their time on this earth to give them that chance. So there will be nobody who just needed a little more time or who died prematurely who would have responded to another chance to receive Christ.

"God is fair. He isn't trying to make it difficult for people. I believe it's certainly possible that those who respond to the light from nature that they have received will either have the message of the gospel sent to them, or else it may be that God will judge them based on his knowledge of what they would have done had they had a chance to hear the gospel. The simple fact is, God rewards those who seek him."[14]

That only dealt with part of the question, however. "Wait a minute," I said. "Wouldn't death and the awareness of the presence or absence of God after you die be a very motivating thing for people?"

"Yes, it would, but in a negative way. First, you've got to realize that the longer people live separated from God, the less likely they are able to exercise their free choice and trust him. This is why most people who come to Christ do so when they're young. The longer you live with a bad habit, the harder it is to turn that habit around. It's not impossible, but it's harder. So what would make people think that, say, a ten-year incubation period of being separated from God would get their attention?

"Besides, that would make life before death utterly irrelevant. Then the question would be, why didn't God create people from the beginning with the incubation period? Why did he create them on earth for seventy-five years and let them die and then put them in the incubation period if it was the incubation period that they really needed in the first place? Here's the truth, Lee: this life *is* the incubation period!

"The next thing you have to keep in mind is that if people saw the judgment seat of God after death, it would be so coercive that they would no longer have the power of free choice. Any 'decision' they made would not be a real genuine free choice; it would be totally coerced.

"It would be like me holding a paddle over my daughter and saying, 'You will say you're sorry to your sister for wearing her dress without asking.' Any apology would not be a real apology; it would just be avoidance. And people who would 'choose' in a second chance would not really be choosing God, his kingdom, or his ways—nor would they be suited for life in his kingdom. They'd be making a prudent 'choice' to avoid judgment only.

"I'll suggest one more thing. God maintains a delicate balance between keeping his existence sufficiently evident so people will know he's there and yet hiding his presence enough so that people who want to choose to ignore him can do it. This way, their choice of destiny is really free."

Objection #9: **Isn't Reincarnation More Rational Than Hell?**

Hindus reject the idea of hell. Instead, they believe in reincarnation, where people return to this world in another form after their death and are given another opportunity to work off the bad karma they generated in their past life and move toward enlightenment.

"Wouldn't reincarnation be a rational way for a loving God to give people a fresh start so that they might repent the next time around and he wouldn't have to send them to hell?" I asked. "Wouldn't this be preferable to hell?"

"Remember, we don't decide what's true based on what we like or don't like. We have to consider the evidence. I don't know any other way to decide whether something's true except by looking at the evidence," came Moreland's reply.

"Yes," I said, "but isn't there evidence for reincarnation—specifically, individuals who have memories of prior lives or even speak in languages that they wouldn't otherwise know?"

"I think the evidence for reincarnation is weak for several reasons," he said. "For example, it's incoherent. Let me give you an illustration of why. The number two is essentially even. If you were to tell me you're contemplating the number two but it's an odd number, I would tell you, 'You may be thinking about three or five, but you can't be thinking of two, because I'll tell you one thing that's essential to it—it's got to be an even number.'

"Now, it's not essential to me that I'm five-foot-eight. It's not essential to me that I weigh one hundred sixty-five pounds. But it *is* essential to me that I'm a human.

"If you were to say, 'J. P. Moreland is in the other room, and he has lost five pounds,' most people would say, 'Good for him.' What if you said, 'J. P. Moreland is in the other room, and guess what? He's an ice cube.' Most people would say, 'That can't be J. P. Moreland, because if there's one thing I know about him, it's that he's human. He's not an ice cube.'

"Well, reincarnation says I could come back as a dog, as an amoeba—heck, I don't know why I couldn't come back as an ice cube. If that's true, what's the difference between being J. P. Moreland and anything else? There's nothing *essential* to me. And just like being even is essential to the number two, so being human is essential to me—and reincarnation says that what is essential to me isn't really essential after all."

"Therefore," I interjected, "it's incoherent."

"Exactly," Moreland said. "Another reason I don't believe in reincarnation is that most of these evidences you've suggested—things like supposed memories of past lives—can be better explained by other means.

"There can be psychological explanations—people seem to

remember certain details, but they're vague or lucky guesses, or there could be demonic explanations for some of this activity. Actually, when you carefully examine the research, you find it fails to support reincarnation.[15]

"Finally, I don't believe in reincarnation because there's an expert on this question, and he's Jesus of Nazareth. He's the only person in history who died, rose from the dead, and spoke authoritatively on the question. And Jesus says reincarnation is false and that there's one death and after that comes the judgment. His apostles, whom he instructed carefully, reiterated his teachings on this."

Instead, Jesus taught about the reality of hell. In fact, he discussed the subject more than anyone else in the Bible. "It's ironic," I pointed out, "that many atheists embrace Jesus as having been a great teacher, and yet he's the one who had the most to say about hell."

"Yes," said Moreland, "and remember this: the evidence is that Jesus and his followers were virtuous people. If you want to know how to view the poor, you ask someone who's like Mother Teresa. You don't ask Hugh Hefner, because a person like Mother Teresa has more character than he does. If you want to know whether hell is ultimately fair, you ask Jesus. And here's the thing: he saw no problem with the doctrine.

"I think we're on thin ice when we compare our moral sentiments and moral intuitions with Jesus'. We're saying we have greater insight into what's fair and what isn't than he does. And I think that's not the kind of arena we want to step into."

The Truth about Hell

I leaned back on the couch and thought for a moment. Moreland had adroitly responded to the toughest objections to the issue of hell. I had to admit that when I took all of his answers together, they did seem to provide a reasonable rationale for the doctrine.

Yet that didn't remove my discomfort. And I was in good company. C. S. Lewis once said the doctrine of hell is "one of the chief grounds on which Christianity is attacked as barbarous and the goodness of God impugned."[16]

As for Moreland, he had spoken as a philosopher and theologian, but I was curious about his personal reaction to this issue. "What about you, J. P.?" I asked. "You've woven some convincing arguments in favor of the doctrine, but be honest—don't you have times when you feel terribly uncomfortable about the existence of hell?"

Moreland removed his silver-rimmed glasses and rubbed his eyes before speaking. "Absolutely," he said. "No question. But, again, feeling uncomfortable about something is not the same thing as having a rational, considered judgment that it's wrong. I believe that hell is morally justifiable, but I don't feel comfortable about it because it's sad."

He paused and then continued. "Keep in mind that God doesn't feel comfortable about it either. He doesn't like it. So what's the proper response to feeling uncomfortable? It's not to try to create a view of the afterlife that keeps me from feeling uncomfortable. That's a terrible way to approach truth. The proper thing to do is to admit that hell is real and to allow our feelings of discomfort to motivate us to action.

"For those who don't know Christ, it should motivate them to redouble their efforts to seek him and to find him. For those of us who know him, it should cause us to redouble our efforts to extend his message of mercy and grace to those who need it.

"And we need to keep the right perspective through it all. Remember that hell will forever be a monument to human dignity and the value of human choice. It is a quarantine where God says two important things: 'I respect freedom of choice enough to where I won't coerce people, and I value my image bearers so much that I will not annihilate them.'"

"Can you see how the doctrine of hell can be a stumbling block for spiritual seekers?"

"Yes, I can, and I'd like to say something about that. Whenever you're trying to start a friendship with any person, you don't understand everything about them and you don't necessarily agree or feel good about every view they hold. But you have to ask, on balance, do you trust this person enough to want to enter a friendship with them?

"The same is true with Jesus. Every single issue isn't going to be resolved before we enter into a relationship with him. But the question is, on balance, can you trust him?

"I'd encourage any seeker to read the gospel of John and then ask, 'Can I trust Jesus?' I think the answer is yes. And I believe that, over time, as we develop our relationship with him, we'll even come to trust him in those areas where, right now, we lack complete understanding."

"What Is God to Do?"

I let Moreland's words take root for a moment before standing and thanking him for his time and expertise. "This was a tough topic," I said. "I appreciate your willingness to talk about it."

He nodded and smiled. "No problem," he said. "I hope it was helpful."

He walked with me outside, where we shook hands and I climbed into the car to head back toward the airport. The heavy traffic didn't bother me; I had plenty of time before my flight. In fact, I appreciated the leisurely drive because it gave me an opportunity to reflect on the interview.

 Was hell the only option open to God? Is it just and moral? Is the doctrine logically consistent? Clearly, Jesus thought it was. And I believed that Moreland's analysis, overall, was sufficient to knock down hell as an obstacle.

That didn't mean I was totally comfortable with every single nuance of the points he had made. But it did mean his explanations, when taken as a whole, were strong enough that I wasn't going to let this issue derail my spiritual journey.

While entangled in the inevitable Los Angeles traffic jam, I reached into my briefcase and rummaged around for the research materials I had compiled in preparation for my talk with Moreland. Finally, I managed to pull out the tape of a previous interview about hell I had conducted with renowned theologian D. A. Carson.

Popping it into my tape player, I fast-forwarded to some remarks that seemed to be an apt conclusion for the afternoon:

> Having said that, hell is not a place where people are consigned because they were pretty good blokes but just didn't believe the right stuff. They're consigned there, first and foremost, because they defy their Maker and want to be at the center of the universe. Hell is not filled with people who have already repented, only God isn't gentle enough or good enough to let them out. It's filled with people who, for all eternity, still want to be at the center of the universe and who persist in their God-defying rebellion.
>
> What is God to do? If he says it doesn't matter to him, God is no longer a God to be admired. He's either amoral or positively creepy. For him to act in any other way in the face of such blatant defiance would be to reduce God himself.[17]

Deliberations
Questions for Reflection or Group Study

1. What was your concept of hell before you read this chapter? How has Moreland's analysis either reinforced or challenged those beliefs?
2. Mark Twain once quipped, "Heaven for climate, hell for company."[18] In light of Moreland's description of hell, how would you respond to someone who offered that observation?
3. Has the doctrine of hell been a stumbling block to you as a spiritual seeker or a believer in Christianity? In what specific ways has Moreland dealt with the concerns that held you back in your spiritual journey?

For Further Evidence
More Resources on This Topic

Chan, Francis, and Preston Sprinkle. *Erasing Hell: What God Said about Eternity, and the Things We've Made Up*. Colorado Springs: Cook, 2011.

Gomes, Alan W. *Forty Questions about Heaven and Hell*. Grand Rapids: Kregel Academic, 2018.

Gregg, Steve. *All You Want to Know about Hell: Three Christian Views of God's Final Solution to the Problem of Sin*. Nashville, TN: Nelson, 2013.

Lewis, C. S. *The Great Divorce: A Dream*. 1946. Reprint, New York: Harper Collins, 2000.

Peterson, Robert A. *Hell on Trial: The Case for Eternal Punishment*. Phillipsburg, NJ: P&R, 1995.

Sprinkle, Preston, gen. ed. *Four Views on Hell*. 2nd ed. Grand Rapids: Zondervan, 2016.

Strobel, Lee. *The Case for Heaven: A Journalist Investigates Evidence for Life after Death*. Grand Rapids: Zondervan, 2021.

Walls, Jerry. *Hell: The Logic of Damnation*. South Bend, IN: University of Notre Dame Press, 1992.

Church History Is Littered with Oppression and Violence

Christianity has (by certain people) been used throughout history as an excuse for some of the most brutal, heartless, and senseless atrocities known to man. The historical examples are not difficult to recall: the Crusades; the Inquisitions; the witch-burnings; the Holocaust . . . I did not see much in Christianity that I considered to be worth the having.

KEN SCHEI, ATHEIST

Christianity has been a boon to mankind . . . [and] has had a beneficent effect upon the human race . . . Most people today who live in an ostensibly Christian environment with Christian ethics do not realize how much we owe Jesus of Nazareth . . . What goodness and mercy there is in this world has come in large measure from him.

D. JAMES KENNEDY, CHRISTIAN

Wayne Olson was always the life of the party. An imposing, avuncular judge with pale blue eyes and a crown of white hair, Olson would regale everyone with sidesplitting stories from his often-bizarre experiences at Cook County Criminal Court. He had a keen wit, a prodigious capacity for booze, and the backslapping friendliness of an old-time Chicago alderman.

Olson was an undistinguished but seemingly conscientious jurist. He especially liked to see his name in the paper, so he would frequently slip me stories when I was the *Chicago Tribune*'s reporter at the Criminal Courts building on Chicago's West Side.

At the end of the day, sometimes we would lounge around his chambers and swap jokes. Occasionally we'd have some laughs over drinks at Jean's, a popular hangout down the block, where he would entertain everyone with stories about how he worked his way through law school as a drummer in a polka band. An inveterate extrovert, he couldn't stand to be alone.

Once he called the pressroom and invited me to a wedding. I went up to his chambers and found a jovial Olson presiding over the impromptu marriage of a handcuffed burglar—whom he had just sentenced to three years in prison—and his very pregnant girl-friend. Olson instantly designated me as the best man.

"Sorry," he said with a smile as deputies led away the groom after a two-minute ceremony. "No honeymoon."

As a narcotics judge hearing routine criminal cases, Olson wasn't in a position to pave any new judicial paths. At least not on purpose. However, on Thanksgiving weekend 1980, Olson unwit-tingly became entangled in an incident that was unprecedented in American jurisprudence.

After Olson had driven away from the courthouse, anticipating a restful four-day vacation, a team of FBI agents surreptitiously broke into his darkened chambers and planted a judicially approved listening device. This marked the first time in United States his-tory that federal investigators had bugged the chambers of a sitting judge—an honor that Olson, had he known, would have gladly relinquished to someone else.

Terrence Hake, the prosecutor assigned to work in Olson's courtroom, actually was an undercover agent who was part of a clandestine government investigation called "Operation Greylord." After Olson returned from the holiday, whenever anyone under sur-veillance would walk into his chambers, Hake would use a hidden transmitter to send a coded message to an FBI agent stationed in a car parked outside. The agent would then signal another investigator to activate the bug so that agents could eavesdrop on what transpired behind the closed doors.[1]

In all, more than 250 hours of conversations were secretly recorded—and they confirmed government suspicions that the judge had been leading a double life. The likable, easygoing Olson—Mr. Popularity of the county courthouse—turned out to be a thoroughly corrupt extortionist who was cynically selling justice to the highest bidder.

Preserved forever on tape was Olson taking kickbacks from attorneys and perverting justice at every turn. At one point, he was overheard to say, "I love people that take dough because you know exactly where you stand."[2] In fact, within days after the bug was planted, agents listened in astonishment as Olson brazenly fixed a narcotics case with a crooked lawyer:

> **Olson:** I'm a coin collector.
> **Attorney:** Is two [hundred dollars] enough—sufficient, judge?
> I cleared seven hundred sixty-five [dollars] for the day.
> **Olson:** Well, I made a deal with somebody, but I'd rather give it to you; you'd do a better job.
> **Attorney:** I gave you a deuce [two hundred dollars]. If it's not enough, just tell me. Whatever the deal is . . .
> **Olson:** I like the guy that gives me half of . . . what he gets . . . It's just that some days I get nothing. It's a shame to have a guy come here and not have anything.[3]

I had already left the *Tribune* to edit another newspaper when the stunning news broke. Olson had been indicted on fifty-five counts of bribery, extortion, and racketeering. I shook my head. He had deceived me, his colleagues, and the public for so many years. I felt betrayed and angered over his cavalier trashing of the very laws he had sworn to uphold. It was an incredible reversal of fortune—the judge who had once presided so regally over the fate of others now found himself sentenced to twelve years in a federal penitentiary.

And he didn't go to prison alone. Dozens of other crooked judges and lawyers also found themselves swept up in the net of Operation Greylord, the most successful undercover probe in the history of the Cook County court system—and an investigation which raised questions that, by analogy, also are relevant to Christianity.

Corrupt to the Core?

One of the issues that surfaced through Operation Greylord was this: When the history of Chicago is written, will the crimes of Wayne Olson and other corrupt court officials be seen as anomalies in an otherwise honest system of justice? In other words, is the criminal justice apparatus fundamentally untainted and impartial, except for those rare blemishes that occurred when a rogue judge tried to cash in for himself?

Or are Olson and his cronies symptomatic of widespread and systematic corruption that has corroded the very DNA of justice in Cook County? Is the court system compromised to its core by extortion and favoritism, so that Olson's case was actually a window into "business as usual" among the local judiciary?

Essentially these same questions could be asked about Christianity. Christians tend to see the instances of church abuse and violence through the centuries as anomalies in an otherwise positive institution. Critics, however, are more apt to see travesties like the Crusades, the Inquisition, and the Salem witch trials as illustrative of a deeper problem: that Christianity itself is tainted to its core by a power-hungry desire to impose its will on others—even through violence and exploitation, if necessary. One of modern history's most famous atheists, Bertrand Russell, said this was inevitable:

> As soon as absolute truth is supposed to be contained in the
> sayings of a certain man, there is a body of experts to interpret

his sayings, and these experts infallibly acquire power, since they hold the key to truth. Like any other privileged caste, they use their power for their own advantage . . . They become necessarily opponents of all intellectual and moral progress.[4]

Certainly the atrocities committed in the name of Jesus have been lightning rods for opponents to the faith. Said Nobel Prize–winning physicist Steven Weinberg, "With or without religion, good people can behave well and bad people can do evil; but for good people to do evil, that takes religion."[5]

Abuses by the church were one factor that prompted Ken Schei to take the oxymoronic step of founding an organization called "Atheists for Jesus," which endorses what it calls Jesus' "message of love and kindness" without embracing him as God or the church as his institution.

Charles Templeton's distaste for much of what has happened through churches was evident in our conversation as well as in his writings. While conceding that organized religion has done "immeasurable good," he charged that it "has seldom been at its best. Too often it has been a negative influence . . . Across the centuries and on every continent, Christians—the followers of the Prince of Peace—have been the cause of and involved in strife."[6] For example, he likened the church during the Middle Ages to "a terrorist organization."[7]

Is that assessment warranted by the historical data? Is it possible for Christians to defend themselves against the brutal bloodbath of the Crusades and the cruel torture of the Inquisition? Do these examples of violence and exploitation represent a persistent pattern of behavior that should justifiably prompt spiritual seekers to steer clear of organized religion?

These are troubling questions, but fortunately I didn't have to travel very far to get some answers. One of Christianity's leading historians lived less than an hour from my home when I resided in suburban Chicago.

The Seventh Interview: John D. Woodbridge, PhD

After receiving his master's degree in history from Michigan State University, the bilingual Woodbridge earned his doctorate at the University of Toulouse in France. He has received a Fulbright Fellowship and grants from the National Endowment for the Humanities and the American Council of Learned Societies, and has taught at a number of secular universities, including in the Religious Sciences section at École pratique des hautes études, at the Sorbonne, Paris. Currently, he is a research professor of church history at Trinity Evangelical Divinity School in Deerfield, Illinois.

Woodbridge's numerous history-related books include such technical works as *Revolt in Prerevolutionary France: The Prince de Conti's Conspiracy against Louis XV, 1755–1757* and more popular-level efforts, including *Great Leaders of the Christian Church*, *More Than Conquerors*, and *Ambassadors for Christ*. He also has written books on theology and biblical studies, such as *Hermeneutics, Authority, and Canon* and *Scripture and Truth*, both coauthored with D. A. Carson, and *Biblical Authority*. In addition, he served as senior editor of *Christianity Today* for two years.

Woodbridge is a member of several key historical societies in the United States and France, including the American Catholic Historical Association, American Society of Church History, American Society of Eighteenth Century Studies, the Société française du XVIII siècle, and the Société d'histoire moderne et contemporaine.

When I met Woodbridge at his traditionally decorated Dutch colonial home, I experienced a bit of déjà vu. Only later did I realize that he bears an uncanny resemblance to the actor Peter Boyle. The fifty-nine-year-old, balding father of three was wearing a white fisherman net sweater over a blue button-down shirt. We sat across from each other at his dining room table, which was strewn with papers for a book he was completing while on a sabbatical.

There was no way to ease into our discussion. Not with this

topic. Although our interview took place a few months before Pope John Paul II made his historic public confession and asked God's forgiveness for sins committed or condoned by the Roman Catholic Church during the last two millennia,[8] I pulled out a newspaper clipping about an earlier admission by the pope and pointed to it as I posed my first challenge.

Confessing the Church's Sins

"As far back as 1994," I began, "Pope John Paul II called on the church to acknowledge 'the dark side of its history' and said, 'How can one remain silent about the many forms of violence perpetrated in the name of the faith—wars of religion, tribunals of the Inquisition and other forms of violations of the rights of persons?'[9] Isn't it true that the church through the centuries has intentionally glossed over these instances of abuse?"

As he listened, Woodbridge sat with his elbows on the table and his hands laced together in front of him. He analyzed my question for a few moments before responding.

"I think the pope's statement is courageous," he replied, "because he is acknowledging that the Roman Catholic Church has glossed over some things that have been done in the name of Christ and that are obviously fodder for criticism of Christianity in general.

"I would quickly add, though, that we should be careful in using the expression 'the church,' because that gives the impression there has only been one representative institution of Christianity. I would make a clear line of demarcation between people who are part of 'the church'—people who are the sheep who hear the shepherd's voice and would be true Christians—and the institutional churches," he said, emphasizing the plural of that last word.

"Now, obviously," he added, "there are many, many true Christians who are in the visible churches, but just because a person is part of a church doesn't necessarily mean they are a follower of Jesus. Some people are *cultural* Christians but not *authentic* Christians."

I squinted with skepticism. "Isn't that a bit of twenty-first century revisionism?" I asked. "That makes it rather easy to look back and say that all of the atrocities committed in the name of Christianity were actually perpetrated by those who said they were Christians but who really weren't. That seems like a convenient escape hatch."

"Oh, no, this distinction isn't new," he insisted. "In fact, it goes back to Jesus himself." He reached for his Bible, which was hidden beneath some stray papers, and read the words of Jesus from the gospel of Matthew:

> "Not everyone who says to me, 'Lord, Lord,' will enter the kingdom of heaven, but only the one who does the will of my Father who is in heaven. Many will say to me on that day, 'Lord, Lord, did we not prophesy in your name and in your name drive out demons and in your name perform many miracles?' Then I will tell them plainly, 'I never knew you. Away from me, you evildoers!'"[10]

Looking up from the book, Woodbridge said, "So Jesus talked about this distinction two millennia ago. And certainly through the centuries much has been done in the name of Christianity that does not reflect his teachings.

"For example, Adolf Hitler tried to color his movement as being Christian, but obviously he didn't represent what Jesus stood for. Theologian Karl Barth was once asked to begin a lecture in Germany by saying, 'Heil Hitler.' 'It would be bad taste,' he told them, 'to begin a commentary on the Sermon on the Mount with Heil Hitler.'"[11] Those two things just don't go together. So if we accept this distinction, then we can more accurately analyze some of the things that have been attributed to the Christian faith."

I remained dubious. "So you're saying that if something bad was done in history, it couldn't have been committed by authentic Christians?"

"No, no, I'm not suggesting that," Woodbridge replied. "The Bible makes it clear that because of our sinful nature, we continue to do things as Christians that we shouldn't. We're not perfect in this world. And unfortunately, some of the evil deeds committed through history may have, indeed, been committed by Christians. When that has happened, they've acted in ways that are contrary to the teachings of Jesus.

"At the same time, we should recognize that there has often been a minority voice that has spoken out against the abuses that some institutional churches have perpetrated. For instance, I was just reading this morning that during Spain's colonization of Latin America, there were Roman Catholics who were appalled at the way native peoples were being exploited for economic purposes in the name of Christ. They said, 'No, you can't do that!' These Christians were willing to speak out against abuses by representatives of the state or church."

"Let's get back to the pope's statement," I said. "Is it appropriate at this point in history to be confessing the past sins of the church?"

"Yes, it's totally appropriate to admit that some things Christians have done are, in fact, sins. The Bible tells us to confess our sins. Confession should be one of the hallmarks of Christians—a willingness to admit fault, seek forgiveness, and endeavor to change our ways in the future. In fact, it's not just the pope who is doing this. In the Southern Baptist Convention, there was a recent initiative to acknowledge that early Southern Baptists had badly erred regarding the issue of slavery, and a few years ago a Canadian Lutheran group apologized to Jews for anti-Semitism in Martin Luther's writings."

"As a historian, can you see why skeptics seize on the abuses from church history as arguments against Christianity or as a way to attack the faith?"

"Oh, yes, I can understand that," he replied. "Unfortunately, certain incidents in history have created cynicism in some people toward Christianity. At the same time, there are a number of misleading stereotypes about what Christians have and haven't done.

Some critics have attacked a cultural Christianity, failing to grasp that it is not an authentic Christianity.

"This has been one of our problems for centuries. Voltaire was a major critic of Christianity, yet when he went to England, he ran into some Quakers and Presbyterian Christians and was very impressed by their faith. So there can be an institutional form of Christianity that sometimes repels people, while authentic expressions of faith can be quite attractive when non-Christians encounter them."

With that background, I decided to go back to the dawning of Christianity and then move ahead through history by hitting some of the most disturbing episodes that have been attributed to the faith.

Why Christianity Spread

Historians have long marveled at—and theorized about—the amazing speed with which Christianity spread throughout the Roman Empire despite brutal persecution. I asked Woodbridge to assess the comment made by atheist-turned-Christian Patrick Glynn: "Part of the reason for Christianity's rapid spread, historians have remarked, was simply that the early Christians were such nice people. The very kindness of the Christians and their service to the poor and downtrodden attracted new adherents. 'Christians astounded the ancients with their charity,' as one historian [E. Glenn Hinson] has put it."[12]

Woodbridge nodded in response. "Yes, I think Glynn's reference to the rapid spread of Christianity is accurate," he said. "Tertullian writes at the end of the second century, 'We are but of yesterday, and we have filled every place among you—cities, islands, fortresses . . . palace, senate, forum, we have left nothing to you but the temples of your gods.'[13] So in a hundred fifty years, Christianity spread very, very quickly.

"One explanation of its rapid spread, as Glynn indicated, is that many Christians were not just taking care of their own, but they were caring for neighbors, the poor, widows, and the hurting, and they were basically very loving. They showed compassion toward children, who were often treated very callously by the Romans and Greeks at birth, especially baby girls. The lifestyle of Christians matched their teachings, so that many early Christians were not afraid to say, 'Imitate us as we imitate Christ.'"

Having said that, Woodbridge added a bit sheepishly: "Unfortunately, in contemporary evangelicalism people sometimes say, 'Don't look at us; look at Christ,' because we're worried what people will find if our own lives are scrutinized. That wasn't true of many of these early Christians—there was consistency between their beliefs and behavior."

Woodbridge pulled out a piece of paper. "We can also gain some insights into why Christianity grew so quickly from a few early non-Christians," he said, reading aloud the observations of Lucian, a second-century Greek satirist and critic of Christianity:

> These misguided creatures start with the general conviction that
> they are immortal for all time, which explains the contempt of
> death and voluntary self-devotion which are so common among
> them; and then it was impressed on them by their original
> lawgiver that they are all brothers, from the moment that they
> are converted, and deny the gods of Greece, and worship the
> crucified sage, and live after his laws. All this they take quite on
> faith, with the result that they despise all worldly goods alike,
> regarding them merely as common property.[14]

"He's confirming the fact that Christians treated each other as brothers and sisters and freely shared their possessions with each other. Add to that another important factor to which he alludes: Christians believed that to die is to be with Christ. Justin Martyr, in the *First Apology*, says: 'You can kill, but not hurt us.'[15] Most of us think killing is a big-time hurt, but from their point of view, being killed doesn't matter too much. As Paul said, 'To live is Christ and to die is gain.'[16]

"So when you take into consideration the early Christians' fearless devotion to the faith, their willingness to testify through their own martyrdom to the truth of Christ, their humble and compassionate lifestyle, their care for each other and the helpless and hurting and disenfranchised in the community, their commitment to prayer, and their empowerment by the Holy Spirit, you can begin to understand why the faith spread so rapidly."

"Ultimately," I asked, "was it a good or bad thing for Christianity that it was adopted as the state religion of the Romans?"

"On one hand, it was very nice to have the persecutions cease, so that was a good thing," Woodbridge said with a smile. "But as the church became closely related to the state, the church began to use the state as a persecuting agency, and that became a very bad thing. Also, worldliness swept into the church."

"How so?" I asked.

"The rumor was abroad that Constantine promised if you became a Christian, you'd get a beautiful robe and pieces of gold. Well, those aren't very good reasons to become a Christian. So the door was opened wide to persons who may have professed Christianity but who didn't really embrace Jesus."

"In other words, cultural Christians rather than authentic followers of Jesus?"

"Exactly," he said.

With the groundwork concerning early Christianity having been established, I turned the page in my list of questions and began to focus on the five major blots on Christian history that troubled me the most when I was a skeptic—the Crusades, the Inquisition, the Salem witch trials, exploitation by missionaries, and anti-Semitism. Unquestionably, it was an unsavory and unholy litany.

Sin #1: The Crusades

"Let's skip ahead," I said to Woodbridge. "Christian crusaders tried for two centuries to expel the Muslims from the Holy Land." I opened a history book and paged through it until I found the right entry. "One horrific account described the crusaders' entry into Jerusalem in the First Crusade this way," I said, reading to Woodbridge the following description from an eyewitness:

> Some of our men . . . cut off the heads of their enemies; others shot them with arrows, so that they fell from the towers; others tortured them longer by casting them into the flames . . . It was necessary to pick one's way over the bodies of men and horses. But these were small matters compared to what happened at the Temple of Solomon [where] . . . men rode in blood up to their knees and bridle reins. Indeed it was a just and splendid judgment of God that this place should be filled with the blood of the unbelievers, since it had suffered so long from their blasphemies.[17]

Slamming the book shut with disgust, I looked hard at Woodbridge and asked in a voice laden with sarcasm: "Do you agree that the Crusades were 'just and splendid'?"

Woodbridge pursed his lips. "That kind of bloodshed is repugnant and abhorrent," he said firmly. "Did it happen? Yes, it did. Is it heartbreaking to contemplate? Yes, it is. I'm not going to try to excuse it or rationalize it away. However, your question—were the Crusades just or not?—demands an either-or answer, and I think it might be more helpful to provide a little broader context."

I sat back in my chair. "Go ahead," I said.

"Pope Urban II launched the First Crusade in 1095, when he gave a very famous sermon and the crowds responded by declaring, 'God wills it!'" Woodbridge began. "The Crusades continued until the loss of the last Christian stronghold in the Holy Land in 1291, when a town called Acre was taken over once again by Muslims. Jerusalem was back in the hands of the Muslims by 1187.

"The pope called on barons and others to go to the Holy Land and retrieve it from the Muslims who were occupying it and who were thought to be the foes of Christ. So if we put ourselves back into the shoes of those early crusaders, we can understand that they thought they were doing something magnificent for Christ. But when you study the details of what actually happened, you become deeply troubled. In fact, in one Crusade, the Fourth, the participants didn't even make it to the Holy Land. They got as far as Constantinople, seized it, and set up their own kingdom. Tremendous bloodshed ensued. Western Christians killed Eastern Christians.

"In addition to the violence, another major problem was the motivation of some who went. In 1215, Pope Innocent III actually instructed people that if they went on the Crusades, this could earn their salvation. And if they sent someone to fight in their place, this, too, would earn their salvation. This counsel was an obvious distortion of true Christianity. It makes a mockery of the teachings of the Bible and can't in any way be squared with historic Christian beliefs.

"The motivations of the crusaders become more difficult to assess after the Muslims took back Jerusalem. Some of the later Crusades involved Christians going to the Holy Land in an attempt to save other Christians who were in desperate straits. All in all, though, it's fair to say that despite anyone's intentions, the general avarice and slaughter associated with the Crusades have created an ugly stain on the reputation of the Christian faith.

"And that's not just a liberal, twenty-first-century perspective. In the early part of the thirteenth century, a number of Christians were saying the same thing. One reason the crusading ideal disintegrated was due to the enormous travesties associated with the Crusades. Popes tried in later centuries to launch crusades, but they couldn't gain political and popular support. The genuine discrepancy between authentic Christianity and the reporting of what the Crusades had been like contributed to this loss of interest or enthusiasm for new crusades.

"This takes us back to the distinction between things done in the name of Christ and those things that really represent Jesus' teachings. When you try to mesh Jesus' teachings with the slaughter of the Crusades—well, there's no way they can be reconciled."

I asked: "What do you say to a non-Christian who says the Crusades just show that Christians want to oppress others and are as violent as anybody else is?"

Woodbridge pondered the question for a moment before answering. "I would say that there is some truth in that statement as it relates to the Crusades," he began. "There have been people who have done things in the name of Christ they never should have done. Then I would point out that not everything done in the name of Christ should, in point of fact, be attributed to Christianity.

"But I would not try to dodge the point that terrible things occurred during the Crusades. They need to be confessed as being totally contrary to the teachings of the One the crusaders were supposedly following. It's important to remember that Jesus' teachings aren't at fault here; it's the actions of those who, for whatever reason, greatly strayed from what he clearly taught: we are to love our enemies. A 'just war' theory must interact with this principle.

"Nobody was more outspoken against hypocrisy or cruelty than Jesus. Consequently, if critics believe that aspects of the Crusades should be denounced as hypocritical and violent—well, they'd have an ally in Christ. They'd be agreeing with him."

Sin #2: The Inquisition

The Inquisition began in 1163 when Pope Alexander III instructed bishops to discover evidence of heresy and take action against the heretics. What developed was a campaign of terror, with secret proceedings, supreme authority vested in the inquisitor, and a complete lack of due process, where the accused didn't know the names of their accusers, there was no defense attorney, and torture was used to extract confessions. Those who refused to repent were turned over to the government to be burned at the stake.

"What precipitated the Inquisition?" I asked. "And more important, how could authentic Christians participate in such atrocities?"

"The roots of the Inquisition can be traced back to the papacy's deep concern about the problem of heresy, especially in southern France among the Albigenses," Woodbridge explained. "Actually, there's no question that the Albigenses were proponents of heretical teachings and practices. Traditional means of persuasion—for instance, sending them missionaries—didn't work. The Inquisition was an alternative approach or tactic to try to prevent this heresy from spreading. And there were political factors at work too—the northern French were looking for any excuse to intervene in southern provinces."

"So that was the first phase of the Inquisition?" I asked.

"Yes, it was," he said. "There were basically three waves of Inquisitions. First, the one I just mentioned. The second one began in 1472 when Isabella and Ferdinand helped establish the Spanish Inquisition, which also had the Pope's authority behind it.[18] The third wave began in 1542 when Pope Paul III determined to hunt down Protestants, especially Calvinists."

"So," I said, "you have Catholics who call themselves Christians persecuting Protestants who call themselves Christians."

"Yes, this shows once again that you can't really talk about the 'one church,'" he replied. "And things get more complicated because contemporaries often identified heresy with political sedition. If a person was deemed to be a heretic, they were also thought to be politically seditious. For instance, in the trial of Michael Servetus, the state ultimately put him to death. One accusation was that he was a heretic, but what was possibly the state's great fear? It's that he was also politically seditious. Religion and politics were bound up together."

"Is it possible that some authentic Christians were actually the victims of the Inquisition? We typically think of Christians as perpetrating the terror and wonder how true Christians could torture anyone, but could it be that the true Christians really were the ones being killed?"

"Yes, it's very possible," he said. "We don't know the identities of all those who died, but it's likely many were the ones upholding the true faith. Certainly there's evidence that the Catholic Church had lost its way in launching these inquisitions. Protestants sometimes used inappropriate tactics to suppress heresy as well."

"Was the Inquisition an anomaly or part of a broader pattern of abuse and oppression by churches through history?"

"I think that the Inquisition is a tragedy that Christians cannot run away from. But I don't think that it's representative of the history of the Christian churches. It's too much of an extrapolation to say that this kind of hateful activity is part of a pattern.

"For much of their existence, many Christian churches have been in a minority situation and therefore not even in a position to persecute anyone. In fact, talk about persecution—millions of Christians themselves have been victims of brutal persecution through the ages, continuing to the present day in some places. In fact, there were apparently more Christian martyrs in the twentieth century than in any other. To this very day, Christians are being killed for their faith around the world. So, no, the Inquisition is by far an exception in church history, not the norm."

Woodbridge's remarks reminded me of a magazine column about Christians being on the receiving end of persecution. While most people think of the average Christian today as being a United States resident living far away from any danger for their faith, journalist David Neff set the record straight. "The typical Christian," he said, "lives in a developing country, speaks a non-European language, and exists under the constant threat of persecution—of murder, imprisonment, torture, or rape."[19]

Sin #3: The Salem Witch Trials

The Salem witch trials at the end of the 1600s are frequently cited as a kind of Christian hysteria. In all, nineteen people were hanged and one pressed to death for refusing to testify.[20]

"Isn't this another example of how Christian beliefs can result in the trampling of the rights of others?" I asked.

"Yes, it's an example—if, in point of fact, true Christianity is involved here. When you unpack the episodes leading to the trials, you see many factors that precipitated them. There are issues related to people scheming to get land from other people; there are issues related to hysteria; there are issues of believing in astral appearances, whereby people testify that somebody did something even when they were in another place. When you study the legal context for the trials, there are variables that take you into issues unrelated to Christianity."

"Are you saying the churches were innocent?"

"This may not be a total exculpation of Christianity's influence in the trials, but historians who work with matters of this sort know that you should not be monocausational in sorting out such events. Life is more complex than just saying Christianity was responsible. Although there were witch trials in Europe, this was an aberration, not part of a bigger pattern in the colonies. You have to question the psychological equilibrium of some of the people who were involved in the witch trials and consider their false reporting of things.

"Again, we have to emphasize that the Salem witch trials constituted a terrible episode. I'm not trying to downplay their seriousness. But historians recognize that the story line is considerably more complicated than merely blaming the churches."

"One of the presuppositions at the time was that witches exist," I pointed out. "How about you? Do you believe there are witches?"

"Yes, I believe that they do exist," he replied. "In fact, a number of years ago I was watching French television when Robert Mandrou, a very distinguished historian, was proposing that once people become enlightened, they don't believe in witches anymore. Then a woman called to say, 'Mr. Mandrou, I'm very impressed by all you've said, but I just want to tell you that I'm a witch.' And, indeed, witchcraft is practiced in France, the United States, and elsewhere.

"So part of the problem in dealing with the Salem witch trials is the assumption that all of this was totally hokum, that there's no such thing as witches and witchcraft. The hard-core reality is that there is; even many non-Christians recognize that.

"Does this excuse what happened at Salem? No, of course not. But when you sort through the complexities, this situation can't be simply written off as an example of Christianity having run amok. Life—and history—isn't that simple."

"What ended the trials?" I asked.

"This isn't commonly known," he said, "but it was a Christian who played the key role. A Puritan leader named Increase Mather spoke out forcefully against what was happening, and that was the beginning of the end. Ironically, it was a Christian voice that silenced the madness."

Sin #4: Exploitation by Missionaries

The missionaries arrive uninvited. Despite noble intentions, they are ignorant of the place where they set up shop and indifferent to the hearts and values of the people they have come to help. They meddle in things which are none of their business. They assume that the natives' traditional spirituality is defective, even devilish. They bribe or coerce the people to abandon their traditional ways until, in the process of trying to "save" the people, the missionaries wind up destroying them.[21]

I read that accusation to Woodbridge, following it with these questions: "Haven't missionaries through history contributed to the demise of native cultures? Haven't they ended up exploiting the very people they claimed they wanted to help? On balance, haven't missionaries done more harm than good?"

This issue struck close to home for Woodbridge, whose family has a long tradition of serving on the mission field. But he didn't seem to take the challenge personally, responding instead with his characteristic evenhandedness and balance.

"Let me start with the Spanish incursion into Latin America as an example, because it illustrates how complicated this issue can become," he said.

When I nodded my assent, he continued. "Was there exploitation and abuse of native people there? Yes, unfortunately, there was. But was this the result of the missionaries? Well, history tells us that the missionary movement was often associated with an economic policy of the colonial powers known as mercantilism."

"Could you define that?"

"Mercantilism was the belief that the country with the most gold would be the most powerful. The political balance of power in Europe was thought to be in part determined by which country successfully explored Latin America and elsewhere. As a result, mercantilist motivations became, unfortunately, mixed with missionary enterprises. It is, indeed, true that the Spanish did horrible things in Latin America, but much of it was instigated by adventurers and mercantilist types while many missionaries did praiseworthy things."

Woodbridge opened a book sitting nearby. "In fact, historian Anthony Grafton of Princeton University talks about the valuable things that the missionaries did," he said, reading from the book *New Worlds, Ancient Texts*: "The Roman church insisted on the humanity of the Indians, and large numbers of missionaries—especially idealistic mendicant friars bent on bringing what they saw as the simple, incorrupt people of the New World to Christ—arrived. They built churches and religious communities."[22]

"Now, Grafton is not an evangelical," Woodbridge continued, "but he has carefully studied the missionary movement and acknowledges the enormous amount of good that the missionaries did. Unfortunately, missionaries as a group get discussed as agents of mercantilism, and so they often get blamed for some of the horrible things the Spanish did in Latin America.

"And as I noted earlier, in the sixteenth century there were debates in Spain about whether what was going on in Latin America was Christian. There were major defenders of the Indians who insisted they shouldn't be exploited. One key figure, Bartolomé de las Casas, was driven to his reforming attitude after reading a passage in Ecclesiasticus in the Roman Catholic Bible, which says: 'The bread of the needy is their life. He that defraudeth him thereof is a man of blood.'[23] Having read this, he and other Roman Catholics opposed the malevolent things that were taking place in Latin America."

His comments triggered my memory of seeing a statue outside the United Nations building in New York City a number of years earlier. Now I understood the background: Francisco de Vitoria, the founder of international law, had been one of the theologians who had argued for the full dignity of the New World Indians and who had fearlessly opposed their exploitation at the Spanish Court.

"So while it is indeed true that sometimes 'Christian civilization' has done some of the things you pointed out earlier, there have also been thousands of acts of charity that have been God-honoring. The Catholic Church has an impressive record of taking care of the poor during the Middle Ages. In California, their missions all up the coast took care of people. When you read the journals of a number of Protestant missionaries who went to other lands, it's very difficult to conclude that they were self-consciously determined to oppress or destroy all aspects of native cultures."

While Woodbridge's answer was providing some context, I wanted to press him further for a more personal response. "Your family has included missionaries," I said. "What were their experiences?"

"Well, I've read the diary of my grandfather, who was one of the earliest Protestant missionaries to China. I certainly didn't get the sense that he was doing what you said earlier. Instead, he had a burning desire that the Chinese people come to know Christ, and he was very concerned about the poverty of the Chinese people and about some of their practices that were very detrimental to the humanity of individuals. He respected aspects of their culture and wore a pigtail on occasion so that he would be accepted by them.

"It has to be pointed out that sometimes the critics of missionaries have almost a Rousseauist idealism that native peoples were always happy and living perfect lives and that none of the demonic or negative spiritism was going on in their cultures. But when you read the accounts of people going into certain regions, you see that some of these native people were in dire physical and spiritual circumstances and that the missionaries greatly helped them.

"I've also read letters written by my mother, who worked as a missionary in Africa when she was single. She would ride a motorcycle deep into the jungles, going from village to village. She worked in a leper colony taking care of the sick. She desired to show them the love of Christ and to serve them and to see them healed. She served even at great personal risk due to malaria and other dangers associated with living in a jungle.

"So, yes, sometimes there can be a transformation of a culture, but often that transformation brought about some good. When native people became Christians, they experienced the love and joy of Christ. That's a wonderful thing. It's when other motivations creep into the minds of those seeking to change a culture, like a quest for economic gain or a twisted sense of racial superiority, that very bad things result."

"Perhaps," I observed, "some critics of missionaries see no value in the Christian message and therefore no benefit to the people who become followers of Jesus."

"Right!" he declared. "Often that's the underlying presupposition. But if a person has the presupposition that the gospel is the power of God that brings salvation, then the gain to the various cultures of the world that hear the gospel is incalculable.

"I have a colleague who is a leading African theologian. He's had to battle the literature that says Christianity is a Western imperialist ideology bent on destroying African religions. His perspective is quite different. He sees the wonderful contributions that Christianity has made to African societies. It's brought hope and redemption, and countless Africans are very grateful for the gospel. At the same time, he does not deny that the bearers of the Christian message sometimes did not live up to the teachings of Christ in their dealings with Africans."

Sin #5: Anti-Semitism

One of the ugliest blights on Christianity's history has been anti-Semitism—certainly an ironic circumstance, since Jesus was Jewish and claimed to be the long-awaited Messiah of Israel and the world. His disciples were Jewish, and Jews also wrote the entire New Testament, with the exception of Acts and the third gospel, which were authored by the physician Luke.

In 1998, the Roman Catholic Church apologized for "errors and failures" of some Catholics for not aiding Jews during the Nazi Holocaust, while Cardinal John O'Connor of New York expressed "abject sorrow" for anti-Semitism in churches through the years, saying, "We most sincerely want to start a new era."[24]

Woodbridge readily conceded that, regrettably, anti-Semitism has soiled Christian history. The key question was why it happened in the first place.

"One factor was this: most Jews didn't think Jesus was the Messiah. The Jews' refusal to accept him often transformed Jews in the minds of some Christians into foes of Christ," he said. "Add to this that the Jews were thought to be responsible for Jesus' crucifixion, and you have two powerful components of 'Christian' anti-Semitism."

That wasn't sufficient for me. "There has to be more to it than that," I insisted.

"Yes, I believe there is," he replied. "Heiko Oberman, the distinguished historian at the University of Arizona, has tried to identify a number of the other factors. For example, by the time you get to the Middle Ages and the Reformation, there were abundant false rumors about Jews that added even more fuel to the anti-Semitic fires."

"What kind of rumors?"

"That they had been involved with the poisoning of wells at the time of the Black Death of 1348, that they desecrated Christian sacraments when they could, that they privately had sacrificial deaths, that they tampered with Christian Scriptures, and so forth.

Now, keep in mind that these accusations weren't true. Nevertheless, they did stoke feelings of anger and resentment."

Yet that didn't seem to satisfy Woodbridge. He gazed off to the side as if he were searching for another explanation, finally turning to me in obvious frustration.

"It seems to me that this doesn't totally handle the issue," he said. "One would have thought—or should I say, one would have *hoped*—that Christians by the Middle Ages and going up to Martin Luther's day would have realized that the teachings of Jesus absolutely forbade them from doing and saying some of the things that were said and done in his name."

"You mentioned Luther," I said. "His own anti-Semitism is well documented. Where did that come from?"

"Obviously, he knew some of the rumors about Jews. Early in his life, however, he was apparently philo-Semitic—a lover of Jews—and because of this love, he hoped there would be a mass conversion in which they would embrace Jesus as their Messiah. When they didn't, particularly as Luther became more irritable in his later years, he said some very ugly things about them."

His answer puzzled me. "I was under the impression that his anti-Semitism was a lifelong affliction," I said.

"Some scholars contend there's a continuity of his views about Jewish people all throughout his life, but I would argue that Luther's most virulent statements of hostility come toward the end of his life. Perhaps he was saying them out of deep-seated frustration because they didn't come to Christ.

"All that being said, though, some of his statements are so horrific that it is totally appropriate for Lutherans to repudiate them and for all Christians thoroughly to reject them. Christians simply cannot be anti-Semitic. It should be unthinkable to any follower of Jesus.

"Now, on the other side of the coin, in contemporary times, evangelical Christians have often been some of Israel's greatest friends. And the general attitude I see in many churches toward Jewish people today is one of respect."

"What do you say to a Jewish person who says to you that they could never even consider Christianity because of its anti-Semitic history?"

Woodbridge nodded slightly. "I've been hit by that before," he said with sadness in his voice. "I was teaching at a secular university, and a young Jewish student said, 'I want to do a paper on Luther. My grandmother told me he hated Jews. Is that true?' I said, 'It probably is, but go ahead and do the paper.' She came back with research that just made me weep. She found things I didn't even know Luther had said; it's *that* bad."

"What can you say to someone like her?"

"That I'm very, very sorry for what Luther said; those things are absolutely out of line with the teachings of Christ, and this is one of the problems that we as Christians face—we don't always live up to the ideals of Jesus. And I would say, 'I realize how difficult this is, but I hope you would think through what Jesus said and did and examine Christianity on the merits of what it actually teaches.'"

Woodbridge tried to elaborate but apparently could think of nothing else to add that would be very helpful. "I'm afraid that's not very elegant," he conceded. "But that's what I'd say from my heart."

"Some Jewish people believe Hitler was a Christian—" I began, but Woodbridge jumped in and cut me off.

"Oh, yes, that's exactly right," he said. "Again, that's why we have to make the distinction between cultural and authentic Christianity. During the rise of the National Socialists, Hitler tried to wrap himself around Christianity and Martin Luther. It was a clever ideological ploy. But Christian critics, like Karl Barth and others, didn't buy for a moment that Hitler represented orthodox Christianity.

"Let me give you another historical illustration. Many Jewish people in 1665 and 1666 believed that a certain individual was the Messiah. But then he converted to Islam, which dashed the aspirations of a lot of Jewish folks. Now, if I said to a Jewish historian today, 'Do you want to identify that man as the Messiah?' He'd say, 'Of course not. He was a fraud.'

"Well, in a similar fashion, we Christians would say that Hitler was not any sort of Christian Messiah. People often claim things that are false. He was a fraud, an evil individual, who could not have been an authentic Christian, much less a representative of true Christian teachings."

A Portrait of Christianity

We could have gone on to discuss other historical blots on Christianity, including the oppression of women, which has occurred despite Jesus' countercultural attitude toward them, and the way many people in the South once quoted the Bible in a twisted attempt to justify racism and slavery. But I had already spent a long time grilling Woodbridge. Without trying to defend the indefensible, he had sought to provide some context and explanations. In order to establish whether these episodes were exceptions or the norm for Christianity, it was time to explore the other side of Christian history.

"Given all we've talked about," I said, "what's the bottom line? Is the world worse off or better off because of Christianity?"

Woodbridge sat bolt upright in his chair. "Better off," he insisted. "No question about it. These are regrettable historical instances that shouldn't be swept under the rug. We should apologize for them and efforts should be made to make sure they don't ever happen again. At the same time, though, the vast sweep of Christian history has been very beneficial to the world."

"I suppose it's easy in talking about the sins of Christianity to forget the role of atheism in trampling human rights," I observed. I took out a book and read Woodbridge some remarks by prominent Christian Luis Palau:

> Nevertheless, the seismic shock of out-and-out atheism sent tidal waves across Europe and beyond, accounting directly for the annihilation and butchering of more than 100 million people this past century alone.

Humanity has paid a steep, gruesome price for the awful experiments in deliberate antitheism carried out by Lenin, Adolf Hitler, Joseph Stalin, Mao Tse-tung and others—each of whom was profoundly influenced by the writings of the apostles of atheism . . .

After watching atheism proliferate, and witnessing the tragic results, it's clearer than ever that . . . without God, we're lost.[25]

"I agree that without God, we're lost," Woodbridge responded. "That's not to say an atheist could never govern well, because, from the Christian point of view, the atheist benefits from God's common grace. But given the lack of framework in atheism for making moral decisions, it's easy to see why the world has experienced the horrors of these regimes. Where there's no absolute moral standard, raw power often wins."

"What would you say are the positive ways Christianity has contributed to civilization?"

Woodbridge settled deeper into his chair. He ruminated on my question for a few moments and then answered in a voice whose sincerity and wonder and enthusiasm conveyed his deeply felt love for the church.

"I see Christianity's influence as a resplendent mural with many scenes, each depicted in bright, brilliant, and beautiful colors," he said. "Without Christianity, there would be an awful lot of grays and only a few scattered and disconnected lines here and there giving any sense of meaning. But Christianity adds so much meaning, so much hope and beauty and richness to the picture."

Intrigued by the imagery, I asked, "What would the painting show?"

"The very center scene would portray the story of Jesus and his redemption for our sins. Finally, once and for all, he dealt with the issues of our guilt, our loneliness, and our alienation from God. Through his atoning death and resurrection, he opened up heaven for everyone who follows him. That's the greatest contribution

Christianity ever could have made. It's summarized in John 3:16: 'For God so loved the world that he gave his one and only Son, that whoever believes in him shall not perish but have eternal life.'

"Also, Christianity provides us a revelation as to the meaning of life and the existence of universal morality. Without that revelation, it's very difficult to have any sense of what meaning is. You end up like Albert Camus, who said in the opening paragraph of *The Myth of Sisyphus* that we all must answer "the fundamental question of philosophy": Is life worth or not worth living?²⁶ Well, Christianity explains why it is. It gives us a frame of reference for living, for following a moral path, for relating to God and others in a healthy and deeply meaningful way.

"Brushstrokes in the painting would depict scenes revealing vast humanitarian impulses that have been inspired by Jesus' life and teaching. Roman Catholics, Orthodox, Protestants—all have been deeply involved in helping the poor, the disadvantaged, the disenfranchised. They've been willing to work against their own personal interests to serve others. Losing all of that—all the missionary work, all the hospitals, all the homeless shelters, all the rehabilitation programs, all of the orphanages, all the relief organizations, all the selfless feeding of the hungry and clothing of the poor and encouraging of the sick—would be a devastating blow to the world.

"In addition, the impact of Christian thought adds other scenes and gives shading and nuance and depth to the painting. Christians have given their minds to God, and their literary, musical, architectural, scientific, and artistic contributions, if taken away, would render the world much duller and shallower. Think of all the great educational institutions that Christians built, including Harvard, Yale, and Princeton, which were originally conceived and constructed to advance the gospel.

"Finally, there's the power of the Holy Spirit that colors everything good. Can you imagine what the world would be like if the Holy Spirit were withdrawn? I mean, talk about your local horror show! It's bad enough the way things are now, but if the restraining power of the Holy Spirit were not here, the horrible side of life would emerge even more graphically than it already does."

"As you look at this painting of history," I asked, "do you see the positives of Christianity overwhelming the negative instances we've discussed?"

"Yes, I do," he said without hesitating. "I'm heartsick about the times when we as Christians have not lived according to Jesus' teachings and thereby created barriers to the faith. But I'm just so grateful for the nameless men and women who have humbly and courageously upheld the faith through the centuries, who have served in obscurity, who have given their lives to help others, who have left the world a far better place, and who have struggled to do the right thing despite incredible pressure to do otherwise.

"When I think of Christian history," he concluded, "they're the first to come to my mind. They're the heroes who are too often forgotten."

He stopped. Then with a wistful smile, he gave them his greatest tribute: "They're what Jesus envisioned."

The Gifts of Christianity

Woodbridge's impassioned words were still ringing in my mind when I arrived back home, exhausted from a long day. I collapsed into my favorite chair and picked up a magazine to thumb through. There, quite by coincidence, I encountered an article in which several scholars, writing in the waning days of the twentieth century, speculated about where civilization would have been without Christianity. Their observations picked up right where Woodbridge had left off.

Michael Novak extolled Christianity's gift of dignity. "Both Aristotle and Plato held that most humans are by nature slavish and suitable only for slavery," he wrote. "Most do not have natures worthy of freedom. The Greeks used 'dignity' for only the few, rather than for all human beings. By contrast, Christianity insisted that every single human is loved by the Creator, made in the Creator's image, and destined for eternal friendship and communion with him."[27]

He pointed to the civilizing ideas of liberty, conscience, and truth that can be traced to Christianity. "Without the Christian foundations laid for us in the high Middle Ages and again in the sixteenth century our economic and political life together would not only be far poorer," he contended, "but far more brutal as well."

David N. Livingstone, a professor in the School of Geosciences at the Queen's University of Belfast, Northern Ireland, focused on Christianity's gift of science. "The idea that Christianity and science have constantly been at loggerheads is a gross distortion of the historical record," he wrote. "Indeed, Robert Boyle, the great English student of chemistry, believed that scientists more than anyone else glorified God in the pursuit of their tasks because it was given to them to interrogate God's creation."[28]

He pointed out that those in the Reformation "believed that God has revealed himself to humanity in two ways—in Scripture and in nature. This enabled them to engage in the scientific investigation of the natural world." The results have been sweeping contributions by scientists who were spurred on by their Christian faith.

David Lyle Jeffrey, a professor of English literature at the University of Ottawa, described Christianity's gift of literacy. "It would hardly be too much to say that literary culture in Europe, much of Africa and the Americas is inseparable from the culturally transformative power of Christianity," he said. "In most of Europe, as in Africa, South America, and in many other parts of the world, the birth of literacy and literature essentially, not accidentally, coincides with the arrival of Christian missionaries."[29]

Perhaps most captivating, however, was historian Mark Noll's exploration of Christianity's gift of humility, a little-noted contribution that had special relevance in light of my discussions with Woodbridge about the ugly side of Christian history. Wrote Noll:

Over the long course of Christian history, the most depressing thing—because repeated so often—has been how tragically far short of Christian ideals we ordinary Christians so regularly fall. Over the long course of Christian history, the most remarkable thing—because it is such a miracle of grace—is how often believers have acted against the pride of life to honor Christ. Of all such "signs of contradiction," the most completely Christlike have been those occasions when believers who are strong—because of wealth, education, political power, superior culture, or favored location—have reached out to the despised, the forsaken, the abandoned, the lost, the insignificant, or the powerless.[30]

Power, he said, nurtures the idolatry of self. It corrupts and almost never apologizes. But then Noll went on to recount several episodes through history in which powerful people, in whole or in part because of their Christian faith, willingly humbled themselves in public repentance for their abuse of power—an enduring and countercultural testimony to the power of the gospel.

One story particularly piqued my interest because it concerned an obscure but illuminating incident at the conclusion of an episode that Woodbridge and I had discussed—the Salem witch trials.

One of the judges, a prominent Puritan named Samuel Sewall of Boston, became terribly distressed over the role he had played in that debacle. His Christian conscience was finally moved to action when he heard his son recite a familiar Bible passage: "But if ye had known what this meaneth, I will have mercy and not sacrifice, ye would not have condemned the guiltless."[31] The words broke Sewall's heart.

At church services on January 14, 1697, he gave his pastor a statement to read as a contrite Sewall stood ashamed before the congregation. The statement confessed Sewall's guilt for much of what had happened, saying that he "desires to take the Blame and shame of it, Asking pardon of men, And especially desiring prayers that God, who has an Unlimited Authority, would pardon that sin and all other sins."[32] His humble act of sorrow and repentance prompted several other jurors to confess their failures too.

I shut the magazine and tossed it onto the coffee table. *That, I thought to myself, is perhaps one of Christianity's most amazing legacies—the willingness of the mighty to bend the knee of repentance when wrongs have been committed.* It was yet another reminder of the power of faith to change lives—and history—for the good.

Deliberations
Questions for Reflection or Group Study

1. Before reading this chapter, what aspect of Christian history bothered you the most? If it was addressed by Woodbridge, how well did he deal with the issue? Is your opinion about that episode the same or different now?

2. Do you think the historical sins discussed by Woodbridge are anomalies in church history or reflective of something that's terribly wrong in the very DNA of the faith? What facts helped you form your opinion?

3. Has the world been better-off because of Christianity? Why or why not? On balance, have the contributions of atheism been positive or negative for humankind?

For Further Evidence
More Resources on This Topic

Carroll, Vincent, and David Shiflett. *Christianity on Trial: Arguments against Anti-Religious Bigotry.* San Francisco: Encounter, 2001.

Dickerson, John S. *Jesus Skeptic: A Journalist Explores the Credibility and Impact of Christianity.* Grand Rapids: Baker, 2019.

Dickson, John. *Bullies and Saints: An Honest Look at the Good and Evil of Christian History.* Grand Rapids: Zondervan Reflective, 2021.

Ganssle, Gregory E. *Our Deepest Desires: How the Christian Story Fulfills Human Aspirations.* Downers Grove, IL: IVP Academic, 2017.

Johnston, Jeremiah. *Unimaginable: What Our World Would Be Like without Christianity.* Minneapolis: Bethany House, 2019.

Shelley, Bruce. *Church History in Plain Language.* 5th ed. Grand Rapids: Zondervan Academic, 2021.

Stark, Rodney. *For the Glory of God: How Monotheism Led to Reformations, Science, Witch-Hunts, and the End of Slavery.* Princeton, NJ: Princeton University Press, 2004.

———. *God's Battalions: The Case for the Crusades.* New York: HarperOne, 2010.

Wright, Bradley R. E. *Christians Are Hate-Filled Hypocrites . . . and Other Lies You've Been Told: A Sociologist Shatters Myths from the Secular and Christian Media.* Minneapolis: Bethany House, 2010.

I Still Have Doubts,
So I Can't Be a Christian

*In their most inner thoughts, even the most devout
Christians know that there is something illegitimate
about belief. Underneath their profession of faith
is a sleeping giant of doubt . . . In my experience,
the best way to conquer doubt is to yield to it.*

DAN BARKER, PASTOR-TURNED-ATHEIST

*Those who believe they believe in God but without passion
in the heart, without anguish of mind, without uncertainty,
without doubt, and even at times without despair, believe
only in the idea of God, and not in God himself.*

MADELEINE L'ENGLE, CHRISTIAN

The lawyer had a tip for me—a human-interest story, he said.
The tale of a reformed gang member. An inspiring yarn about
a former street terrorist who had found religion and gone straight.
It will be heartwarming, he promised. A good Sunday read.

I rolled my eyes. The story sounded much too saccharine for
me. I was on the prowl for something hard-hitting, something gritty,
something that would land me on the front page of the weekend
Tribune. I wasn't interested in a naive fairy tale about some flaky
born-again fugitive.

But the weekend was approaching fast, and the story leads I had been pursuing had taken me down nothing but blind alleys. So I reluctantly wrote down the lawyer's tip. *Who knows?* I thought. *Maybe I can expose this con man's phony story and get the kind of article I'm after.*

I picked up the telephone and started calling my police sources. Had anyone ever heard of this Ron Bronski character? Sure enough, my contacts in the Gang Crimes Unit were well acquainted with him. He was the street-toughened second-in-command of the Bel-Airs, a gang that terrorized parts of Chicago's Northwest Side. He was dangerous and violent, they said. He had a hair-trigger temper, an appetite for illicit drugs, and an encyclopedic arrest record.

"The guy's a sociopath," said one investigator. Another snorted at the mention of his name and then dismissed him with a single word: "Garbage."

They told me there was a warrant out for his arrest on a charge of aggravated battery for shooting a rival gang member in the back. I scrawled the word *coward* in my notebook.

"We haven't seen him around for a long time," one undercover cop told me. "We figure he fled the city. The truth is, we don't care where he is as long as he's not around here."

Then I called some church leaders in Portland, Oregon, where the lawyer told me Bronski had been living for the last couple of years. While working at a metal shop, he had met some Christians and supposedly abandoned his life of crime, married his live-in girlfriend, and become a devout follower of Jesus.

"Ron is one of the most beautiful, loving people I know," his pastor told me. "He's totally committed to Christ. We pray together several times a week, and he's always doing things like visiting the sick and praying with them, and using his street knowledge to preach to troubled kids. I guess people would call him a 'Jesus freak.'"

He said that Bronski had been reconciled with God but not with society. "He knew there was still a warrant out for his arrest," he said, "so he saved his money and took the train to Chicago to turn himself in."

That piqued my curiosity. A guilty plea to aggravated battery could bring twenty years in the penitentiary. I decided I would go the next step in my research by interviewing Bronski as soon as his lawyer could arrange a meeting.

That night, I was sitting at our kitchen table, mulling the conflicting portraits that the police and pastor had painted of Bronski. "On the surface, it sounds like a miraculous change," I commented to Leslie as she stood at the stove, brewing her evening tea.

"On the surface?" she asked.

"Yeah," I said. "When I dig deeper, I'll find out his scam."

She eased into the chair across from me and sipped from a mug. "The police weren't hunting for him, but he gave himself up anyway. What would motivate him to do that?"

"That's what I'm going to find out," I said. "He's probably pretending he's reformed so he'll get a lighter sentence. Or his lawyer is trying to cut some sort of deal with the prosecutor. Or he knows the witnesses are all dead and they can't convict him anyway. Or he's hoping to get some positive publicity to influence the judge. Or he's setting up an insanity defense . . ."

I went on and on, my hypotheses getting more and more outlandish as I speculated about the real reason he was turning himself in. I considered every far-out possibility—except that his life had legitimately changed and that he had decided to do the right thing by facing the consequences for his crime.

Finally, Leslie put up her hand. "Whoa, whoa," she said. "Those are pretty bizarre theories." She put down her cup and looked me in the eyes. "Tell me something," she said with an edge to her voice. "Are you trying to poke holes in his story because you really think he's a con man? Or are you raising objections because you don't want his story to be true?"

I jumped on the defensive. "Hey," I shot back, "it's my job to be skeptical!"

But she had struck a nerve. To be honest, I didn't want to believe that Christianity could radically transform someone's character and values. It was much easier to raise doubts and manufacture outrageous objections than to consider the possibility that God actually could trigger a revolutionary turnaround in such a depraved and degenerate life.

Piercing the Smoke Screen

As it turned out, Ron Bronski survived my cynical attempts to skewer his story. The street-savvy police detectives were absolutely convinced that the changes in his life were authentic. So was the prosecutor. After hearing the evidence, the judge agreed, and instead of sentencing him to the penitentiary, he set him free on probation. "Go home and be with your family," he told a surprised and grateful Bronski.

Today, more than twenty years later, Bronski is still a minister to street kids in the inner city of Portland—and he remains a close friend of mine.[1]

My initial attitude toward Bronski was reminiscent of the doubts I had raised as a spiritual skeptic. At first, I had heartfelt and thoughtful objections to the Christian faith. But over time, after I began finding adequate answers to those issues, I started to bring up new and increasingly marginal challenges.

Then one day I remembered Leslie's comment about Ron Bronski, and I imagined how she might confront me again with similar words: "Lee, are you trying to poke holes in Christianity because you really think it's an illusion—or are you raising objections because you don't *want* it to be true?"

That stung. Admittedly, I had a lot of motivation to find faults with Christianity when I was an atheist. I knew my hard-drinking, immoral, and self-obsessed lifestyle would have to change if I ever became a follower of Jesus, and I wasn't sure I wanted to let go of that. After all, it was all I knew. Consequently, instead of trying to find the truth, I found myself attempting to fend off the truth with fabricated doubts and contrived objections.

I don't think I'm alone in doing this. Many spiritual seekers have legitimate questions concerning Christianity and need to pursue answers that will satisfy their heart and soul. Yet I think some seekers get to the point where they are subconsciously raising smoke screens to mask their deep-seated motivations for rejecting the faith.

The same is true for Christians who fall prey to doubts about their beliefs. Often, they're having a bout of sincere misgivings about some aspect of their faith; other times, however, their professed doubts may actually be a subtle defense mechanism. They may think they're hung up over an objection to some part of Christianity, when the reality is that they're actually just casting around for some excuse—*any* excuse—not to take Jesus more seriously.

For many Christians, merely having doubts of any kind can be scary. They wonder whether their questions disqualify them from being a follower of Christ. They feel insecure because they're not sure whether it's permissible to express uncertainty about God, Jesus, or the Bible. So they keep their questions to themselves—and inside, unanswered, they grow and fester and loom until they eventually succeed in choking out their faith.

"The shame is not that people have doubts," Os Guinness once wrote, "but that they are ashamed of them."[2]

At the same time, many Christians have a completely different perspective. They believe that having doubts isn't evidence of the absence of faith; on the contrary, they consider them to be the very essence of faith itself. "The struggle with God is not lack of faith," said André Resner. "It *is* faith!"[3]

Do spiritual seekers have to resolve each and every one of their questions before they can follow Jesus? Can a person be a Christian and nevertheless have reservations or doubts? What can people do if they want to believe in Christ—much like Charles Templeton professed he did in my interview—but they feel that questions about Christianity are blocking their way? Is there a process for resolving doubts when they arise? And is there hope for those whose melancholy personality seems to draw them inexorably toward uncertainty in matters of faith?

Scholars have wrestled with these issues for years, but I didn't want to talk with some professor whose interest in doubt was merely antiseptic and academic. I wanted to get answers from someone who has personally known the confusion, the guilt, the maddening ambiguity of uncertainty—and that lured me to Dallas to interview a Christian leader whose faith journey has repeatedly taken him on torturous detours through the valley of the shadow of doubt.

The Eighth Interview: Lynn Anderson, DMin

Outside his 1929-vintage house, filled with primitive typewriters, quaint candlestick telephones, and other antiques from that era, Lynn Anderson works in a cozy office above his garage. His working space has a rustic feel, with Indian and Western art on the walls, wooden bookcases from floor to ceiling, and a photo of the cabin where he was born in Saskatchewan sixty-three years ago. There was no electricity on the homestead where he grew up, just one beloved battery-powered radio that kept the family connected to the outside world.

Anderson has an easygoing cowboy charm that belies his deep intellect and impressive accomplishments. He has a master's degree from the Harding Graduate School of Religion and a doctor of ministry degree from Abilene Christian University, where he has been an adjunct professor for more than two decades. Anderson was a senior pastor for thirty years at churches in Canada and the United States, leaving the pulpit in 1996 to found Hope Network Ministries, through which he coaches, mentors, and equips church leaders.

He has written a number of books, including *Navigating the Winds of Change, Heaven Came Down, In Search of Wonder, The Shepherd's Song,* and *They Smell Like Sheep.*

The book that especially grabbed my attention, however, was the provocatively titled, *If I Really Believe, Why Do I Have These Doubts?* It was this candid and astute book that disclosed Anderson's recurring personal battles with uncertainty.

After chatting for a while to get to know each other, Anderson and I sat down in straight-backed chairs at an austere wooden table underneath a ceiling fan that gently washed us with cool air. Anderson has rugged good looks, with rusty-colored hair, a ruddy complexion, and gold-rimmed glasses.

He's demonstrative as he speaks, his arms reaching out at times for understanding and expression. His voice, rich with rough-hewn honesty and sincerity, would occasionally dip to a sandpapery whisper, as if he were confiding some embarrassing secret to me.

My opening questions took Anderson back to his childhood experiences in rural western Canada as I searched for the genesis of his chronic uncertainties. I suspected that many who wrestle with doubts could relate to his story.

The Roots of Doubt

Anderson was the son of committed Christians who were part of a small, tight-knit church in an area largely devoid of Christians. He said he derived his identity and sense of value from his family and church community, but even so, his doubts about Christianity started early.

"Even as a little kid, I had a melancholy, contemplative personality," he began. "I brooded a lot. I was always looking at the underside of things, not taking anything at face value, always questioning, always probing one level deeper. I've never been able to totally shake that."

I smiled. I've often been accused of asking too many questions myself. "When did you become a Christian?" I said.

"I made a profession of faith at a summer camp when I was eleven, but I felt unclean afterward. I was supposed to have committed my life to Jesus, but I wasn't even sure there was a Jesus. I felt deceptive."

"Did you mention your feelings to anyone?"

"I talked with a minister, but he didn't seem to understand," he said. "I just kind of swallowed it. But of course I still prayed for things. I remember praying and praying that I'd get a bike, and I never got one. That made me feel like God wasn't connected to me. I thought, *Let's get real. When you pray, there's nothing up there but blue sky.*"

I asked if he only felt doubt or whether there were eras when his faith flourished.

"Sometimes I would really sense God's presence," he told me. "I would ride home from school in a snowstorm at twilight, singing hymns and feeling I was in God's hands. But much of the time, I didn't believe in him—at least not like my church peers did."

"Were you afraid they might find out?"

"Absolutely, because I had an enormous need to be loved and accepted and have status in that believing community. I was scared that they'd think I was bad, they'd be angry, they'd think my parents were spiritual failures. I was afraid my parents would be disappointed or ashamed."

Obviously, parents can play a significant role in shaping a child's view of God. In fact, one study showed that most of history's most famous atheists—including Bertrand Russell, Jean-Paul Sartre, Friedrich Nietzsche, Albert Camus, Sigmund Freud, Madalyn Murray O'Hair, and Karl Marx—had a strained relationship with their father or their dad died early or abandoned them at a young age, thus creating difficulty in them believing in a heavenly Father.[4] So I decided to probe in this area with Anderson.

"Tell me a little about your parents," I said a bit tentatively, hoping I wasn't getting too personal.

Anderson removed his glasses and laid them on the Bible that sat open in front of him. "In retrospect," he said, "I guess some of my doubts might have stemmed from the parenting style of my mother. She loved me more than life but had no emotional tools to show it. Her way of getting us to improve was to show what we did wrong. She was taught that mothers aren't supposed to show physical affection to sons or it might make them homosexual, and that you don't affirm people because that could give them a big head."

"Did that color your view of God?"

"As you know, people often define God as a parent image. And for good reason—the Bible calls him a father and even a mother sometimes. So part of the distance I felt from God might have been the distance I felt from my mother. On the other hand, my father was an outgoing, affectionate, affirming person, but I think there's something in our fallen nature that hears the bad news come through the good news."

"And so what was the basic Christian message that you perceived in your early years?" I asked.

"It was, 'If you don't meet this standard, you're lost—but nobody can meet this standard, especially you.' As a result, the closer I would get to God—when I'd start believing and get serious about connecting with him—the more hopeless I felt because I couldn't meet his expectations. Then I would think, *This is sick! Why would I believe in something that's going to condemn me no matter what I do? Surely if there's a God, he couldn't be like that. Some monster invented this.*"

"Did you think you'd outgrow this?"

"I hoped this was part of being a kid. But at college, the doubts moved from the emotional to the intellectual. I ran into questions about the Bible, and I wondered why there's so much suffering in the world."

He smiled as he recalled a story. "I remember one day a student raised some huge biblical dilemma. The teacher couldn't answer it. Finally, after stumbling around for a while, the teacher said, 'When all the facts are in, we'll see that it underscores the credibility of the Bible.'"

Anderson let out a laugh. "I remember thinking, *Oh, no! This guy's hoping it's true too. If you scratch under the surface, he's as scared as I am!*"

Species of Doubt

Anderson has described himself as being a "congenital doubter," or someone who's always asking, "What if?" Like lawyers and accountants who are trained to identify what could possibly go wrong, congenital doubters are drawn like magnets to uncertainties and questions. They may be filled with angst or have a melancholy personality. For them, faith doesn't come naturally.

But that's just one species of doubt. I asked Anderson for examples of others.

He leaned back in his chair, lifting the front two legs slightly off the floor and then rocking gently back and forth. "Oh, there are lots of different kinds," he said. "Some doubters are rebellious, even though they may not identify themselves that way. They have the attitude, *I'm not going to let somebody run my life or do my thinking.* This can take the form of an arrogant pride. Sometimes a young person wants to rebel against their parents, and one way to do that is to rebel against the God their parents believe in.

"Then there are people whose doubts stem from their disappointment with God. Like the girl I visited with yesterday. God says, 'Seek and ask,' but she's asked and he hasn't given. So she's wrestling with uncertainty. Was God serious? Was he even there?

"Others have personal or family wounds. I talked a few weeks ago with a woman who underwent physical abuse from her mom and dad who were deeply religious—they'd make her kneel by the bed and pray, and then they'd beat her. I can see why she's got a problem with God! Others have been personally hurt in the sense of being rejected by a mate or their business has gone south or their health has gone bad. They're wondering, *If there's a God, why does this stuff happen?*

"Then there are the intellectual doubts. This was where I was at. I was doing my best to intellectually undergird my faith, but there were people a lot smarter than me who didn't believe in God. I started to think, *Is faith only for the brilliant? How can faith be so important to God, and yet you've got to have an IQ of 197 to hang on to it?*"

I wondered whether there are some factors that can accentuate doubt in people. I asked Anderson, "What things contribute to doubt, even though a person may not be aware of it?"

"Seasons of life can make a big difference," he replied. "Sometimes people are great believers while in college, but when they're young parents with their second baby and working sixty to eighty hours a week and their wife is sick all the time and the boss is on their back—they simply don't have time to reflect. And I don't think faith can develop without some contemplative time. If they don't make room for that, their faith is not going to grow and doubts will creep in.

"Another factor can be making comparisons with the faith of others. I met with a young woman who said, 'I hate to go to church because I hear all these claims that I'm not experiencing. I believe, I study the Bible, I pray, I work as hard at ministry as any of them do, but I don't get this joy, I don't get my prayers answered, I don't get a great sense of peace, I don't feel like I'm in the hands of a God who's guiding me down the road and is going to take care of me.' People like this begin to think, *What's wrong with God that he won't give me those things?*"

I was curious about how he handled her situation. "What did you say to her?" I asked.

"I encouraged her to read the psalms, because that will alter her perspective on what normal faith looks like. We like to focus on the upbeat psalms, but 60 percent of them are laments, with people screaming out, 'God, where are you?' Normal faith is allowed to beat on God's chest and complain."

"There's a lot of fear of commitment in our culture," I pointed out. "Does that affect a person's willingness to have faith in God?"

"Yes, it can," he replied. "In this narcissistic country, our definition of freedom is the freedom to get our own way and keep our options open. Some young people are afraid to get married because it's a lifetime commitment. Well, the ultimate commitment is to God. We have a Baskin-Robbins culture where the most-dreaded sentence would be to serve a life with no options. And I do think that contributes to people's fear of committing themselves to Christ."

What Faith Isn't

I knew that misconceptions about faith often open the door to doubts because they can create false expectations or misunderstandings about the nature of God. For instance, if people incorrectly think God has promised to heal everyone or make everyone wealthy if they just exhibit sufficient faith, they can fall prey to doubts when illness strikes or bankruptcy looms. In order to arrive at an accurate view of faith, I decided to first clear out the theological underbrush by defining what faith *isn't*.

"What are some common misunderstandings about faith?" I asked.

"People mix up faith and feelings," Anderson replied. "For example, some people equate faith with a perpetual religious high. When that high wears off, as it inevitably does, they start to doubt whether they have any faith at all."

I interrupted. "Are you saying there's no connection between feelings and faith?"

"No," he said. "Feelings are connected with some dimensions of faith, but a lot of that has to do with people's temperaments. Some folks are just not wired to feel very much, even though they may have strong values and convictions."

"How about you?" I asked.

He chuckled. "I tend to be emotionally up and down. It took me years to figure out that this is not a fluctuation of faith. That's why we have to be careful about our feelings—they can be fickle. Let me give you an example.

"A guy once told me, 'I don't like my wife anymore.' My response was to tell him, 'Go home and love her.' But he said, 'You don't understand—I have no feelings for her anymore.' I said, 'I wasn't asking how you felt. I was saying, 'Go home and love her.' Then he said, 'But it would be emotionally dishonest for me to treat my wife that way when I don't feel it.'

"So I asked, 'Does your mother love you?' That seemed to

insult him. He said, 'Yeah, of course.' I said, 'About three weeks after she had brought you home from the hospital and you were screaming and she had to wake up dog-tired and put her bare feet on the cold floor, clean up your miserable diapers, and feed you a bottle—did you think she really got a kick out of that?' He said, 'No.' I said, 'Well, then, I think your mother was being emotionally dishonest.'

"Here was the point I was making: the measure of her love wasn't that she felt good about changing his diaper, but that she was willing to do it even when she wasn't feeling particularly happy about it. And I think we need to learn that about faith. Faith is not always about having positive emotional feelings toward God or life."

"Okay, that's one misconception," I said. "What about the idea that faith is the absence of doubt?"

"Yes, some people think that faith means a lack of doubt, but that's not true," he said. "One of my favorite Bible texts is about the man who comes to Jesus with his demon-possessed son, hoping that the boy would get healed. Jesus says all things are possible to those who believe. And the man's response is so powerful. He says, and I paraphrase, 'I believe, but would you help me with my unbelief?'"[5]

Anderson slapped his knee. "Oh, man!" he exclaimed. "I can really connect with that!"

"So doubt and faith can coexist?" I asked.

"Yeah, it means you can have doubts even when you believe. That was even true of Abraham. He clearly believed, but at the same time, he had doubts. You can see that by what he did at times and what he said. Now, I don't know where you cross the line into corrosive, eroding, negative doubt, but I do believe that where there's absolutely no doubt, there's probably no healthy faith."

"So doubt can actually play a positive role?"

"I think so. I always get a little nervous at what I call the 'true believer mentality'—people with bright smiles and glassy eyes who never have a doubt in the world, who always think everything's wonderful, everything's great. I don't think they run in the same world I do. I'm afraid of what's going to happen to them when something bad occurs.

"For example, I know a physician whose four-year-old child was stricken with cancer. I remember many nights when forty or fifty people would jam into a house to fervently pray for that child. Some of them thought, *Of course he's going to be healed because we prayed.* And when he wasn't, it devastated them.

"Their theology had been misguided and unexamined. It had never been challenged by doubts or thoughtful questions. Doubts could have helped them develop a more substantial and realistic faith—to trust God in the face of death and not just in the face of healing."

Anderson's eyes bored into me as if to emphasize his next words. "You see," he stressed, "a faith that is challenged by adversity or tough questions or contemplation is often a stronger faith in the end."

Delving beneath the Surface

Admittedly, doubts can sometimes serve a positive purpose. I have learned through the years, however, that it can be deceiving to take all doubts at face value. Like my first response to the Ron Bronski story, skepticism can at times be subtly used as a shield to keep people away from deeper motivations. I didn't want to invalidate the legitimacy of people seeking answers to their sincere obstacles to God, but I needed to get to the root of why some individuals raise smoke-screen issues.

"In your experience," I said to Anderson, "do some people claim to have intellectual objections, even though their doubts have another underlying source?"

"Yes, that's certainly true," he said as he nodded and planted the front feet of his chair firmly on the floor once again. "In fact, I personally think all unbelief ultimately has some other underlying reason. Sometimes a person may honestly believe their problem is intellectual, but actually they haven't sufficiently gotten in touch with themselves to explore other possibilities."

"Can you give me an example?" I asked.

It only took him a moment to come up with one. "When I was a youngster, a brilliant novelist—an atheist from an atheistic, Communist family—came to our little town in Canada to gather local color for a book he was writing. One day he was visiting with our family, and he got real serious. He said, 'Can I ask you questions about your religion?' Even though I had been wrestling with doubts from time to time, I said yes.

"He asked, 'Do you really believe there's a God who knows my name?' I said, 'Yeah, that's what I believe.' He said, 'Do you believe the Bible is true? Babies born from virgins, dead people coming out of the cemetery?' I said, 'Yes, that's what I believe.'

"Then he said with great emotion, 'I'd give *anything* to believe that because I've traveled all over the world and I've seen that most people are miserable. The only people who really seem to be getting out of life what they want are the people who say they believe what you believe. But I just can't believe because my head keeps getting in the way!'"

Anderson's eyes got wide. "I was blown away, Lee. I didn't know what to say next because his head was a lot smarter than mine!"

Then Anderson leaned closer to me. "But in retrospect, I don't think his head was the real problem," he said. "I started thinking about what he would lose if he followed Jesus. He was part of a guild of brilliant writers who all think religion is a total crock. I really believe his professional pride and the rejection of his peers would have been too high a price for him to pay."

He let the story soak in. "Let me give you another example," he offered.

"I was talking once with an ex-Marine who said, 'I'm miserable. I've got a wife and kids, and I'm making more money than I can spend with both hands, and I'm sleeping with every woman in town—and I hate myself. You've got to help me, but don't give me any of that God-talk because I can't believe that stuff.'

"We talked for hours. Finally, I said, 'Maybe you think you're shooting straight with me, but I'm not sure you are. I don't think your problem is that you *can't* believe; I think it's that you won't believe because you're afraid to give up the things that help get you through the night.'

"He thought for a while and then said, 'Yeah, I guess that's true. I can't imagine sleeping with just one woman. I can't imagine making do with less money than I make—which I'd have to do because I lie to get it.' He was finally trying to be honest."

With that, Anderson's voice dropped to an intense whisper. "And here's my point," he said. "That man would argue and argue for hours about his cerebral doubts. He would convince people that he couldn't believe because he had too many intellectual objections. But they were just a smoke screen. They were merely a fog he used to obscure his real hesitations about God."

Anderson leaned back in his chair. "I talked with another girl who had been sexually abused," he continued. "Every way God had been represented to her, as filtered through her parents' religion, was horrible. I don't blame her for having trouble believing. But her arguments were always in the intellectual realm. When you tried to dig deeper into her real obstacles, she didn't want to go through the pain of facing them. She used intellectual doubts to deflect people.

"Then there was the time I had a conversation about God with a guy in the Pacific Northwest. He was raising all kinds of intellectual issues. But when we got beneath that, it turned out he didn't want to believe in God because he didn't want to sell his topless bar. The money was too good, and he was having too much fun making it.

"Here's my experience," Anderson said in summary. "When you scratch below the surface, there's either a will to believe or there's a will not to believe. *That's* the core of it."

I stroked my chin in thought. "So you're saying faith is a choice," I said.

Anderson nodded in agreement. "That's exactly right," he replied. "It's a choice."

The Decision to Believe

When I asked Anderson to elaborate on the roles of faith and the will, he immediately brought up the Old Testament character Abraham as an illustration.

"He was called the 'father of the faith,'" said Anderson, "but it wasn't that he never doubted; it wasn't that he always did the right thing; it wasn't that his motives were always pure. He failed on all three counts. But listen—*Abraham never gave up on his will to follow God*. He said, 'I'm going to trust him—will not the Judge of all the earth do right?'[6] He wouldn't give up on God. And one definition of faith is that it's the will to believe. It's the decision to follow the best light you have about God and not quit.

"The idea of choice runs all the way through Scripture. Look at Joshua. He says to choose this day for yourselves whom you're going to serve, but as for him and his household, they will serve the Lord.[7] So faith, at its taproot, is a decision of the will."

I lifted my hand to stop him. "But isn't there also a sense in which faith is a gift from God?" I asked.

"Yes," he conceded, "and that raises a big mystery about choice and free will. But I look at it like the power steering on a car. Good luck trying to move the car's tires without it. But with one finger you can supply the impulse of request, and the power steering will empower you to turn the wheels. In a similar way, our wills make the decision to put our trust in Christ, and God empowers us."

Anderson reached over to remove his glasses from atop his Bible. He slipped them on and then rustled through the book's wafer-thin pages until he came to the gospel of John.

"Listen to John 7:17," he said, clearing his throat. "Jesus says, 'Anyone who chooses to do the will of God will find out whether my teaching comes from God or whether I speak on my own.' So, somehow, if we have the will to believe, God then confirms that Jesus is from God."

He turned a few pages to John 12:37. "The Bible elaborates on this when it says, 'Even after Jesus had performed so many signs in their presence, they still *would not* believe in him.' Then two verses later, it says, 'For this reason they *could not* believe.'[8]

"In other words, they made a decision of the will to deny the message of the miracles—the evidence that Jesus is God—because they wouldn't pay the price, which would be seeing their whole religious system being blown out of the water," he explained. "And they had made this decision not to believe for so long that they had dismantled their capacity to believe. Consequently, at its core, faith is a decision of the will that we keep on making, but we're given that option by God's grace. We're empowered to keep making it by his Spirit."

"And," I observed, "it's a choice we must make without having all the complete information we'd like to have."

"That's right. Otherwise what we would have is knowledge, not faith."

"Talk about the difference."

Anderson laid the Bible back on the table and scanned the room in a search of an impromptu illustration. Apparently unable to find a suitable prop, he reached into his pocket and withdrew his hand. "Okay," he said, "I'm holding something. Do you know what it is?"

I ventured a guess. "A coin."

"But you don't know for sure," he said. "That's your opinion. Our faith is not our opinion. Let me tell you I've got a quarter in my hand. Do you believe that?"

"Sure," I said.

"I'm telling you it's true, but you haven't seen it. That's faith. Hebrews says faith is the evidence of things we do not see."[9]

Anderson smiled. "Watch as I completely destroy your faith." With that, he opened his hand to reveal a quarter. "Now it's no longer faith; it's knowledge."

He tossed the quarter on the table. "Sometimes people think that faith is knowing something is true beyond any doubt whatsoever, and so they try to prove faith through empirical evidence," he said. "But that's the wrong approach."

He gestured toward the coin. "You can see and touch that quarter, so you don't need faith. God, for his own reasons, has not subjected himself to that kind of proof.

"Instead, people should do what you did in *The Case for Christ*—you relied on corroborative evidence. You showed how various strands of evidence point convincingly toward God. And that does something very important—it leaves room for us to make a choice by taking a step of faith in the same direction that the evidence is pointing."

Dealing with Doubt

The afternoon was wearing on, but I didn't want to end our conversation without getting advice from Anderson on how people can deal with the doubts that may be plaguing them. I knew there was no simple formula for overcoming uncertainty; at the same time, people can take some steps to help ease their doubts. And everything begins with the will.

"When you teach on this topic, you tell people that initially they need to decide whether or not they really want to believe," I said. "Why do you start there?"

"Because some people say they want to believe when they really don't. As I said earlier, they raise intellectual issues when they're just trying to deflect attention away from why they really don't want to believe. For instance, a college girl told me, 'It looks to me like this whole Christian crock is invented by people who have a psychological need to believe.'

"My answer was, yes, people have a psychological need to believe—just as some people have psychological needs *not* to believe. I said to her, 'What's the reason you don't want to believe? Is it because you don't want the responsibility faith brings with it? Is it because of despair over your own incorrigibility? Or is it because you don't want to give up going to parties?'

"She was startled. She said, 'Who told you that? It's a little bit of all three.' Okay, she's got emotional reasons for not wanting to believe. Other people have different reasons.

"But people really have to decide why they want to believe. Is it because they've seen some evidence that Christianity is true? Or because they're desperate without God? And if they don't want to believe, why not?

"If they have intellectual doubts, that's fine, but don't stop there. They need to go deeper into what really may be driving them to back away from God. For ten years I've been visiting a young girl whose family had been abusive, and she has just finally admitted to me that it's not God she has trouble with. It's not her questions; it's her scars, her emotions. She needs to start there."

"Assuming a person wants to believe," I said, "what do you recommend as a next step?"

"I suggest they go where faith is. If you want to grow roses, you don't buy an acre at the North Pole. You go where roses grow well. If you're going to do faith, you probably don't want to join American Atheists, Inc. Get around people you respect for their life, their mind, their character, and their faith, and learn from them. Watch their life.

"And I encourage people to put faith-building materials into their mind. By that, I mean books, tapes, and music that build strong motivation for faith, that clarify the nature of God, that examine the evidence pro and con, that deal intelligently with the critics of the faith, that give hope that you can connect with God, that give you tools to develop your spirituality."

These suggestions made sense. But something was missing. "Faith for the sake of faith is meaningless," I said. "Isn't it important to establish exactly where you're putting your faith?"

"Precisely, which is why the next step is to clarify the object of your faith," Anderson replied. "We Canadians know there are two kinds of ice: thick and thin. You can have very little faith in thick ice and it will hold you up just fine; you can have enormous faith in thin ice and you can drown. It's not the amount of faith you can muster that matters up front. It may be tiny, like a mustard seed. But your faith must be invested in something solid.

"So people need to clarify their reasons for believing. Why should they believe in Jesus rather than the Maharishi? Why do they believe in crystals or in Oriental mysticism? Where's the substance?" Anderson gestured toward the leather-bound Bible on the table. "Obviously, I'm prejudiced," he said, "but when it comes right down to it, the only object of faith that is solidly supported by the evidence of history and archaeology and literature and experience is Jesus."

The Faith Experiment

Deciding to believe, going where faith is, consuming faith-building materials, clarifying the object of faith—certainly these were all good recommendations. But something still seemed to be absent. "At some point, the faith journey needs to begin," I said. "How does that happen?"

"Sitting and brooding over faith and doubt will never make a believer out of anybody," came Anderson's response. "Neither will reading all the right books or hanging out with the right people or even making the decision to believe. Ultimately, you must embark on your experiment of faith by doing what faith would do.

"Jesus said that if we continue in his word—that is, continue doing what Jesus says—then we are truly his disciples.[10] Being a disciple means you're a 'following learner.' And when you're a following learner, you will know the truth, and the truth will set you free.

"Knowing the truth doesn't mean filling your head with knowledge; this is the Hebrew *know*, which isn't gathering information. It's experiential knowledge. Like Adam knew Eve—he didn't just know her name and address; he experienced her.

"To experience the truth and be set free, you have to be a following learner. In other words, do what Jesus says, and you'll experience the validity of it. It's kind of like riding a bicycle. You can't watch a video or read a book about it; you've got to get on one and get the feel of it."

"How does a person do that?" I asked.

"You say, 'I've heard some things that Jesus taught. They sound like good ideas to me, but I don't know if they're true. For instance, I've heard Jesus say it's more blessed to give than to receive.[11] How can I know if that's true?' Well, a thousand debates won't prove it. But when you become generous, you'll realize this is truth. You might say, 'Oh, maybe Jesus accidentally guessed right about that one.' Then just keep going. You'll be amazed at how often he 'guessed' right!"

I reached over to pick up Anderson's Bible, rummaging through it until I came to Psalm 34:8. "King David said, 'Taste and see that the LORD is good,'" I said. "Is that what you're talking about?"

"That's the idea. The more you do this," he said with conviction, "the more you will experientially be woven into a web of faith."

I expected Anderson to elaborate, but he momentarily stopped with that comment. He glanced off to the side as he gathered his thoughts. Then he went on to talk movingly about the experience of faith.

Faith as a Verb

"I know, Lee, that you're a former atheist," Anderson said. "You could probably come up with a hundred questions about God that I wouldn't know how to answer. But do you know what? It doesn't matter, because I've discovered that this is true.

"I didn't develop a silly grin and glassy eyes. I've discovered it is more blessed to give than it is to receive. I've walked and walked with this. Every time I discover a new insight, every time Jesus speaks to me personally in ways I can't even articulate, every time I practice his teachings and experience the results—well, after a while I don't care how many intellectual questions you have about why this can't be true. I *know* it's true.

"It's like you say, 'Prove to me that a rainbow is beautiful.' I say, 'Well, it's red and green.' But you say, 'I don't like green and red together.' I'd say, 'But the way they're together in the rainbow, it's beautiful!' I've never heard of anyone who thought a rainbow was ugly. When you are able to actually look at it for yourself, then I don't need to say any more. You've seen it, you've experienced it, and you *know* it's beautiful.

"I think faith is like that. Eventually, you have to move out and do it. By the way, in the gospel of John, faith is never a noun; it's always a verb. Faith is action; it's never just mental assent. It's a direction of life. So when we begin to do faith, God begins to validate it. And the further we follow the journey, the more we know it's true."

While his analysis had appeal, nevertheless there was an apparent loophole. "If faith is experiential, you could get into Buddhism and find that meditation lowers your blood pressure and makes you feel good," I pointed out. "But that doesn't necessarily mean Buddhism is true."

"But remember that experience is just one avenue of evidence," he cautioned. "You also have to clarify the object of your faith, to determine if there are valid reasons for believing it's true. But the ultimate test of the pudding is in the eating. Buddhism does work for some things; atheism works for some things. But if you pursue the whole Jesus journey, you find that his teachings work consistently because they're true. Christianity isn't true because it works; it works because it's true."

I smiled. "It sounds like you're speaking from experience."

"Well, I'll tell you what—my faith is a lot better than it was thirty years ago. Do I have it all together? That would be stretching it. But I am so much more at peace with who God is. I'm so much more confident that I'm in his arms, and I believe that he accepts my feeble attempts to glorify him with my life."

"Do you ever have moments when you still doubt?" I asked.

"Oh, man, yeah!" he exclaimed. "I struggle with why I don't

make more progress in overcoming my pet sins. Surely this can't be God's fault—but on the other hand, why is he making it so hard for me? I have those kind of doubts. I struggle with the horrible things happening in Kosovo and Indonesia and parts of Africa, where whole races are being annihilated—some of it in the name of religion. Why doesn't a loving God deal with this? I'm not saying I don't believe in him. I'm saying I don't have the complete and final answer to that question."

"Is there hope for congenital doubters like yourself?"

Anderson was adamant. "Yes, yes," he insisted. "Absolutely. When I say I struggle with my doubts and sins, I don't want to sound like someone who is being defeated or who has no hope. One guy from my church read my book on doubt and said, 'Oh, no! You mean you don't really believe?' I told him, 'No, I really *do* believe—but would you help me with my unbelief?'

"These days, I'm experiencing God more than ever. I can even see God's grace in those times when he feels absent from me, just like the attributes of my wife seem more real when I'm away from her because I long for her. I pray more these days, and I see more of God's response to prayer than I ever have in my life. I feel less need to control other people or outcomes because I know God is in control.

"And ironically, I feel less equipped to answer all the objections that come from brilliant skeptics. But do you know what? That doesn't matter to me like it used to. Because I know this is true. I see it.

"I see it in my life. I see it in my marriage. I see it in my children. I see it in my relationships. I see it in other people's lives when they're changed by the power of God, when they're renewed by him, when they're freed by his truth."

Anderson's voice had an undercurrent of confident authority. Then with a ring of finality, he declared, "Lee, I've tasted. I'm telling you—I've tasted! And I have seen that the Lord is good."

My mind flashed back to the image of a rural Canadian youngster in anguish over his doubts, desperately searching for solid spiritual ground to build his life on. And now—*not despite the doubts but because of them*—he's found it. His personal experience with God is confirming to him over and over what no empirical evidence could ever prove.

I reached over and turned off my tape recorder. "Thanks, Lynn," I said, "for being so honest."

Having Faith in Doubt

I continued to replay the mental tape of my interview with Anderson as I flew back to Chicago on a half-empty flight that night. I found myself agreeing with his evaluation of the role of doubt. While it can be disconcerting and although it can eventually become destructive if left untended, doubt clearly can have benefits.

I resonated with the view of Gary Parker in his book *The Gift of Doubt*: "If faith never encounters doubt, if truth never struggles with error, if good never battles with evil, how can faith know its own power? . . . In my own pilgrimage, if I have to choose between a faith that has stared doubt in the eye and made it blink, or a naive faith that has never known the firing line of life, I will choose the former every time."[12]

I would too. I knew that my fundamental trust in Jesus would be stronger, surer, more confident, more steadfast because it had been refined through the purifying fire of doubt. In the end, despite questions, challenges, and obstacles, my faith would not just survive, but it would thrive.

Then my thoughts wandered to Charles Templeton. Were his intellectual objections to God really responsible for dismantling his faith—or was there something lurking beneath those doubts, some unspoken, subterranean motivation that was secretly fueling his challenges to Christianity? There was no way for me to be sure. I had no desire to poke around in his private life to try to find out.

At this point, the best I could do would be to continue to take his objections at face value.

There was another important implication of Anderson's interview. If doubt and faith can coexist, then this means people don't have to fully resolve each and every obstacle between them and God in order to have an authentic faith.

In other words, when the preponderance of all the evidence tilts decisively in God's favor, and a person then makes the rational choice to put their trust in him, they can hold some of their more peripheral objections in tension until the day comes when they're resolved.

In the meantime, they can still make the choice to believe—and ask God to help them with their unbelief.

Deliberations
Questions for Reflection or Group Study

1. What part of Anderson's story could you especially relate to? In what ways is your spiritual journey different or similar to his?
2. What kind of doubts do you wrestle with? Is it possible that they're fueled by a motivation not to believe? If so, can you pinpoint why you're reluctant to pursue faith in Christ?
3. How has your picture of God been affected by the family in which you grew up or the church you attended as a child? In retrospect, did you grow up with a biblically accurate view of God?
4. Anderson offered several suggestions for getting off dead center in your spiritual journey—making the decision to believe, going where faith is, consuming faith-building materials, clarifying the object of your faith, and experimenting with following Jesus' teachings. Which of these steps do you believe would be most helpful to you and why?

For Further Evidence
More Resources on This Topic

Anderson, Lynn. *If I Really Believe, Why Do I Have These Doubts?* West Monroe, LA: Howard, 2000.

Conway, Bobby. *Doubting toward Faith: The Journey to Confident Christianity.* Eugene, OR: Harvest House, 2015.

Guinness, Os. *God in the Dark: The Assurance of Faith beyond a Shadow of Doubt.* Wheaton, IL: Crossway, 1996.

Habermas, Gary R. *The Thomas Factor: Using Your Doubts to Draw Closer to God.* Nashville, TN: B&H, 1999.

McGrath, Alister E. *Doubting: Growing through the Uncertainties of Faith.* Downers Grove, IL: InterVarsity, 2006.

Mittelberg, Mark. *Confident Faith: Building a Firm Foundation for Your Beliefs.* Carol Stream, IL: Tyndale, 2013.

Rota, Michael. *Taking Pascal's Wager: Faith, Evidence, and the Abundant Life.* Downers Grove, IL: IVP Academic, 2016.

Sharp, Mary Jo. *Why I Still Believe: A Former Atheist's Reckoning with the Bad Reputation Christians Give a Good God.* Grand Rapids: Zondervan, 2019.

CONCLUSION

The Power of Faith

Somebody, somewhere, love me!
WRITTEN REPEATEDLY IN THE DIARY OF THE
LATE ATHEIST MADALYN MURRAY O'HAIR

*What is faith? My broad definition is beliefs and
actions that are based on something considered to be
trustworthy—even on the absence of absolute proof.*
MARK MITTELBERG, CHRISTIAN

It had taken me all day to get back from my interview in Texas. My flight was delayed because of stormy weather and then cancelled due to mechanical problems, and I had to be rerouted through two other cities in order to get home. The flights were bumpy and crowded. Physically, I was exhausted—but my mind was working overtime.

I had finally finished retracing and expanding on my original spiritual journey by interviewing experts about "The Big Eight" objections to Christianity. Once again, Faith had stared Doubt squarely in the eye—and the only question was which one would blink.

I sank into my favorite overstuffed chair, my mind whirring as it sought to assimilate all the data, opinions, and evidence I had been gathering for the previous year. I had filled a stack of legal pads with research. My collection of interview tapes overflowed two shoe boxes. My office was choked with books.

All eight obstacles to faith raised troublesome issues. The experts I interviewed, however, had been masterful in providing satisfying answers. In several matters they were able to offer clear-cut explanations that definitively settled the issue in my mind. For some subjects that didn't lend themselves to that kind of decisive resolution, the scholars managed to dilute the potency of the objections by providing important context and insights. Misconceptions were cleared away and increased clarity achieved, and in the end the sting of each challenge had been successfully eased.

For me personally, two of the obstacles—the existence of suffering and the doctrine of hell—proved to be the most vexing. The more I would delve into them, the more I found myself in jeopardy of losing my perspective. As I closed my eyes and thought about the investigation, looking for overarching themes that would help me make sense of it all, three distinct scenes came into my mind— starting with a short discussion in which J. P. Moreland had helped me regain my equilibrium.

Scene #1: Finding Perspective

I was about to leave Moreland's home on the day of our interview about the doctrine of hell. I knew he needed to get to the seminary, so I thanked him for his time and started packing my recording equipment. But something was still nagging at him. As we stood, he asked if he could make one more point.

"Lee, there's something else I need to mention," he said as he searched his mind for the right way to say it. He sighed, seemingly frustrated about how to sum it up. Then as I leaned against his doorframe and listened intently, he described an analogy that created an "aha!" moment for me.

"When we're trying to make a decision about something and weighing the evidence for and against it, it's important to consider all the relevant evidence and not just a little piece of it," he began.

That made sense, but I asked why he felt compelled to say it.

"Because," he explained, "we've been focusing on one common objection to Christianity—namely, the existence of hell. If you just concentrate on one obstacle, though, you're missing the big, overarching picture.

"Let me give an illustration. Suppose I saw my wife holding hands with another man at the mall. Would it be reasonable to conclude she was cheating on me? Well, it depends on what evidence I consider. If the only evidence I weigh is what I saw at the mall, then I'd say to myself, *I don't see anything to indicate she's not cheating.* But that leaves something out, doesn't it?

"It ignores a huge chunk of evidence that has nothing to do with the mall situation but has everything to do with the last quarter-century I've spent with her. I've known her well enough, day by day, to be confident she could never cheat on me like that. So if I'm allowed to bring in that lifetime of evidence, I'd say, *On the surface it looks like something's funny, but it simply can't be true that she's cheating. There's got to be another explanation.*

"Now, suppose that unbeknownst to me she had received a call from a person she had helped become a Christian twenty years earlier. He happened to be in town and she hadn't seen him in two decades, so they got together at the mall and were showing each other family pictures and reminiscing. He was getting ready to leave for a foreign country, and she might never see him again. And so, like a brother and sister, they innocently held hands and talked at the mall.

"Well, this is similar to our examination into the rationality of hell. You may be asking yourself, *Do I buy hell or not?* If the only evidence you're factoring into your deliberation is the pros and cons of hell by itself, that's like deliberating about my wife's situation and only allowing the evidence for and against what I saw at the mall.

"I want to submit that there's a lot of other evidence you should consider that has nothing to do with hell per se, but it's relevant. What is that? It's all the evidence that there's a God, that he created you, that the New Testament is historically trustworthy, that Jesus performed miracles and rose from the dead, that God wants to spend eternity with you in heaven.

"When you factor all of that in, you might say to yourself, *Even though I might not have a completely good explanation at this point for why there's a hell, I know there's got to be one because I have too much evidence that Jesus Christ really is the Son of God and he taught about it. And because I can trust him and his deep love for people—as demonstrated by his death for us on the cross—I can have confidence that hell will eventually make sense, that I'll see its fairness, and that I will ultimately recognize it as being the best moral alternative.*"

A Litany of Evidence

Moreland's simple illustration was extremely helpful to me. As I delved into the most troublesome obstacles to faith, they tended to loom so large in my mind that they crowded out other relevant information. And maybe as you've focused on an issue that's particularly nettlesome for you, the same phenomenon has occurred.

Debunking Christianity takes more than just trying to poke a hole in it by raising an objection. That's because there's a backdrop of other relevant evidence that creates a strong presumption in favor of faith in Jesus Christ. Simply examining individual challenges isn't enough; this broad sweep of evidence must be kept in mind as each individual objection is weighed.

What kind of evidence? My interviews with the experts elicited these persuasive facts that point powerfully toward the existence of God and his unique Son, Jesus Christ:

- *The big bang.* William Lane Craig, coauthor of *Theism, Atheism, and Big Bang Cosmology*, showed that the universe and time itself had a beginning at some point in the finite past. Scientists refer to this as the big bang. Craig argued that whatever begins to exist has a cause; the universe began to exist; and therefore the universe has a cause—that is, a creator who is uncaused, changeless, timeless, and immaterial.

Even renowned atheist Kai Nielsen once said, "Suppose you suddenly hear a loud bang . . . and you ask me, 'What made that bang?' and I reply, 'Nothing, it just happened.' You would not accept that."[1] To which Craig said that if there is obviously a cause for a little bang, doesn't it also make sense that there would be a cause for a big bang?

- *The fine-tuned universe.* In the past thirty-five years, scientists have been stunned to discover how life in the universe is astoundingly balanced on a razor's edge. The big bang was actually a highly ordered event that required an enormous amount of information, and from the moment of inception, the universe was finely tuned to an incomprehensible precision for the existence of life like ourselves. An infinitesimal difference in the rate of the universe's initial expansion, the strength of gravity or the weak force, or dozens of other constants and quantities would have created a life-prohibiting rather than a life-sustaining universe. All of this contributes to the conclusion that there's an Intelligent Designer behind creation.

- *The moral law.* Without God, morality is simply the product of sociobiological evolution and basically a question of taste or personal preference. For instance, rape may become taboo in the course of human development because it's not socially advantageous, but it's also conceivable that rape could have evolved as something that's beneficial for survival of the species. In other words, without God there is no absolute right or wrong that imposes itself on our conscience. But we know deep down that objective moral values *do* exist—some actions like rape and child torture, for example, are universal moral abominations—and therefore this means God exists.

- *The origin of life.* Darwinism can offer no credible theory for how life could have emerged naturally from nonliving chemicals. Earth's early atmosphere would have blocked the development of the building blocks of life, and assembling even the most primitive living matter would be so outrageously difficult that it absolutely could not have been the product of unguided or random processes. On the contrary, the vast amount of specific information contained inside every living cell—encoded in the four-letter chemical alphabet of DNA— strongly confirms the existence of an Intelligent Designer who was behind the miraculous creation of life.

• *The Bible's credibility.* Scholar Norman Geisler convincingly argued that there's more evidence that the Bible is a reliable source than there is for any other book from the ancient world. Its essential trustworthiness has been corroborated repeatedly by archaeological discoveries, "and if we can trust the Bible when it's telling us about straightforward earthly things that can be verified, then we can trust it in areas where we can't directly verify it in an empirical way," Geisler said. Further, the Bible's divine origin has been established in two ways. First, in defiance of all mathematical odds, dozens of ancient prophecies about the Messiah—including the precise time frame in which he would appear—were miraculously fulfilled in only one person throughout history: Jesus of Nazareth. Second, biblical prophets performed miracles to confirm their divine authority. Jesus' own miracles were even acknowledged by his enemies. By contrast, in the Qur'an when unbelievers challenged Muhammad to perform a miracle, he refused and merely told them to read a chapter in the Qur'an, even though he conceded, "God hath certainly power to send down a sign."[2]

• *The resurrection of Jesus.* Craig built a compelling case that Jesus Christ returned from the dead in the ultimate authentication of his claim to divinity. He presented four facts that are widely accepted by New Testament historians from a broad spectrum. First, after being crucified, Jesus was buried by Joseph of Arimathea in a tomb. This means its location was known to Jew, Christian, and Roman alike. Second, on the

Sunday after the crucifixion, the tomb was found empty by a group of his women followers. Indeed, nobody claimed the tomb was anything but vacant. Third, on multiple occasions and under various circumstances, different individuals and groups experienced appearances of Jesus alive from the dead. This is not likely to be legendary because of the extremely early date of these accounts. Fourth, the original disciples suddenly and sincerely came to believe that Jesus was risen from the dead despite their predisposition to the contrary. They were willing to go to their death proclaiming that Jesus was resurrected and thus proved he was the Son of God—and nobody knowingly is willing to die for a lie.

In addition, the thirteen scholars and experts I interviewed for my previous book, *The Case for Christ*, established that the biographies of Jesus in the New Testament stand up to intellectual scrutiny, that they were reliably passed down to us through history, that there's corroborating evidence for Jesus outside the Bible, that Jesus wasn't psychologically imbalanced when he claimed he was God, and that he fulfilled all the attributes of deity. See "Appendix: A Summary of *The Case for Christ*" at the back of this book for an overview of these findings.

Accounting for the Evidence

Every single one of "The Big Eight" objections needs to be weighed in light of this overwhelming positive evidence for the existence of God and the deity of Jesus Christ. For example, as Peter Kreeft conceded in our interview, the suffering in this world does constitute some evidence against the existence of God—but in the end it's buried by an avalanche of *other* evidence that he does exist, that he does love us, and that he can even redeem our suffering and draw good from it. This mountain of evidence can give us confidence that even though we may not fully understand why there's suffering or why hell exists, we can trust that God is just, that he is acting appropriately, and that someday we'll have a deeper explanation.

While each of these eight obstacles is serious, none of them were able to overcome the other data that persuasively points toward Christianity as being true. When I was an atheist, I realized I would need to do more than merely raise random objections in order to cripple Christianity; I would have to come up with a nontheistic scenario that would better accommodate all of the facts that I've just listed. But atheism cannot credibly account for the big bang, the fine-tuning of the universe, the emergence of life, the existence of moral laws, the supernatural confirmation of the Bible, and the resurrection. The only hypothesis that explains them all is that there's a divine creator whose unique Son is Jesus of Nazareth.

I had examined each obstacle on its own merits, interviewing experts who were able to provide satisfying explanations and analysis. Then I evaluated each of the objections in the context of the convincing evidence that Christianity is true and that therefore God is ultimately trustworthy and loves us deeply.

My conclusion is that Christianity emerged unscathed. After spending a year investigating "The Big Eight" objections, I remained utterly convinced that the most rational and logical step people can take is to invest their faith in Jesus of Nazareth.

Scene #2: Making a Choice

At the University of Southern California, inside a red brick building with the words "Truth Shall Make You Free" etched in its exterior, Leslie and I found ourselves sitting in an office that looked like the aftermath of a tornado in a trailer park. Surrounding us—on the desk and floor and spare chairs—were papers piled high. Shelves were bursting with heavy books, dog-eared journals, and a variety of mementos. And sitting serenely in the midst of it all was philosopher Dallas Willard, one of the most influential Christian thinkers of our day.

It was a rare opportunity to talk with the author of two of the most celebrated Christian books of recent decades: *The Spirit of the Disciplines* and *The Divine Conspiracy*. Our conversation with the gray-haired, bespectacled professor of philosophy was centering on how faith is exercised through prayer.

At one point, as we discussed how people respond to God, Willard made an especially interesting observation: "The issue is, what do we want? The Bible says that if you seek God with all your heart, then you *will* find him.[3] It's the person who wants to know God that God reveals himself to. And if a person doesn't want to know God—well, God has created the world and the human mind in such a way that he doesn't have to."

He reached over and dug through a stack of papers on his desk, withdrawing a single sheet. "This is a handout I gave to the students in my class," he said. I took the paper and read the words:

> Suppose, however, next Tuesday morning, just after break-fast, all of us in this one world will be knocked to our knees by a percussive and ear-shattering thunderclap. Snow swirls, leaves drop from trees, the earth heaves and buckles, buildings topple and towers tumble. The sky is ablaze with an eerie silvery light, and just then, as all the people of this world look up, the heavens open, and the clouds pull apart, revealing an unbelievably radiant and immense Zeus-like figure towering over us like a hundred Everests. He frowns darkly as lightning plays over the features of his Michelangeloid face, and then he points down, at me, and explains for every man, woman, and child to hear, "I've had quite enough of your too-clever logic chopping and word-watching in matters of theology. *Be assured, N. R. Hanson, that I do most certainly exist!*"[4]

"So," said Willard, "I asked the class, 'If this really happened, how would Hanson respond?'"

I said, "You think he'd explain it away."

"Absolutely!" Willard replied. "It's very unfortunate, but I think he'd explain it away. We need to be alert to the fact that, in nearly every case imaginable, answered prayer can be explained away if you want to. And that's what people normally do. They say, 'Well, I'm very smart; I can't be fooled by all these things.'"

I could relate to that. I told Willard about the time my newborn daughter was rushed into intensive care because of a mysterious illness that was threatening her life. The doctors weren't able to diagnose it. Even though I was an atheist, I was so desperate that I actually prayed and implored God—if he existed—to heal her. A short time later, she astounded everyone by suddenly getting completely better. The doctors were left scratching their heads.

"My response," I told Willard, "was to explain it away. I said, 'What a coincidence! She must have had some bacteria or virus that spontaneously disappeared.' I wouldn't even consider the possibility that God had acted. Instead, I stayed in my atheism."

Willard smiled at the story. "I don't mean to diagnose your case in your presence," he said gently, "but might it be that your pride got in the way? You were too smart! You weren't going to be taken in by this. Let all the little old ladies be fooled, but not you. As long as a person has that attitude, that's their response."

Bingo! He was right on target. Even if there had been a proliferation of corroborating evidence that God had intervened, I would have come up with *any* explanation—no matter how bizarre, no matter how nonsensical—other than the possibility that he had answered my prayer. I was too proud to bend the knee to anyone and too enmeshed in my immoral lifestyle to want to give it up.

"I guarantee you," continued Willard, "that it wouldn't take five minutes to explain away a clear-cut miracle like the fire that came down out of the heavens to consume the altar in the case of Elijah in the Old Testament.[5] And do you know what? People *did* explain it away! If they hadn't, the history of Israel would have been very different from what it was.

"And God has set up prayer in such a way that if you want to explain it away, you can. That's the human mind. God set it up like that for a reason, which is this: *God ordained that people should be governed in the end by what they want.*"

A Will to Believe

That insight from Dallas Willard cut to the heart of my spiritual journey. If I wanted to, I could continue to try to explain away the words of the experts I had interviewed, no matter how outlandish or nitpicky my arguments would eventually become. And believe me, my mind is quite capable of manufacturing all kinds of elaborate rebuttals, excuses, and counterarguments—even in the face of obvious truth.

Ultimately, though, faith isn't about having perfect and complete answers to every single one of "The Big Eight" objections. After all, we don't demand that level of conclusive proof in any other area of life. The point is that we certainly do have sufficient evidence about God on which to act. And in the end, *that's* the issue. Faith is about a choice, a step of the will, a decision to want to know God personally. It's saying, "I believe. Please help me with my unbelief!" As Willard said, "It's the person who wants to know God that God reveals himself to." Or as Lynn Anderson had told me, "When you scratch below the surface, there's either a will to believe or there's a will not to believe. *That's* the core of it."

I was thankful that I didn't have to throw out my intellect to become a Christian. The positive evidence for Jesus being the unique Son of God and the convincing answers to "The Big Eight" objections cleared the way for me to take that step. But I *did* have to overcome my pride. I *did* have to drive a stake through the egoism and arrogance that threatened to hold me back. I *did* have to conquer the self-interest and self-adulation that were keeping my heart shut tight from God.

To apply Willard's words to myself, the biggest issue was, "What did I want?" Did I *want* to know God personally—to experience release from guilt, to live the way I was designed to live, to pursue his purposes for my life, to tap into his power for daily living, to commune with him in this life and for eternity in the next? If so, there was plenty of evidence on which to base a rational decision to say yes to him.

It was up to me—just as it's up to you. As William Lane Craig expressed it:

> If God does not exist, then life is futile. If the God of the Bible does exist, then life is meaningful. Only the second of these two alternatives enables us to live happily and consistently. Therefore, it seems to me that even if the evidence for these two options were absolutely equal, a rational person ought to choose biblical Christianity. It seems to me positively irrational to prefer death, futility, and destruction to life, meaningfulness, and happiness. As [Blaise] Pascal said, we have nothing to lose and infinity to gain.[6]

Scene #3: Changing a Life

This third episode occurred after my Atlanta interview with Craig about the issue of miracles. I got into my rental car and took a leisurely drive up Interstate 75 to Rome, Georgia. The next morning was cool but sunny, and I got dressed and headed to a church for the Sunday morning service.

Outside, politely greeting everyone with a handshake as they arrived, was William Neal Moore, looking handsome in a tan suit with dark stripes, a crisp white shirt and a brown tie. His face was deep mahogany, his black hair was close-cropped, but what I remember most was his smile: it was at once shy and warm, gentle and sincere, winsome and loving. It made me feel welcome.

"Praise the Lord, Brother Moore!" declared an elderly woman as she grasped his hand briefly and then shuffled inside.

Moore is an ordained minister at the church, which is sandwiched between two housing projects in the racially mixed community. He is a doting father, a devoted husband, a faithful provider, a hardworking employee, a man of compassion and prayer who spends his spare time helping hurting people everyone else seems to have forgotten. In short, a model citizen.

But turn back the calendar to May 1984. At that time, Moore was locked in the deathwatch cell at the Georgia State Penitentiary, down the hallway from the electric chair where his life was scheduled to be snuffed out in less than seventy-two hours.

This was not the case of an innocent man being railroaded by the justice system. Unquestionably, Moore was a murderer. He had admitted as much. After a childhood of poverty and occasional petty crimes, he had joined the army and later became depressed by marital and financial woes. One night he got drunk and broke into the house of seventy-seven-year-old Fredger Stapleton, who was known to keep large amounts of cash in his bedroom.

From behind a door, Stapleton let loose with a shotgun blast, and Moore fired back with a pistol. Stapleton was killed instantly, and within minutes Moore was fleeing with $5,600. An informant tipped off the police, and the next morning he was arrested at his trailer outside of town. Caught with the proceeds from the crime, Moore admitted his guilt and was sentenced to death. He had squandered his life and turned to violence, and now he himself would face a violent end.

But the William Neal Moore who was counting down the hours to his scheduled execution was not the same person who had murdered Fredger Stapleton. Shortly after being imprisoned, two church leaders visited Moore at the behest of his mother. They told him about the mercy and hope that is available through Jesus Christ.

"Nobody had ever told me that Jesus loves me and died for me," Moore explained during my visit to Georgia. "It was a love I could feel. It was a love I wanted. It was a love I *needed*."

On that day, Moore said yes to Christ's free gift of forgiveness and eternal life, and he was promptly baptized in a small tub used by prison trusties. And he would never be the same.

For sixteen years on death row, Moore was like a missionary

among the other inmates. He led Bible studies and conducted prayer sessions. He counseled prisoners and introduced many of them to faith in Jesus Christ. Some churches actually sent people to death row to be counseled by him. He took dozens of Bible courses by correspondence. He won the forgiveness of his victim's family. He became known as "The Peacemaker," because his cellblock, largely populated by inmates who had become Christians through his influence, was always the safest, the quietest, the most orderly.

Meanwhile, Moore inched closer and closer to execution. Legally speaking, his case was a hopeless cause. Since he had pleaded guilty, there were virtually no legal issues that might win his release on appeal. Time after time, the courts reaffirmed his death sentence.

"A Saintly Figure"

So profound was the depth of Moore's transformation, however, that people began to take notice. Mother Teresa and others started campaigning to save his life. "Billy's not what he was then," said a former inmate who had met Moore in prison. "If you kill him today, you're killing a body, but a body with a different mind. It would be like executing the wrong man."[7]

Praising him for not only being rehabilitated but also being "an agent of the rehabilitation of others," an editorial in the *Atlanta Journal and Constitution* declared, "In the eyes of many, he is a saintly figure."[8]

Just hours prior to Moore's being strapped into the electric chair, shortly before his head and right calf would be shaved so that the lethal electrodes could be attached, the courts surprised nearly everyone by issuing a temporary halt to his execution.

Even more amazingly, the Georgia Board of Pardons and Paroles later voted unanimously to spare his life by commuting his sentence to life in prison. But what was *really* astounding—in fact, unprecedented in modern Georgia history—was when the board decided that Moore, an admitted and once-condemned armed robber and murderer, should go free. On November 8, 1991, he was released.

As I sat with Moore in his home overlooking a landscape of lush pine trees, I asked him about the source of his amazing metamorphosis.

"It was the prison rehabilitation system that did it, right?" I asked.

Moore laughed. "No, it wasn't that," he replied.

"Then it was a self-help program or your positive mental attitude," I suggested.

He shook his head emphatically. "No, not that either."

"Prozac? Transcendental Meditation? Psychological counseling?"

"Come on, Lee," he said. "You know it wasn't any of those."

He was right. I knew the real reason. I just wanted to hear him say it. "Then what was responsible for the transformation of Billy Moore?" I asked.

"Plain and simple, it was Jesus Christ," he declared adamantly. "He changed me in ways I could never have changed on my own. He gave me a reason to live. He helped me do the right thing. He gave me a heart for others. He saved my soul."

That's the power of faith to change a human life. "Therefore," wrote the apostle Paul, "if anyone is in Christ, the new creation has come: The old has gone, the new is here!"[9]

Billy Moore the Christian is not the same as Billy Moore the killer. God intervened with his forgiveness, with his mercy, with his power, with the abiding presence of his Spirit. That same kind of transforming grace is available to everyone who acts on the ample evidence for Jesus Christ by making the decision to turn away from their sins and embrace him as their forgiver and leader.

It's awaiting all those who say yes to God and his ways.

Reaffirming the Faith

Those three scenes summarized my yearlong quest for answers to "The Big Eight." The first scene emphasizes the magnitude of the overall case for Christ and the availability of solid responses to the toughest questions about the Christian faith. In other words, there's ample justification for a thinking person to put their trust in Jesus. The second scene highlights our human tendency to explain away that evidence out of pride or self-interest. In the end, faith is a step of the will; God will give us what we want. The third scene uses one radical example to illustrate God's willingness to change the lives of those who respond to the evidence, overcome their pride, and open their hearts to him.

All of this can be boiled down to a three-word process— *investigation . . . decision . . . transformation*—that I experienced in my spiritual journey. It was in 1981 when I originally responded to the evidence by deciding to abandon atheism and cling to Christ. And like Moore, I've never been the same. Opening my life wider and wider to God and his ways, I've found that my values, my character, my priorities, my attitudes, my relationships, and my desires have been changing over time—for the better.

Today, having now retraced my original investigation, my confidence in that 1981 decision has only been reinforced. Asking uncomfortable questions hasn't diminished my faith; it has strengthened it. Probing the "soft spots" of Christianity has reaffirmed for me the fundamental soundness and logical integrity of the faith. Refined by the rigors of intellectual scrutiny, my faith has emerged deeper, richer, more resilient, and more certain than ever.

Yet as I reclined on that chair in my living room and mentally reviewed my investigation, I realized that my task was not quite complete. Preacher-turned-skeptic Charles Templeton, who resolutely denied the existence of a loving God but who wept out of his longing for Jesus, provided much of the impetus for this flurry of interviews about "The Big Eight" obstacles to faith.

The intention of my investigation was to get answers to the issues that had most troubled me in my spiritual journey, not to try to spell out a point-by-point rebuttal of Templeton and his writings. But there was considerable overlap between the issues that blocked his path to faith and the topics that disturbed me when I was a spiritual seeker.

How, I wondered, would Templeton have reacted to my interviews with these eight experts? Would he have been receptive to their evidence and arguments? Or would the inexorable advance of Alzheimer's disease have already robbed him of the capacity to rethink spiritual issues anew?

A Note of Hope

It was mid-afternoon on a bright spring day in Orange County, California, where Leslie and I had recently moved. I had just printed out the nearly five hundred pages of the manuscript of this book and was in the midst of packing them into a box when Leslie poked her head into my office.

"What are you doing?" she asked.

I gestured toward the manuscript. "There's someone I want to send this to," I replied.

Leslie put down her cup of tea and walked over to put her arm around my shoulder. "Chuck Templeton, right?" she said. "I think about him from time to time. In fact, I've been praying for him."

That didn't surprise me. "Praying what?" I asked.

"That he'd still be healthy enough to reconsider his conclusions about God. That he'd be open to the explanations you've received from the experts. That he'd respond to that tug inside him that seems to be pulling him toward Jesus."

I nodded. I had been praying too. "I talked to his wife on the phone a few minutes ago," I said. "She told me the Alzheimer's hasn't been very kind to Chuck and that now he has some other health problems. When I got a chance to talk to Chuck and ask him how his Alzheimer's was, he answered with just one word in a very despondent voice—he said, '*Devastating.*'"

"Oh, I'm so sorry," Leslie said quietly.

"Me too," I sighed. "It's very sad." I put some more pages into the box. "She also said Billy Graham came to see Chuck a few months ago."

Leslie's eyes widened. "Really?" she said. "What happened?"

"They hadn't seen each other in quite a while. She said when Chuck recognized him, it was as if a chill went through him and he started crying and threw his arms around Billy and hugged him. She couldn't say enough wonderful things about how kind and loving Billy was. They visited for a while and ate together. Billy prayed before the meal—she said, 'That's the first time grace has ever been said at our table.' Then before he left, Billy prayed for Chuck."

I could see that Leslie's eyes were moist. "I'm so glad they were able to spend some time together," she said. "Maybe something will come out of it."

I nodded and turned to resume packing the manuscript. "Madeleine said she was anxious to see my book and promised to read it to Chuck," I said. "I just hope his mind will be clear enough to understand what these scholars have said. But I feel like I've got to send it—just in case."

With that, I sat down to write him a letter, wishing him well and encouraging him, as best he can, to keep an open mind and take a fresh look at the evidence for Jesus. I signed my name and put down the pen, but I hesitated to fold the letter. I wanted to write something else; I just wasn't sure what was left to say.

I glanced out the window. Saddleback Mountain was majestic against the deep blue sky. For a while I was lost in thought. And then, suddenly, words flooded into my mind. I picked up the pen, and with Leslie peering over my shoulder, quickly added this postscript:

> Chuck, I hope you'll take to heart what Proverbs 2:3–5 says:
> "If you scream for insight and call loudly for understanding,
> if you pursue it like you would money and search for it as you
> would hidden treasure, then the Lord will be awesome to you,
> and you will come into possession of the knowledge of God."[10]

I sealed the note in an envelope, tossed it into the box, and picked up the car keys.

"Let's go mail this," I said.

Epilogue

Several weeks after sending my manuscript to Templeton, I received a warm handwritten note from Madeleine. She said her husband had been too ill to read the book himself, so she read the entire manuscript to him aloud. She thanked me on his behalf, saying Templeton deeply appreciated what I had written.

I put down the note and said to Leslie, "I'm glad he liked the book, but I wish there had been more."

She cocked her head. "Did you expect he'd agree with everything you wrote?"

"No," I said, "but I like him so much that I hoped, well, that he would have reached out to the Jesus he talked about so tearfully."

Over the following months, I couldn't get Templeton out of my mind. I wanted one more chance to dialogue with him. My friend Mark Mittelberg and I began planning to fly to Toronto for one final conversation with him when we heard the news: Templeton died of Alzheimer's. The date was June 7, 2001.

It felt like a punch to the gut. And yet stories soon began to leak out that bolstered my optimism.

It seems that one of Templeton's unlikely friends was a Salvation Army officer named Beverly Ivany. Dressed in her uniform, she attended Templeton's wake. That's where she learned what Templeton had declared shortly before he died in a Toronto hospital, as reported by his wife.

An excited Templeton had exclaimed to her, "Madeleine, do you see them? Do you *hear* them? The angels! They're calling my name! I'm going home!"[1]

An article in the *Toronto Star* elaborated. "Suddenly, Madeleine said, he became very agitated, looking intensely toward the ceiling of the room, his eyes 'shining more blue than I'd ever seen before.' He cried out: 'Look at them, look at them. They're so beautiful. They're waiting for me. Oh, their eyes, their eyes are so beautiful!' Then, with great joy in his voice, he said, 'I'm coming!'"[2]

The news nearly took my breath away. What was happening? Ivany thinks she knows. "I really believed he finally made peace, in his own very private way, with God—and that he *was* going home to be with Jesus."

In fact, she added, Templeton would be one of the first people she would look for when she got to heaven.[3]

Me too, I thought as I read her words. Me too.

I especially want to hear the story of how Templeton was greeted by Jesus himself—the forgiving and gracious Redeemer whose love is so deep that it would extend even to an adamant agnostic if he turned to him in his final breaths on earth.

I'm not sure how that encounter would play out, but I'm pretty confident it would involve a lot of tears—perhaps on both sides.

APPENDIX

A Summary of
The Case for Christ

I n *The Case for Christ*, I retraced and expanded on my 1980–81 journey from atheism to Christianity by interviewing thirteen leading experts on the historical evidence for Jesus Christ. Below is a summary of the answers to the issues I investigated.

Can the Biographies of Jesus Be Trusted?
I once thought the Gospels were merely religious propaganda, hopelessly tainted by overactive imaginations and evangelistic zeal. But Craig Blomberg of Denver Seminary, one of the country's foremost authorities on the biographies of Jesus, built a convincing case that they reflect eyewitness testimony and bear the unmistakable earmarks of accuracy. So early are these accounts of Jesus' life that they are highly unlikely to be the product of legendary invention. "Within the first two years after his death," Blomberg said, "significant numbers of Jesus' followers seem to have formulated a doctrine of the atonement, were convinced he had been raised from the dead in bodily form, associated Jesus with God, and believed they found support for all these convictions in the Old Testament."

Do Jesus' Biographies Stand Up to Scrutiny?
Blomberg argued persuasively that the gospel writers intended to preserve reliable history, were able to do so, were honest and willing

to include difficult-to-explain material, and didn't allow bias to unduly color their reporting. The harmony among the Gospels on essential facts, coupled with divergence on some incidental details, lends historical credibility to the accounts. What's more, the early church is not likely to have taken root and flourished right there in Jerusalem if it had been teaching facts about Jesus that his own contemporaries could have exposed as exaggerated or false. In short, the Gospels were able to pass all eight evidential tests, demonstrating their basic trustworthiness as historical records.

Were Jesus' Biographies Reliably Preserved for Us?

World-class scholar Bruce Metzger, professor emeritus at Princeton Theological Seminary, said that compared with other ancient documents, there is an unprecedented number of New Testament manuscripts and that they can be dated extremely close to the original writings. No major Christian doctrines are in doubt due to any variances between the manuscripts. The criteria used by the early church to determine which books should be considered authoritative have ensured that we possess the best records about Jesus.

Is There Credible Evidence for Jesus outside His Biographies?

"We have better historical documentation for Jesus than for the founder of any other ancient religion," said Edwin Yamauchi of Miami University, a leading expert on ancient history. Sources from outside the Bible corroborate that many people believed Jesus performed healings and was the Messiah, that he was crucified, and that despite this shameful death, his followers, who believed he was still alive, worshiped him as God. One expert documented thirty-nine ancient sources that corroborate more than one hundred facts concerning Jesus' life, teachings, crucifixion, and resurrection. Seven secular sources and several early Christian creeds concern the deity of Jesus, a doctrine "definitely present in the earliest church," according to Dr. Gary Habermas, the scholar who wrote *The Historical Jesus*.

Does Archaeology Confirm or Contradict Jesus' Biographies?

John McRay, a professor of archaeology for more than fifteen years and author of *Archaeology and the New Testament*, said there's no question that archaeological findings have enhanced the New Testament's credibility. No discovery has ever disproved a biblical reference. Further, archaeology has established that Luke, who wrote about one-quarter of the New Testament, was an especially careful historian. Concluded one expert, "If Luke was so painstakingly accurate in his historical reporting [of minor details], on what logical basis may we assume he was credulous or inaccurate in his reporting of matters that were far more important, not only to him but to others as well?" Like, for instance, the resurrection of Jesus—the event that authenticated his claim to being the unique Son of God.

Is the Jesus of History the Same as the Jesus of Faith?

Gregory Boyd, a Yale- and Princeton-educated scholar who wrote the award-winning *Cynic Sage or Son of God?*, offered a devastating critique of the Jesus Seminar, a group that questions whether Jesus said or did most of what's attributed to him. He identified the Seminar as "an extremely small number of radical-fringe scholars who are on the far, far left wing of New Testament thinking." The Seminar ruled out the possibility of miracles at the outset and employed questionable criteria, and some participants have touted myth-riddled documents of extremely dubious quality. Further, the idea that stories about Jesus emerged from mythology fails to withstand scrutiny. Said Boyd, "The evidence for Jesus being who the disciples said he was . . . is just light-years beyond my reasons for thinking that the left-wing scholarship of the Jesus Seminar is correct." In sum, the Jesus of faith is the same as the Jesus of history.

Was Jesus Really Convinced He Was the Son of God?

By going back to the very earliest traditions, Ben Witherington III, author of *The Christology of Jesus*, was able to show that Jesus had a supreme and transcendent self-understanding. Based on the evidence, Witherington said, "Did Jesus believe he was the Son of God, the anointed one of God? The answer is yes. Did he see himself as the Son of Man? The answer is yes. Did he see himself as the final Messiah? Yes, that's the way he viewed himself. Did he believe that anybody less than God could save the world? No, I don't believe he did." Scholars said that Jesus' repeated reference to himself as the Son of Man was not a claim of humanity but a reference to Daniel 7:13–14, in which the Son of Man is seen as having universal authority and everlasting dominion and receives the worship of all nations. Said one scholar, "Thus, the claim to be the Son of Man would be in effect a claim to divinity."

Was Jesus Crazy When He Claimed to Be the Son of God?
Gary Collins, a professor of psychology for twenty years and author of forty-five books on psychology-related topics, said Jesus exhibited no inappropriate emotions, was in contact with reality, was brilliant and had amazing insights into human nature, and enjoyed deep and abiding relationships. "I just don't see signs that Jesus was suffering from any known mental illness," he concluded. In addition, Jesus backed up his claim to being God through miraculous feats of healing, astounding demonstrations of power over nature, unrivaled teaching, divine understanding of people, and with his own resurrection, which was the ultimate evidence of his deity.

Did Jesus Fulfill the Attributes of God?
While the incarnation—God becoming man, the infinite becoming finite—stretches our imaginations, prominent theologian D. A. Carson pointed out there's lots of evidence that Jesus exhibited the characteristics of deity. Based on Philippians 2, many theologians believe Jesus voluntarily emptied himself of the independent use of his divine attributes as he pursued his mission of human redemption. Even so, the New Testament specifically confirms that Jesus ultimately possessed every qualification of deity, including omniscience, omnipresence, omnipotence, eternality, and immutability.

Did Jesus—and Jesus Alone—Match the Identity of the Messiah? Hundreds of years before Jesus was born, prophets foretold the coming of the Messiah, or the Anointed One, who would redeem God's people. In effect, dozens of these Old Testament prophecies created a fingerprint that only the true Messiah could fit. This gave Israel a way to rule out imposters and validate the credentials of the authentic Messiah. Against astronomical odds—by one estimate, one chance in a trillion, trillion, trillion, trillion, trillion, trillion, trillion, trillion, trillion, trillion, trillion—Jesus, and only Jesus throughout history, matched this prophetic fingerprint. This confirms Jesus' identity to an incredible degree of certainty. The expert I interviewed on this topic, Louis Lapides, is an example of someone raised in a conservative Jewish home who came to believe Jesus is the Messiah after a systematic study of the prophecies. Today, he's the pastor of a church in California and former president of a national network of fifteen messianic congregations.

Was Jesus' Death a Sham and His Resurrection a Hoax?

By analyzing the medical and historical data, Dr. Alexander Metherell, a physician who also holds a doctorate in engineering, concluded Jesus could not have survived the gruesome rigors of crucifixion, much less the gaping wound that pierced his lung and heart. In fact, even before the crucifixion he was in serious to critical condition and suffering from hypovolemic shock as the result of a horrific flogging. The idea that he somehow swooned on the cross and pretended to be dead lacks any evidential basis. Roman executioners were grimly efficient, knowing that they themselves would face death if any of their victims were to come down from the cross alive. Even if Jesus had somehow lived through the torture, his ghastly condition could never have inspired a worldwide movement based on the premise that he had gloriously triumphed over the grave.

Was Jesus' Body Really Absent from His Tomb?

William Lane Craig, who has earned two doctorates and written several books on the resurrection, presented striking evidence that the enduring symbol of Easter—the vacant tomb of Jesus—was a historical reality. The empty grave is reported or implied in extremely early sources—Mark's gospel and a creed in 1 Corinthians 15—that date very close to the event. The fact that the Gospels report that women discovered the empty tomb bolsters the story's authenticity, because the testimony of women lacked credibility in the first century and thus there would have been no motive to report they found the empty tomb if it weren't true. The site of Jesus' tomb was known to Christians, Jews, and Romans, so it could have been checked by skeptics. In fact, nobody—not even the Roman authorities or Jewish leaders—ever claimed that the tomb still contained Jesus' body. Instead, they were forced to invent the absurd story that the disciples, despite having no motive or opportunity, had stolen the body—a theory that not even the most skeptical critic believes today.

Was Jesus Seen Alive after His Death on the Cross?

The evidence for the post-resurrection appearances of Jesus didn't develop gradually over the years as mythology distorted memories of his life. Rather, said renowned resurrection expert Gary Habermas, Jesus' resurrection was "the central proclamation of the early church from the very beginning." The ancient creed from 1 Corinthians 15 mentions specific individuals and groups who encountered the risen Christ, and Paul even challenged first-century doubters to talk with these individuals personally to determine the truth of the matter for themselves. The book of Acts is littered with extremely early affirmations of Jesus' resurrection, while the Gospels describe numerous encounters in detail. Concluded British theologian Michael Green, "The appearances of Jesus are as well authenticated as anything in antiquity . . . There can be no rational doubt that they occurred."

Are There Any Supporting Facts That Point toward the Resurrection?

Professor J. P. Moreland presented circumstantial evidence that provided strong corroboration for the resurrection. First, the disciples were in a unique position to know whether the resurrection happened, and they were willing to suffer and even go to their deaths proclaiming it was true. Nobody knowingly is willing to die for a lie. Second, apart from the resurrection, there's no good reason why such skeptics as Paul and James would have been converted and would have died for their faith. Third, within weeks of the crucifixion, thousands of Jews became convinced Jesus was the Son of God and began following him, abandoning key social practices that had critical sociological and religious importance for centuries. They believed they risked damnation if they were wrong. Fourth, the early sacraments of the Lord's Supper and baptism affirmed Jesus' resurrection and deity. And fifth, the miraculous emergence of the church in the face of brutal Roman persecution "rips a great hole in history, a hole the size and shape of the Resurrection," as C. F. D. Moule put it.[1]

Taken together, I concluded that this expert testimony constitutes compelling evidence that Jesus Christ is who he claimed to be—the one and only Son of God. The atheism I had embraced for so long buckled under the weight of historical truth.

For the details that support this summary, please refer to *The Case for Christ.*

An Interview with
Lee Strobel

For the last twenty years, *The Case for Faith* has been illuminating minds and touching hearts. Now that the book is being updated and expanded, bestselling author Mark Mittelberg turned the tables on Lee Strobel to interview him about the impact of the book through the years. Mittelberg and Strobel have been ministry associates since they first met in 1987. In addition to coauthoring several books with Strobel, Mittelberg has written *Questions Christians Hope No One Will Ask (with Answers)*, the *Contagious Faith* book and training course, and several other books on how to share and defend Christianity.

Q. Why do you think *The Case for Faith* has been so successful?

A. I think it's the result of more and more people having sincere and pressing questions about Christianity. We live in a world that's increasingly skeptical and even hostile toward our faith. In recent years, there has been a proliferation of websites and books attacking Christianity, which has prompted many Christians to seek answers for two reasons. First, because they want to deepen their own faith, and, second, because they have friends and family members they want to help get past the spiritual sticking points that are holding up their journey toward God.

Q. Over the years you've shared with me a number of compelling stories about how God has used this book in people's lives. What's one that stands out in your mind?

A. Oh, yeah, here's one of the classics. I met a young man in Florida who told me he woke up one morning on the beach after getting drunk during spring break. He was depressed, his head was throbbing, he felt full of regret over the aimless life he was living, and he knew he needed a new direction. He wished he could find God, but he had too many questions and objections to be able to do that.

Q. So what happened?

A. Well, as he was walking down the beach, pondering his future, his foot kicked something that was half-buried in the sand. He picked it up and brushed it off—and it turned out to be a well-worn copy of *The Case for Faith*! He said he read it and found good answers to his spiritual questions, and he put his trust in Christ! He later came up to me at an event where I was speaking to tell me how thrilled he is with his new life as a follower of Jesus.

Q. Wow, that's such a great story! Do any others come to mind?

A. On a more somber note, I got an email from a woman named Katie who went through a traumatic event just before she married her husband.

Q. Were they Christians at the time?

A. Yes, for about a decade. Her fiancé's mother had been a drug addict and served time in jail, but her life was radically transformed when she met Jesus. She got sober, earned her degree in the field of substance abuse, and became a much-loved counselor at a facility for people with addictions. As one of her sons said, "She had a knack for helping people. She'd give you the shirt off her back to let you know she loves you." One day in December 2019, a homeless man walked in. She greeted him warmly and invited him to sign up for free counseling—but then he pulled out a knife and brutally stabbed her to death.

Q. That's awful! Did it shake the faith of her son and his fiancée?

A. Absolutely. "For about two months," Katie told me, "we walked around numb. We were trying to remember why on earth we even talked to a God who would let this happen." Fortunately, her future husband picked up a copy of *The Case for Faith* and they read my interview with Dr. Peter Kreeft on why God allows tragedies to occur. "Your chapter on suffering and evil seriously brought me to tears," she said. "I personally didn't think I would ever find resolution of our situation on this side of heaven. The pain is not gone, but the fear of God not being good is. We trust more and more every day, just as my husband's mom would have wanted us to."

Q. That really illustrates the power of providing thoughtful answers to tough questions.

A. I've heard over the years that Dr. Kreeft's interview in the book has helped a lot of people wrestle with the issue of why God allows suffering. I thought he did a tremendous job with the number one most challenging objection to Christianity.

Q. Thinking back, what would you say was your most memorable experience in researching the book?

A. By far, it was the interview with Canadian agnostic Charles Templeton, the former pulpit partner of Billy Graham, who lost his faith while attending a liberal seminary.

Q. I remember how that interview came about. You and I were doing a question-and-answer session in Alberta, Canada, and a skeptic asked whether you had read Templeton's book *Farewell to God*. When you said you had never heard of it, he got really mad! So you went down to a little bookstore in Banff, bought a copy, and decided to interview Templeton about his objections to the faith.

A. Right. I was surprised to find Templeton's phone number on the internet, and I just called him out of the blue. He was very polite and invited me to his place in Toronto. At the time, I didn't have enough money for airfare, so Leslie and I drove there from Chicago. The whole time I was interviewing Templeton, which took several hours, Leslie stayed in the car and prayed! I'm so grateful that her prayers were answered.

Q. What do you remember most about the interview?

A. That moment when Templeton suddenly began to cry because he said he missed Jesus so much. I was stunned! I wasn't sure how to react. Was I a pastor at that moment, or a journalist? Should I comfort him, or push him for details? In the end, he seemed embarrassed and moved on, but it was one of the most poignant moments of any interview I've ever conducted. And I almost missed it.

Q. What do you mean?

A. When I got in the car and went to play the tape for Leslie, I found that the recorder hadn't captured his words. The machine had inadvertently been set to "voice activation," and his voice was too soft to trigger the recorder. I was panic-stricken.

Q. Oh no! What did you do?

A. Fortunately, I had used *two* recorders, and the other one captured everything. I still have that recording to this day. In fact, now when I interview someone for a book—no kidding—I use as many as *six* recorders at the same time!

Q. Sounds like journalistic overkill, but after that scare, it may be a pretty good idea! Do you see changes in the types of questions being asked about God these days?

A. The eight objections covered in this book are still among the most prevalent. Because of cultural trends, people are asking questions about sexuality and gender issues as well. But whatever intellectual or emotional obstacles are blocking people from faith in

Christ, Christians are still called on to help them find answers. First Peter 3:15 says, "But in your hearts revere Christ as Lord. Always be prepared to give an answer to everyone who asks you to give the reason for the hope that you have. But do this with gentleness and respect."

Q. My experience is that a lot of Christians shy away from getting into spiritual conversations because they're afraid they'll be asked a question they can't answer.

A. I agree, but I think that in many cases they're putting undue pressure on themselves. Instead, when a person raises a particularly challenging objection, they can simply reply, "That's a great question! I have no idea how to respond. But let's find an answer together." Then perhaps they can find a relevant book they and their friend can read together and discuss—possibly including *The Case for Faith*. And that opens up even more opportunities to explore spiritual issues with them. Of course, it's always helpful if Christians are equipped to respond to the kinds of questions that are likely to be raised. This can give them the confidence they need to engage in spiritual conversations with others. That's why I'm excited about our new center.

Q. Yes, I'm thrilled to be the executive director of the Lee Strobel Center for Evangelism and Applied Apologetics at Colorado Christian University [StrobelCenter.com], where we offer accredited online courses toward degrees, or where people can take courses just for their own growth.

A. We're glad to have you! We want to nurture and train a whole new generation of Christians who can help people find answers to satisfy their mind and soul. Honestly, I think we're on the verge of a golden era of Christian apologetics, which refers to the practice of providing reasons for why we believe. It started when the so-called New Atheists went on the offensive and thought they had dealt a death blow to the faith. But the opposite happened. They only awakened the church to its historic role of telling others about Jesus and providing evidence and answers to back up our beliefs.

Q. It's an exciting time to launch this important initiative.

A. It certainly is—and it *is* important! Christian apologetics had largely fallen out of favor in the middle of the twentieth century. Now there is a robust community of people committed to sharing the message of Jesus far and wide, offering historical and scientific evidence to back it up, and responding with "gentleness and respect" to the often-tough questions raised by spiritual seekers. This is a great time to be telling others the good news of the gospel and why it makes sense. I'm so glad this updated book can be a part of that endeavor.

Q. Any final words you'd like to share with your readers, Lee?

A. Yes, I'd like to remind them that the case for the Christian faith really is powerful and persuasive. If you keep studying books like this and others in the "Case For" series, along with others I've recommended along the way, then your spiritual confidence will continue to grow, and over time you'll become a formidable force that God can deploy to reach and teach the people around you. And as you stretch out and share the information you've learned, God will use you to impact people with his love and truth—and maybe next time I'll be interviewing *you* about stories of what he has done in and through your efforts. That would be truly rewarding!

Notes

Introduction: The Challenge of Faith

1. William Franklin Graham Jr., "Billy Graham Indiana Crusade" (sermon), RCA Dome, Indianapolis, IN, June 4, 1999.
2. Billy Graham Indiana Crusade, June 4, 1999.
3. See Billy Graham, *Just as I Am: The Autobiography of Billy Graham* (Grand Rapids: Zondervan, 1997), 137–38.
4. Charles Templeton, *Farewell to God: My Reasons for Rejecting the Christian Faith* (Toronto: McClelland & Stewart, 1996), 3.
5. Quoted in Templeton, *Farewell to God*, 11.
6. Cited in Templeton, *Farewell to God*, 9.
7. Templeton, *Farewell to God*, 5–6.
8. Graham, *Just as I Am*, 138.
9. Graham, *Just as I Am*, 139.
10. Templeton, *Farewell to God*, 8.
11. George H. Smith, *Atheism: The Case against God* (Amherst, NY: Prometheus, 1989), 98.
12. W. Bingham Hunter, *The God Who Hears* (Downers Grove, IL: InterVarsity, 1986), 153.
13. Templeton, *Farewell to God*, vii.
14. See Templeton, *Farewell to God*, 200–202.

On the Road to Answers

1. See Lee Strobel, *The Case for Christ: A Journalist's Personal Investigation of the Evidence for Jesus* (Grand Rapids: Zondervan, 1998), 131–43; Ben Witherington III, *The Christology of Jesus* (Minneapolis: Fortress, 1990); William Lane Craig, *Reasonable Faith: Christian Truth and Apologetics* (Wheaton, IL: Crossway, 1994), 233–54.
2. See 1 Corinthians 15:3–8.
3. See Strobel, *Case for Christ*, 35, 208–11, 229–33, 264–65.
4. Jeremiah 29:13.

313

Objection #1: Since Evil and Suffering Exist, a Loving God Cannot

1. See Lee Strobel, "Thanksgiving Near; Only Food Rice," *Chicago Tribune*, November 25, 1974.
2. See Peter Maass, "Top Ten War Crimes Suspects," *George*, June 1999.
3. Sheldon Vanauken, in Peter Kreeft, *Making Sense Out of Suffering* (Ann Arbor, MI: Servant, 1986), viii.
4. Philip Yancey, *Where Is God When It Hurts?* (Grand Rapids: Zondervan, 1990), 15.
5. Yancey, *Where Is God When It Hurts?*, 20, quoting novelist Peter De Vries.
6. OmniPoll, conducted by the Barna Group, January 1999.
7. Charles Templeton, *Farewell to God: My Reasons for Rejecting the Christian Faith* (Toronto: McClelland & Stewart, 1996), 201–2.
8. Matthew 7:7.
9. See Peter Kreeft and Ronald K. Tacelli, *Handbook of Christian Apologetics* (Downers Grove, IL: InterVarsity, 1994), 48–88.
10. C. S. Lewis, *The Problem of Pain* (New York: Macmillan, 1962), 15.
11. See Leo Tolstoy, *A Confession*, trans. Aylmer Maude (Mineola, NY: Dover, 2005).
12. Harold S. Kushner, *When Bad Things Happen to Good People*, 20th anniversary ed. (New York: Schocken, 2001), 60.
13. Quoted in Edith Hamilton, *The Greek Way* (New York: Norton, 1993), 61.
14. See Romans 5:3–4.
15. Hebrews 5:8: "Son though he was, he learned obedience from what he suffered."
16. *The Twilight Zone*, episode 28, "A Nice Place to Visit," directed by John Brahm, written by Charles Beaumont, featuring Larry Blyden and Sebastian Cabot, aired April 15, 1960, on CBS.
17. See 2 Peter 3:9: "The Lord is not slow in keeping his promise, as some understand slowness. Instead he is patient with you, not wanting anyone to perish, but everyone to come to repentance."
18. Lewis, *Problem of Pain*, 93.
19. Matthew 9:12–13.
20. Jeremiah 6:13.
21. Isaiah 64:6.
22. See C. S. Lewis, *Mere Christianity* (New York: Macmillan, 1960), 59.
23. Augustine, *Enchiridion* xi.
24. Templeton, *Farewell to God*, 201.
25. See 2 Corinthians 4:17.
26. Quoted in Kreeft, *Making Sense Out of Suffering*, 139.
27. Philippians 3:8 (KJV): "I count all things but loss for the excellency of

the knowledge of Christ Jesus my Lord: for whom I have suffered the loss of all things, and do count them but dung, that I may win Christ."
28. Yancey, *Where Is God When It Hurts?*, 260.
29. Quoted in Warren W. Wiersbe, *Classic Sermons on Suffering* (Grand Rapids: Kregel, 1984), 92.
30. Corrie ten Boom, *The Hiding Place* (1971; repr., Grand Rapids: Chosen, 2006), 227.
31. Jesus said in John 16:33: "These things I have spoken to you so that in Me you may have peace. In the world you have tribulation, but take courage; I have overcome the world" (NASB).
32. John R. W. Stott, *The Cross of Christ*, 20th anniversary ed. (Downers Grove, IL: IVP Academic, 2006), 326–27, the last sentence quoting P. T. Forsyth, *Justification of God* (London: Duckworth, 1916), 32.

Objection #2: Since Miracles Contradict Science, They Cannot Be True

1. Charles Templeton, *Farewell to God: My Reasons for Rejecting the Christian Faith* (Toronto: McClelland & Stewart, 1996), 21.
2. Max Planck, *Scientific Autobiography and Other Papers* (New York: Philosophical Library, 1950), 155.
3. Richard Dawkins, interview by Margaret Wertheim, *Faith & Reason*, PBS, September 11, 1998, www.pbs.org/faithandreason.
4. Quoted in Dale and Sandy Larsen, *Seven Myths about Christianity* (Downers Grove, IL: InterVarsity, 1998), 86.
5. Michael Ruse, *Darwinism Defended* (London: Addison-Wesley, 1982), 322.
6. See Michael Behe, *Darwin's Black Box: The Biochemical Challenge to Evolution* (New York: Free Press, 1996); William Dembski, *The Design Inference: Eliminating Chance through Small Probabilities* (Cambridge: Cambridge University Press, 1998); and William Dembski, *Intelligent Design: The Bridge between Science and Theology* (Downers Grove, IL: InterVarsity, 1999).
7. Rudolf Bultmann, *Jesus* (Berlin: Deutsche Bibliothek, 1926), 159.
8. George H. Smith, *Atheism: The Case against God* (Amherst, NY: Prometheus, 1989), 215.
9. Archibald Robertson, *The Origins of Christianity* (New York: International Publishers, 1954), 82.
10. Norman L. Geisler writes in *Baker Encyclopedia of Christian Apologetics* (Grand Rapids: Baker, 1999), 512: "Most miracle claims for Muhammad do not occur in the *Qur'an*, the only book in Islam for which divine inspiration is claimed . . . The vast majority of alleged miracles are reported in the *Hadith* (Islamic tradition), considered by Muslims to contain many authentic traditions. There are hundreds of miracle stories in the *Hadith*."

11. See 2 Corinthians 12:7–10.

12. Richard Robinson, "Religion and Reason," in *Critiques of God*, ed. Peter A. Angeles (Buffalo, NY: Prometheus, 1997), 121.

13. Alvin Plantinga, "Two Dozen (or So) Theistic Arguments" (lecture, 33rd Annual Philosophy Conference, Wheaton College, Wheaton, IL, October 23–25, 1986).

14. For a booklet summarizing Craig's five reasons for believing God exists, see William Lane Craig, *God, Are You There?* (Norcross, GA: Ravi Zacharias International Ministries, 1999).

15. Stephen W. Hawking and Roger Penrose, *The Nature of Space and Time* (Princeton, NJ: Princeton University Press, 1996), 20.

16. Anthony Kenny, *The Five Ways: St. Thomas Aquinas' Proofs of God's Existence* (New York: Schocken, 1969), 66.

17. David Hume to John Stewart, February 1754, in *The Letters of David Hume*, ed. J. Y. T. Greig (Oxford: Clarendon, 1932), 1:187.

18. Kai Nielsen, *Reason and Practice: A Modern Introduction to Philosophy* (New York: Harper & Row, 1971), 48.

19. Arthur Eddington, *The Expanding Universe: Astronomy's "Great Debate," 1900–1931* (New York: Macmillan, 1933), 124.

20. See Stephen W. Hawking, *A Brief History of Time* (New York: Bantam, 1988), 123.

21. For a list of examples, see John Leslie, *Universes* (London: Routledge, 1989).

22. See P. C. W. Davies, *Other Worlds: Space, Superspace, and the Quantum Universe* (London: Dent, 1980), 160–61.

23. See Davies, *Other Worlds*, 168–69.

24. See P. C. W. Davies, "The Anthropic Principle," *Progress in Particle and Nuclear Physics* 10 (1983): 28; Patrick Glynn, *God: The Evidence* (New York: Three Rivers, 1999), 29–31.

25. John Polkinghorne, *Serious Talk: Science and Religion in Dialogue* (Harrisburg, PA: Trinity Press, 1995), 6.

26. Glynn, *God: The Evidence*, 53–54, 26.

27. Michael Ruse, "Evolutionary Theory and Christian Ethics," in *The Darwinian Paradigm* (London: Routledge, 1989), 262, 269.

28. John Healey, fundraising letter, 1991.

29. See 1 Corinthians 15:3–8.

30. Gerd Lüdemann, *What Really Happened to Jesus: A Historical Approach to the Resurrection*, trans. John Bowden (Louisville, KY: Westminster John Knox, 1995), 8.

31. Luke Timothy Johnson, *The Real Jesus: The Misguided Quest for the Historical Jesus and the Truth of the Traditional Gospels* (San Francisco: HarperSanFrancisco, 1996), 136.

32. For a list of these historical tests, see C. Behan McCullagh, *Justifying Historical Descriptions* (Cambridge: Cambridge University Press, 1984), 19. To see how the resurrection meets these criteria, see Craig, *God, Are You There?*, 46–47.

33. John Hick, ed., introduction to *The Existence of God* (New York: Macmillan, 1964), 13–14.

34. See William Alston, "Religious Diversity and Perceptual Knowledge of God," *Faith and Philosophy* 5, no. 4 (1988): 433–48.

35. Romans 8:16: "The Spirit himself testifies with our spirit that we are God's children."

Objection #3: Evolution Explains Life, So God Isn't Needed

1. See Charles T. Jones, "DNA Tests Clear Two Men in Prison," *Daily Oklahoman*, April 16, 1999.

2. See Steven Mills and Ken Armstrong, "Convicted by a Hair," *Chicago Tribune*, November 18, 1999.

3. See Mills and Armstrong, "Convicted by a Hair."

4. Patrick Glynn, *God: The Evidence* (New York: Three Rivers, 1999), 2–3.

5. "Iconoclast of the Century: Charles Darwin (1809–1882)," *Time*, December 31, 1999.

6. Charles Templeton, *Farewell to God: My Reasons for Rejecting the Christian Faith* (Toronto: McClelland & Stewart, 1996), 232.

7. Francisco Ayala, "Darwin's Revolution," in *Creative Evolution?!*, ed. John H. Campbell and J. W. Schopf (Boston: Jones and Bartlett, 1994), 4–5.

8. Michael Denton, *Evolution: A Theory in Crisis* (London: Burnett, 1985), 67.

9. Denton, *Evolution*, 66.

10. Douglas J. Futuyma, *Evolutionary Biology* (Sunderland, MA: Sinauer, 1986), 3.

11. Richard Dawkins, *The Blind Watchmaker: Why the Evidence of Evolution Reveals a Universe without Design* (New York: Norton, 1987), 6.

12. Cited in Phillip E. Johnson, *Darwin on Trial*, 2nd ed. (Downers Grove, IL: InterVarsity, 1993), 126–27.

13. Michael Behe, *Darwin's Black Box: The Biochemical Challenge to Evolution* (New York: Free Press, 1996), 232.

14. Behe, *Darwin's Black Box*, 193, 251, 243 (emphasis in original).

15. David M. Raup, "Conflicts between Darwin and Paleontology," *Field Museum of Natural History Bulletin* 50, no. 1 (January 1979): 22–29.

16. Johnson, *Darwin on Trial*, 54.

17. Charles Darwin, *On the Origin of Species*, 6th ed. (New York: New York University Press, 1988), 154.

18. Quoted in George Johnson, "Science and Religion: Bridging the Great Divide," *New York Times*, June 30, 1998.
19. Charles B. Thaxton, Walter L. Bradley, and Roger L. Olsen, *The Mystery of Life's Origin: Reassessing Current Theories* (Dallas, TX: Lewis and Stanley, 1984), back cover.
20. Thaxton, Bradley, and Olsen, *Mystery of Life's Origin*, back cover.
21. Quoted in Francis Darwin, ed., *The Life and Letters of Charles Darwin* (New York: Appleton, 1887), 202.
22. Quoted in R. Vallery-Radot, *The Life of Pasteur*, trans. R. L. Devonshire (New York: Doubleday, 1920), 109.
23. See Robert Shapiro, *Origins: A Skeptic's Guide to the Creation of Life on Earth* (New York: Summit, 1986), 99.
24. William Day, *Genesis on Planet Earth: The Search for Life's Beginning* (East Lansing, MI: House of Talos, 1979), 7.
25. Quoted in Sol Tax, ed., *The Evolution of Life: Its Origin, History, and Future*, Evolution after Darwin, vol. 1 (Chicago: University of Chicago Press, 1960), 57.
26. See Gordon C. Mills, Malcolm Lancaster, and Walter L. Bradley, "Origin of Life and Evolution in Biology Textbooks—A Critique," *American Biology Teacher* 55, no. 2 (February 1993): 78–83, https://doi.org/10.2307/4449589.
27. Ernst Haeckel, *The Wonders of Life: A Popular Study of Biological Philosophy*, trans. J. McCabe (London: Watts, 1905), 111.
28. Klaus Dose, "The Origin of Life: More Questions Than Answers," *Interdisciplinary Science Reviews* 13, no. 4 (1988): 348.
29. Francis Crick, *Life Itself: Its Origin and Nature* (New York: Simon and Schuster, 1981), 88.
30. See "How Did Life Begin?," *Newsweek*, August 6, 1979.
31. See J. Buell and V. Hearn, eds., *Darwinism: Science or Philosophy?* (Dallas: Foundation for Thought and Ethics, 1994), 68–69.
32. See Dean Kenyon and Gary Steinman, *Biochemical Predestination* (New York: McGraw-Hill, 1969).
33. See Randall A. Kok, John A. Taylor, and Walter L. Bradley, "A Statistical Examination of Self-Ordering of Amino Acids in Proteins," *Origins of Life and Evolution of the Biosphere* 18 (1988): 135–42.
34. Ilya Prigogine and Isabelle Stengers, *The End of Certainty: Time, Chaos, and the New Laws of Nature* (New York: Free Press, 1997), 71.
35. H. P. Yockey, "A Calculation of the Probability of Spontaneous Biogenesis by Information Theory," *Journal of Theoretical Biology* 67, no. 3 (August 1977): 380.
36. See Thaxton, Bradley, and Olsen, *Mystery of Life's Origin*, 191–96.
37. See Thaxton, Bradley, and Olsen, *Mystery of Life's Origin*, 194.

38. Johnson, *Darwin on Trial*, 111.

39. Alexandre Dauvillier, *The Photochemical Origin of Life* (New York: Academic Press, 1965), 2.

40. Quoted in Peter Radetsky, "How Did Life Start?," *Discover*, November 1992.

41. Fazale R. Rana and Hugh Ross, "Life from the Heavens? Not This Way," *Facts for Faith* 1 (Q1 2000): 11–15, emphasis in original.

42. Rana and Ross, "Life from the Heavens?," emphasis in original.

43. Quoted in Radetsky, "How Did Life Start?"

44. Quoted in Radetsky, "How Did Life Start?"

45. Quoted in Radetsky, "How Did Life Start?"

46. See A. G. Cairns-Smith, *Genetic Takeover and the Mineral Origins of Life* (New York: Cambridge University Press, 1982).

47. Quoted in Walter L. Bradley and Charles B. Thaxton, "Information and the Origin of Life," in *The Creation Hypothesis: Scientific Evidence for an Intelligent Designer*, ed. J. P. Moreland (Downers Grove, IL: InterVarsity, 1994), 194.

48. Quoted in William A. Dembski, ed., *Mere Creation: Science, Faith, and Intelligent Design* (Downers Grove, IL: InterVarsity, 1998), 46.

49. See Rana and Ross, "Life from the Heavens?"

50. Dose, "The Origin of Life," 348.

51. Shapiro, *Origins*, 99.

52. Crick, *Life Itself*, 153.

53. Quoted in John Horgan, "In the Beginning . . . ," *Scientific American* 264, no. 2 (February 1991): 116.

54. See Stephen Jay Gould, "Will We Figure Out How Life Began?," *Time*, April 2, 2000, http://content.time.com/time/magazine/article /0,9171,42365,00.html.

55. J. F. W. Herschel, *Preliminary Discourse on the Study of Natural Philosophy* (London: Longman, Rees, Orme, Brown and Green, 1831), 149.

56. Carl Sagan, *Broca's Brain: Reflections on the Romance of Science* (New York: Ballantine, 1979), 322.

57. Johnson, *Darwin on Trial*, 103.

58. Quoted in Candace Adams, "Leading Nanoscientist Builds Big Faith," *Baptist Standard*, March 15, 2000.

59. Denton, *Evolution*, 358.

Objection #4: God Isn't Worthy of Worship If He Kills Innocent Children

1. Charles Templeton, *Farewell to God: My Reasons for Rejecting the Christian Faith* (Toronto: McClelland & Stewart, 1996), 71.

2. George H. Smith, *Atheism: The Case against God* (Amherst, NY: Prometheus, 1989), 77.

3. Smith, *Atheism*, 76.
4. Thomas Paine, *The Age of Reason*, part 1 (1794; repr., New York: Freethought Press Association, 1954), 18–19.
5. See Judges 19:25, 29.
6. 2 Samuel 12:31 (KJV).
7. Malachi 3:6.
8. 1 Samuel 15:3.
9. Mark 10:14.
10. See 2 Kings 2:23–25.
11. Walter C. Kaiser Jr. et al., *Hard Sayings of the Bible* (Downers Grove, IL: InterVarsity, 1996), 234, 233.
12. Kaiser Jr., *Hard Sayings of the Bible*, 232; see also 1 Kings 20:14–15.
13. Templeton, *Farewell to God*, 197 (emphasis removed), 198, 199.
14. Genesis 1:29–30. After the flood, God told Noah and his sons in Genesis 9:3: "Everything that lives and moves about will be food for you. Just as I gave you the green plants, I now give you everything."
15. Isaiah 65:17, 25.
16. See C. S. Lewis, *The Problem of Pain* (New York: Macmillan, 1962), 115–16.
17. Proverbs 12:10.
18. Smith, *Atheism*, 210–11.
19. Templeton, *Farewell to God*, 38.
20. John 3:12.
21. See Clifford A. Wilson, *Rocks, Relics, and Biblical Reliability* (Grand Rapids: Zondervan, 1977), 42.
22. William F. Albright, *Archaeology and the Religion of Israel* (Baltimore, MD: Johns Hopkins Press, 1953), 176.
23. See Colin J. Hemer, *The Book of Acts in the Setting of Hellenistic History* (Winona Lake, IN: Eisenbrauns, 1990).
24. William M. Ramsay, *St. Paul the Traveler and Roman Citizen* (1895; repr., Grand Rapids: Kregel, 2001), 19.
25. A. N. Sherwin-White, *Roman Society and Roman Law in the New Testament* (Oxford: Clarendon, 1963), 189.
26. See William F. Albright, "Retrospect and Prospect in New Testament Archaeology," in *The Teacher's Yoke*, ed. E. Jerry Vardaman (Waco, TX: Baylor University Press, 1964), 29.
27. Quoted in Norman L. Geisler, *Baker Encyclopedia of Christian Apologetics* (Grand Rapids: Baker, 1999), 544.
28. See Bertrand Russell, "What Is an Agnostic?," *Look* magazine, 1953, cited in Geisler, *Baker Encyclopedia of Christian Apologetics*, 455–56.
29. See 1 Kings 18.
30. John 10:37.

31. John 3:2.
32. See Qur'an 2:118; 3:181–84; 4:153; 6:8, 9, 37.
33. Qur'an 6:37.
34. Qur'an 6:37.
35. Luke 7:22.
36. Norman Geisler and Thomas Howe, *When Critics Ask: A Popular Handbook on Bible Difficulties* (Grand Rapids: Baker, 1992).
37. Matthew 16:16; Mark 8:29; Luke 9:20.
38. Quoted in Gregory A. Boyd and Edward K. Boyd, *Letters from a Skeptic* (Wheaton, IL: Victor, 1994), 120.
39. Quoted in John Noble Wilford, "Sizing Up the Cosmos: An Astronomer's Quest," *New York Times*, March 12, 1991.
40. Hugh Ross, *The Creator and the Cosmos: How the Latest Scientific Discoveries Reveal God* (1993; repr., Colorado Springs: NavPress, 2001), 12.
41. See Robert Jastrow, "The Secret of the Stars," *New York Times Magazine*, June 25, 1978, 7.
42. Quoted in Tim Stafford, "Cease-fire in the Laboratory," *Christianity Today*, April 3, 1987, 18.
43. Russell, "What Is an Agnostic?"
44. See Boyd and Boyd, *Letters from a Skeptic*, 189.
45. John 6:68.
46. See Francis William Bourdillon, "The Night Has a Thousand Eyes," *The Spectator*, October 1873.
47. John 8:58.

Objection #5: It's Offensive to Claim Jesus Is the Only Way to God

1. Chaplinsky v. State of New Hampshire, 315 U.S. 568 (1942), Legal Information Institute, www.law.cornell.edu/supremecourt/text /315/568.
2. See Robert J. Wagman, *The First Amendment Book* (New York: Pharos, 1991), 106; see also Chaplinsky v. New Hampshire.
3. See Cohen v. California, 403 U.S. 15 (1971).
4. John 14:6.
5. Quoted in John Hick and Paul F. Knitter, eds., *The Myth of Christian Uniqueness* (London: SCM, 1987), 141.
6. Shmuley Boteach, "Should Christians Stop Trying to Convert Jews?," interview by Larry King, *Larry King Live*, CNN, January 12, 2000.
7. Quoted in Paul Copan, *True for You, but Not for Me: Overcoming Objections to Christian Faith* (Minneapolis: Bethany House, 1998), 34.
8. Charles Templeton, *Farewell to God: My Reasons for Rejecting the Christian Faith* (Toronto: McClelland & Stewart, 1996), 27.

9. Acts 4:12.

10. Templeton, *Farewell to God*, 27, emphasis added.

11. Originally, this book featured an interview on this subject with a different philosopher. My discussion with Dr. Paul Copan took place in 2021.

12. I interviewed Dr. Paul Copan on the tendency of people to pick and choose what they want to believe about Jesus (see Lee Strobel, *In Defense of Jesus* [Grand Rapids: Zondervan, 2007]). I also interviewed him on the topic of hell, annihilationism, and universalism for my book on the afterlife (see Lee Strobel, *The Case for Heaven* [Grand Rapids: Zondervan, 2021]).

13. John 14:9 (NASB).

14. See Matthew 7:13–14.

15. Oprah Winfrey, *The Oprah Winfrey Show* (Chicago: Harpo Productions), season 21, episode 83, "Do You Believe?," aired February 15, 2007.

16. See Lee Strobel, *The Case for Christ* (1998; repr., Grand Rapids: Zondervan, 2016); *The Case for Easter* (Grand Rapids: Zondervan, 2003); *The Case for Miracles* (Grand Rapids: Zondervan, 2018); and *In Defense of Jesus*.

17. See Matthew 28:11–15.

18. See 1 Corinthians 15:5–8.

19. See John 7:5; 1 Corinthians 15:7.

20. See 1 Corinthians 15:8–9; Acts 9.

21. For example, see Matthew 7:22–28; Mark 2:7; John 5:18; 10:33.

22. For example, see John 20:28; 1 Corinthians 8:6; Philippians 2:5–11.

23. See Martin E. Marty, *Politics, Religion, and the Common Good: Advancing a Distinctly American Conversation about Religion's Role in Our Shared Life* (San Francisco: Jossey-Bass, 2000), 10.

24. See Ninian Smart, "Towards a Definition of Religion" (unpublished paper, Lancaster University, 1970); Ninian Smart, *The World's Religions*, 2nd ed. (Cambridge: Cambridge University Press, 1998), 20–21.

25. These characteristics are discussed in The Dalai Lama, *Kindness, Clarity, and Insight* (New York: Snow Lion, 1984), 57–62.

26. Dalai Lama, *Kindness, Clarity, and Insight*, 57.

27. Dalai Lama, *Kindness, Clarity, and Insight*, 64.

28. Dalai Lama, *The Bodhgaya Interviews*, ed. José Ignacio Cabezón (New York: Snow Lion, 1988), 22.

29. Boteach, quoted in "Should Christians Stop Trying to Convert Jews?"

30. For some examples, see "Alan Watts," Pantheism.com, https://pantheism.com/about/luminaries/alan-watts. For a response, see David K. Clark, *The Pantheism of Alan Watts* (Downers Grove, IL: InterVarsity, 1978).

31. 1 Corinthians 4:7.
32. Romans 3:27.
33. See Mark 13:6; John 16:2–3.
34. See Matthew 7:22–23.
35. Shirley MacLaine, *Out on a Limb* (New York: Bantam, 1983), 347.
36. See Matthew 12:9–14.
37. John 10:31–33.
38. See John 20:28; 1 Corinthians 8:6.
39. Vernon Grounds, "Called to Be Saints—Not Well-Adjusted Sinners," *Christianity Today*, January 17, 1986, 28, www.christianitytoday.com /ct/1986/january-17/called-to-be-saintsnot-well-adjusted-sinners.html.
40. Krister Sairsingh, "Christ and Karma: A Hindu's Quest for the Holy," in *Finding God at Harvard: Spiritual Journeys of Thinking Christians*, ed. Kelly Monroe (Grand Rapids: Zondervan, 1996), 187.
41. See Philippians 3:6–11.
42. For an example, see B. R. Ambedkar, "Annihilation of Caste: A Reply to Mahatma Gandhi," *Ambedkarite Today*, www.ambedkaritetoday .com/2020/04/annihilation-of-caste-reply-to-mahatma-gandhi-by -ambedkar.html; see also Christopher Hitchens, "The Real Mahatma Gandhi," *Atlantic* (July/August 2011), www.theatlantic.com/magazine /archive/2011/07/the-real-mahatma-gandhi/308550; J. Daryl Charles, "'Peacemaking' and Public Policy: A Recipe for Disaster," *Providence*, November 2, 2020, https://providencemag.com/2020/11/peace making-public-policy-recipe-disaster-book-review-nathan-scot-hosler -hauerwas-peacemaker.
43. Aleksandr I. Solzhenitsyn, *The Gulag Archipelago: 1918–1956*, trans. Thomas P. Whitney (New York: HarperCollins, 2007), 2:312.
44. John Calvin, *Institutes of the Christian Religion*, ed. John T. McNeill (Philadelphia: Westminster, 1960), 3.13.3.
45. See Luke 23:39–43.
46. Unapologetic Book, "Q&A about '*Impenitente*' [*Unapologetic*] (English Version)," Tumblr post, October 11, 2014, https://unapologetic-book .tumblr.com/post/99715799639/qa-about-impenitente-english-version.
47. Luke 11:10: "For everyone who asks receives; the one who seeks finds; and to the one who knocks, the door will be opened."
48. See Amos 1–2.
49. See Romans 1:20.
50. Jeremiah 29:13: "You will seek me and find me when you seek me with all your heart." Hebrews 11:6: "He [God] rewards those who earnestly seek him."
51. See 2 Peter 3:9.
52. See John 3:16–17; 1 Timothy 2:4; 1 John 2:2.

53. See, for example, James Beilby, *Postmortem Opportunity: A Biblical and Theological Assessment of Salvation after Death* (Downers Grove, IL: IVP Academic, 2021).

54. Luther to Hans von Rechenberg, 1522, quoted in Steve Gregg, *All You Want to Know about Hell: Three Christian Views of God's Final Solution to the Problem of Sin* (Nashville, TN: Nelson, 2013), 261.

55. Paul Copan and I further discuss the possibility of postmortem opportunities for redemption in my 2021 book *The Case for Heaven*.

56. See Acts 17:30.

57. See 2 Corinthians 5:17–21.

58. John 16:33.

59. See Justin Brierley, "Why I Changed My Mind about Christian History—Tom Holland & Larry Hurtado," October 8, 2016, in *Unbelievable?*, produced by Premiere Christian Radio, podcast, MP3 audio, www.premierchristianradio.com/Shows/Saturday/Unbelievable/Episodes/Unbelievable-why-I-changed-my-mind-about-Christian-History-Tom-Holland-Larry-Hurtado.

60. See Alisa Childers, *Another Gospel? A Lifelong Christian Seeks Truth in Response to Progressive Christianity* (Carol Stream, IL: Tyndale Momentum, 2020).

61. See Matthew 7:13–14; 10:39.

62. See John Hick, *An Interpretation of Religion: Human Responses to the Transcendent*, 2nd ed. (New Haven, CT: Yale University Press, 2004), 235–36.

63. See C. S. Lewis, *The Lion, the Witch and the Wardrobe*, vol. 2 in The Chronicles of Narnia (1950; repr., New York: HarperCollins, 1994), 80.

Objection #6: A Loving God Would Never Torture People in Hell

1. This story, including the interview with Judge Cortland A. Mathers, originally was reported in an excellent investigation into mandatory sentencing by the *Boston Globe*'s Spotlight Team (see Gerard O'Neill, ed., Dick Lehr and Bruce Butterfield, "A Judgment on Sentences: Some Judges Balk at Preset Penalties," *Boston Globe*, September 27, 1995).

2. B. C. Johnson, *The Atheist Debater's Handbook* (Buffalo, NY: Prometheus, 1979), 237.

3. Ezekiel 33:11: "Say to them, 'As surely as I live, declares the Sovereign Lord, I take no pleasure in the death of the wicked, but rather that they turn from their ways and live.'"

4. Quoted in George H. Smith, *Atheism: The Case against God* (Amherst, NY: Prometheus, 1989), 300.

5. See Alan Gomes, "Evangelicals and the Annihilation of Hell, Part II," *Christian Research Journal* 13 (Summer 1991): 8–13.

6. Luke 10:27.
7. Psalm 37:10, 20, 38.
8. Matthew 13:30, 48; 15:13. See Samuele Bacchiocchi, "Hell: Eternal Torment or Annihilation," *Endtime Issues*, no. 7 (February 2, 1999): 1–8, https://fliphtml5.com/gcpz/ykyp/basic.
9. Daniel 12:2: "Multitudes who sleep in the dust of the earth will awake: some to everlasting life, others to shame and everlasting contempt."
10. David L. Edwards and John Stott, *Evangelical Essentials: A Liberal-Evangelical Dialogue* (Downers Grove, IL: InterVarsity, 1988), 316.
11. See C. S. Lewis, *The Great Divorce: A Dream* (1946; repr., New York: HarperCollins, 2000), 135.
12. See Hebrews 9:27.
13. See 2 Peter 3:9.
14. See Hebrews 11:6.
15. For further analysis of evidence concerning reincarnation, see Gary R. Habermas and J. P. Moreland, *Beyond Death: Exploring the Evidence for Immortality* (Wheaton, IL: Crossway, 1998), 237–53; and Norman L. Geisler and J. Yutaka Amano, *The Reincarnation Sensation* (Wheaton, IL: Tyndale, 1986).
16. C. S. Lewis, *The Problem of Pain* (New York: Macmillan, 1962), 119.
17. Quoted in Lee Strobel, *The Case for Christ* (1998; repr., Grand Rapids: Zondervan, 2016), 165.
18. Mark Twain, *Mark Twain's Notebooks and Journals*, vol. 3 (1883–1891), ed. Frederick Anderson et al. (Berkeley: University of California Press, 1980), 583.

Objection #7: Church History Is Littered with Oppression and Violence

1. See Maurice Possley, "Court Hears How FBI Agents Bugged Judge," *Chicago Tribune*, April 26, 1985.
2. Quoted in Maurice Possley, "Judge Liked 'People Who Take Dough,' Greylord File Shows," *Chicago Tribune*, April 27, 1985.
3. Quoted in Maurice Possley, "Records Charge Deals by Judge; 'We Can Make $1,000 a Week,' Olson Quoted," *Chicago Tribune*, February 21, 1985.
4. Bertrand Russell, *Why I Am Not a Christian* (New York: Touchstone, 1957), 25–26.
5. Steven Weinberg, "A Designer Universe?," PhysLink.com, www.physlink.com/Education/essay_weinberg.cfm. This article is based on a talk given in April 1999 at the Conference on Cosmic Design of the American Association for the Advancement of Science in Washington, DC.
6. Charles Templeton, *Farewell to God: My Reasons for Rejecting the Christian Faith* (Toronto: McClelland & Stewart, 1996), 127, 129.

7. Templeton, *Farewell to God*, 154.
8. See Richard Boudreaux, "Pope Apologizes for Catholic Sins Past and Present," *Los Angeles Times*, March 13, 2000.
9. Quoted in Peggy Polk, "Papal State: Despite His Recent Ills, Pope John Paul II Is Focused on the Future," *Chicago Tribune*, June 5, 1995.
10. Matthew 7:21–23.
11. Karl Barth, *Barth in Conversation*, ed. Eberhard Busch, vol. 1, *1959–1962* (Louisville, KY: Westminster John Knox, 2017), 152.
12. Patrick Glynn, *God: The Evidence* (New York: Three Rivers, 1999), 157.
13. Tertullian, *Apology* 37, www.newadvent.org/fathers/0301.htm.
14. Lucian, *The Death of Peregrine*, in *The Works of Lucian of Samosata*, trans. H. W. Fowler and F. G. Fowler (Oxford: Clarendon, 1949), 4:11–13.
15. Justin Martyr, *First Apology* 2, www.newadvent.org/fathers/0126.htm.
16. Philippians 1:21.
17. Quoted in Bruce L. Shelley, *Church History in Plain Language*, 2nd ed. (Dallas, TX: Word, 1995), 189.
18. As the third millennium approached, Spanish priests and nuns publicly asked forgiveness for "those religious workers who worked closely with the Inquisition and the monks who were soldiers" (see "Catholic Clerics Apologize for Past Cruelties," *Chicago Tribune*, November 14, 1999).
19. David Neff, "Our Extended, Persecuted Family," *Christianity Today*, April 29, 1996, 14, www.christianitytoday.com/ct/1996/april29/6t5014.html.
20. See Mark A. Noll, *A History of Christianity in the United States and Canada* (Grand Rapids: Eerdmans, 1992), 51.
21. Quoted in Dale and Sandy Larsen, *Seven Myths about Christianity* (Downers Grove, IL: InterVarsity, 1998), 110.
22. Anthony Grafton, *New Worlds, Ancient Texts: The Power of Tradition and the Shock of Discovery* (Cambridge, MA: Belknap, 1992), 132.
23. See Grafton, *New Worlds, Ancient Texts*, 136. Ecclesiasticus, or Sirach, is not considered to be divinely inspired Scripture by Protestants, although it is part of the Roman Catholic and Orthodox canons. It is also known as "The Wisdom of Jesus, the Son of Sirach," after its author, a scholar who apparently wrote the book between 195 and 171 BC.
24. Quoted in "Cardinal's Yom Kippur Letter Seeks Atonement for Church Anti-Semitism," *Chicago Tribune*, September 21, 1999.
25. Luis Palau, *God Is Relevant: Finding Strength and Peace in Today's World* (New York: Doubleday, 1997), 23, 82.
26. Albert Camus, *The Myth of Sisyphus and Other Essays* (1955; repr., New York: Vintage, 1991), 3.
27. See Michael Novak, "Where Would Civilization Be without

Christianity? The Gift of Dignity," *Christianity Today*, December 6, 1999, www.christianitytoday.com/ct/1999/december6/9te050.html.

28. David N. Livingstone, "Where Would Civilization Be without Christianity? The Gift of Science," *Christianity Today*, December 6, 1999, www.christianitytoday.com/ct/1999/december6/9te052.html.

29. David Lyle Jeffrey, "Where Would Civilization Be without Christianity? The Gift of Literacy," *Christianity Today*, December 6, 1999, www.christianitytoday.com/ct/1999/december6/9te054.html.

30. Mark Noll, "Where Would Civilization Be without Christianity? The Gift of Humility," *Christianity Today*, December 6, 1999, www .christianitytoday.com/ct/1999/december6/9te056.html.

31. Matthew 12:7 (KJV).

32. Quoted in Noll, "Where Would Civilization Be without Christianity? The Gift of Humility."

Objection #8: I Still Have Doubts, So I Can't Be a Christian

1. See Lee Strobel, "Reformed Hood Comes Back to Pay His Dues," *Chicago Tribune*, October 27, 1977; and Lee Strobel, *God's Outrageous Claims: Discover What They Mean for You* (1997; repr., Grand Rapids: Zondervan, 2005), 75–79.

2. Os Guinness, *In Two Minds: The Dilemma of Doubt and How to Resolve It* (Downers Grove, IL: InterVarsity, 1976), 61.

3. André Resner, "Grief and Faith: Three Profiles of Struggle in the Face of Loss" (lecture, 46th Annual Pepperdine Bible Lectureship, Pepperdine University, Malibu, CA, April 19, 1989), italics in original.

4. See Paul C. Vitz, "The Psychology of Atheism," *Truth: An International Interdisciplinary Journal of Christian Thought* 1 (1985): 29.

5. See Mark 9:14–27.

6. Genesis 18:25, paraphrase.

7. See Joshua 24:15.

8. Emphasis added.

9. See Hebrews 11:1.

10. John 8:31–32: "To the Jews who had believed him, Jesus said, 'If you hold to my teaching, you are really my disciples. Then you will know the truth, and the truth will set you free.'"

11. See Acts 20:35.

12. Gary E. Parker, *The Gift of Doubt: From Crisis to Authentic Faith* (San Francisco: Harper & Row, 1990), 69.

Conclusion: The Power of Faith

1. Kai Nielsen, *Reason and Practice: A Modern Introduction to Philosophy* (New York: Harper & Row, 1971), 48.

2. Qur'an 6:37.
3. See Jeremiah 29:13.
4. Norwood Russell Hanson, *What I Do Not Believe and Other Essays*, eds. S. Toulmin and H. Woolf (New York: Springer, 1971), 313–14, emphasis added.
5. See 1 Kings 18:38.
6. William Lane Craig, *Reasonable Faith: Christian Truth and Apologetics* (Wheaton, IL: Crossway, 1984), 72.
7. Quoted in Bill Montgomery, "U.S. Supreme Court Halts Execution: Even Victim's Family Pleaded for Mercy," *Atlanta Journal and Constitution*, August 21, 1990.
8. "When Mercy Becomes Mandatory," *Atlanta Journal and Constitution*, August 16, 1990.
9. 2 Corinthians 5:17.
10. My paraphrase of Proverbs 2:3–5.

Epilogue

1. Beverly Ivany, "The Pastor and the Agnostic," *Salvationist*, October 17, 2013, https://salvationist.ca/articles/2013/10/the-pastor-and-the-agnostic, italics in original.
2. Tom Harpur, "Charles Templeton," *Toronto Star*, June 24, 2001, 1.
3. Ivany, "The Pastor and the Agnostic," italics in original; see Greg Laurie, *Billy Graham: The Man I Knew* (Washington, DC: Salem, 2021), 159–70. Laurie, a noted pastor and evangelist, is confident that Templeton is in heaven: "I have no doubt that when Billy [Graham] died in 2018, his old and dear friend Charles Templeton was there sitting near the throne of God to welcome him to the Kingdom" (170).

Appendix: A Summary of *The Case for Christ*

1. C. F. D. Moule, *The Phenomenon of the New Testament* (London: SCM, 1967), 3.

Index

Meet Lee Strobel

Atheist-turned-Christian Lee Strobel, the former award-winning legal editor of the *Chicago Tribune*, is a *New York Times* bestselling author of more than forty books and curricula that have sold fourteen million copies in total. He currently serves as founding director of the Lee Strobel Center for Evangelism and Applied Apologetics at Colorado Christian University.

Lee has been described in the *Washington Post* as "one of the evangelical community's most popular apologists." He was educated at the University of Missouri (bachelor of journalism degree) and Yale Law School (master of studies in law degree). He was a journalist for fourteen years at the *Chicago Tribune* and other newspapers, winning Illinois's highest honors for both investigative reporting and public service journalism from United Press International.

After probing the evidence for Jesus for nearly two years, Lee became a Christian in 1981. He subsequently became a teaching pastor at three of America's largest churches and hosted the national network TV program *Faith under Fire*. In addition, he taught First Amendment Law at Roosevelt University and was professor of Christian thought at Houston Baptist University.

In 2017, Lee's spiritual journey was depicted in an award-winning motion picture, *The Case for Christ*, which showed in theaters around the world. Lee won national awards for his books *The Case for Christ*, *The Case for Faith*, *The Case for a Creator*, and *The Case for Grace*. His latest books are *The Case for Miracles* and *The Case for Heaven*.

Lee and Leslie have been married for nearly fifty years. Their daughter, Alison, is a novelist, and their son, Kyle, is a professor of spiritual theology at the Talbot School of Theology at Biola University.

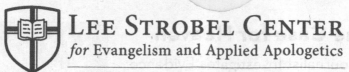

The Case for Heaven

A Journalist Investigates Evidence for Life After Death

Lee Strobel, New York Times bestselling author

Bestselling and award-winning author Lee Strobel interviews experts about the evidence for the afterlife and offers credible answers to the most provocative questions about what happens when we die, near-death experiences, heaven, and hell.

We all want to know what awaits us on the other side of death, but is there any reliable evidence that there is life after death? Investigative author Lee Strobel offers a lively and compelling study into one of the most provocative topics of our day.

Through fascinating conversations with respected scholars and experts—a neuroscientist from Cambridge University, a researcher who analyzed a thousand accounts of near-death experiences, and an atheist turned Christian philosopher—Strobel offers compelling reasons for why death is not the end of our existence but rather a transition to an exciting world to come. Looking at biblical accounts, Strobel unfolds what awaits us after we take our last breath and answers questions like:

- Is there an afterlife?
- What is heaven like?
- How will we spend our time there?
- What does it mean to see God face-to-face?

With a balanced approach, Strobel examines the alternative of hell and the logic of damnation and takes a careful look at reincarnation, universalism, the exclusivity claims of Christ, and other issues related to the topic of life after death. With vulnerability, Strobel shares the experience of how he nearly died years ago and how the reality of death can shape our lives and faith.

Follow Strobel on this journey of discovery of the entirely credible, believable, and exhilarating life to come.

Available in stores and online!

The Case for Miracles

A Journalist Investigates Evidence
for the Supernatural

Lee Strobel, New York Times
bestselling author

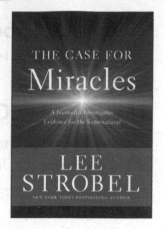

New York Times bestselling author Lee
Strobel trains his investigative sights on a
hot-button question: Is it really credible to
believe God intervenes supernaturally in
people's lives today?

This provocative book starts with an unlikely interview in which
America's foremost skeptic builds a seemingly persuasive case against
the miraculous. But then Strobel travels the country to quiz scholars to
see whether they can offer solid answers to atheist objections. Along
the way, he encounters astounding accounts of healings and other phenomena that simply cannot be explained away by naturalistic causes. The
book features the results of exclusive new scientific polling that shows
miracle accounts are much more common than people think.

What's more, Strobel delves into the most controversial question
of all: What about miracles that don't happen? If God can intervene in
the world, why doesn't he do it more often to relieve suffering? Many
American Christians are embarrassed by the supernatural, not wanting to
look odd or extreme to their neighbors. Yet *The Case for Miracles* shows
not only that the miraculous is possible, but that God still does intervene
in our world in awe-inspiring ways. Here's a unique book that examines all
sides of this issue and comes away with a passionate defense for God's
divine action in lives today.

Also available: *The Case for Miracles* Spanish edition, kids edition, and
student edition.

Available in stores and online!

The Case for Christ

A Journalist's Personal Investigation
of the Evidence for Jesus

Lee Strobel, New York Times
bestselling author

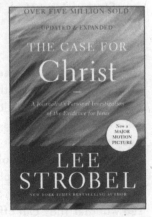

Is there credible evidence that Jesus of
Nazareth really is the Son of God? Former
atheist and *Chicago Tribune* journalist Lee
Strobel takes an investigative look at the evidence from the fields of science, philosophy, and history.

In this revised and updated bestseller, *The Case for Christ*, Lee Strobel
cross-examines a dozen experts with doctorates from schools such as
Cambridge, Princeton, and Brandeis, asking hard-hitting questions—and
building a captivating case for Christ's divinity.

Strobel asks challenging questions like:

- How reliable is the New Testament?
- Does evidence for Jesus exist outside the Bible?
- Is Jesus who he said he was?
- Is there any reason to believe the resurrection was an actual event?

Winner of the Gold Medallion Book Award and twice nominated for
the Christian Book of the Year Award, Strobel's tough, point-blank questions read like a captivating, fast-paced novel. But it's not fiction. It's a
riveting quest for the truth about history's most compelling figure.

This edition includes scores of revisions and additions, including updated material on archaeological and manuscript discoveries, fresh recommendations for further study, and an interview with the author that
tells dramatic stories about the book's impact, provides behind-the-
scenes information, and responds to critiques of the book by skeptics.

Also available: *The Case for Christ* Spanish edition, kids edition, and student edition.